# INSIGHT GUIDE

# Tenerife
## & The Western Canary Islands

Discovery
CHANNEL

**APA** PUBLICATIONS
Part of the Langenscheidt Publishing Group

## INSIGHT GUIDE
# Tenerife
### & the Western Canary Islands

### Editorial
*Project Editor*
**Pam Barrett**
*Managing Editor*
**Dorothy Stannard**
*Editorial Director*
**Brian Bell**

### Distribution

*UK & Ireland*
**GeoCenter International Ltd**
The Viables Centre , Harrow Way
Basingstoke, Hants RG22 4BJ
Fax: (44) 1256-817988

*United States*
**Langenscheidt Publishers, Inc.**
46–35 54th Road, Maspeth, NY 11378
Fax: (718) 784-0640

*Canada*
**Prologue Inc.**
1650 Lionel Bertrand Blvd., Boisbriand
Québec, Canada J7H 1N7
Tel: (450) 434-0306. Fax: (450) 434-2627

*Worldwide*
**Apa Publications GmbH & Co.**
**Verlag KG (Singapore branch)**
38 Joo Koon Road, Singapore 628990
Tel: (65) 865-1600. Fax: (65) 861-6438

### Printing

**Insight Print Services (Pte) Ltd**
38 Joo Koon Road, Singapore 628990
Tel: (65) 865-1600. Fax: (65) 861-6438

©2000  **Apa Publications GmbH & Co.**
**Verlag KG (Singapore branch)**
*All Rights Reserved*

*First Edition 1989*
*Fourth Edition 2000*

**CONTACTING THE EDITORS**
Although every effort is made to
provide accurate information, we
live in a fast-changing world and
would appreciate it if readers
would call our attention to any
errors or outdated information
that may occur by writing to us:
**Insight Guides, P.O. Box 7910,**
**London SE1 1WE, England.**
**Fax: (44 20) 7403-0290.**
**insight@apaguide.demon.co.uk**

# ABOUT THIS BOOK

**T**his guidebook combines the
interests and enthusiasms of
two of the world's best known information providers: Insight Guides,
whose titles have set the standard
for visual travel guides since 1970,
and Discovery Channel, the world's
premier source of nonfiction television programming.

The editors of Insight Guides provide practical advice and general
understanding about a destination's
history, culture, institutions and
people. Discovery Channel and its
Web site, www.discovery.com, help
millions of viewers explore
their world from the com-
fort of their own home and
also encourage them to explore it
first hand.

This completely updated edition of *Insight: Tenerife*
is carefully struc-
tured to convey an understanding of
Tenerife and the smaller western
Canary Islands as well as to guide
readers through their sights and
seasonal activities:

◆ The **Features** section, indicated
by a yellow bar at the top of each
page, covers the history and culture
of the islands in a series of infor-
mative essays.

◆ The main **Places** section, indicated by a blue bar, is a comprehensive guide to all the sights and
areas worth visiting. Places of special interest are coordinated by
number with the maps.

◆ The **Travel Tips**
listings section,
with an orange bar,
provides a handy point of ref-
erence for information on
travel, hotels, shops, restaurants and more.

EXPLORE YOUR WORLD

**Discovery** CHANNEL

◆ **Photographs** are chosen not only to illustrate the islands' geography but also to portray their many faces and moods.

**The contributors**

This edition of *Insight: Tenerife* was revised by **Pam Barrett**, a London-based editor, supervised by managing editor **Dorothy Stannard** at Insight Guides. The book has been completely updated and expanded to take account of the many recent changes on the islands.

The **History** chapters are revised versions of those written for earlier editions by Spanish historian **Felipe Fernandez-Armesto** and Canary-based archaeologist **Mike Eddy**. Several of the original essays in the **Features** section were also contributed by Eddy, while some others are based on pieces by Carolyn

Mowlem, Sarah Simon and Austin Baillon, whose family have lived in Tenerife since 1906.

The **Places** section was updated by **Lindsay Hunt** and **Christopher Catling**, both very familiar with the islands. They built on earlier chapters by Neil Dunkin, Andrew Eames, Paul Murdin and Nigel Tisdall.

Lindsay Hunt updated the pieces on Tenerife itself, and contributed a brand-new chapter on a new area, the Southern Resorts. She also wrote the picture stories on Carnavale and the flora of the Islands.

Christopher Catling revised the chapters on La Palma and La Gomera and the Eastern Islands. Strictly speaking, the latter are outside the province of this book – they are covered in *Insight Guide: Gran Canaria* – but are included to give a taste of their atmosphere, as access is so easy. Catling also wrote the picture story on Canarian Architecture and was responsible for updating the **Travel Tips**, which were originally compiled by **Mary Tisdall**.

The chapter on El Hierro was updated by **Andrew Eames**, who also contributed the piece on the island's giant lizards. Eames, who has worked on numerous Insight Guides and was the Project Editor for the earlier edition of this book, knows the western islands well.

Much of the guide's photography was the work of **Joerg Reuther** and **Gary John Norman,** but valuable contributions were made by many others, including **Marcel Jacquet** and **Sergio Hanquet**, photographers with the Naturpress agency.

Thanks also go to **Sylvia Suddes** for proofreading this latest edition of the book, and to **Isobel McLean** for completing the index.

## Map Legend

| | |
|---|---|
| —  ·  — | International Boundary |
| —  ●  — | National Park/Reserve |
| — — — — | Ferry Route |
| ✈ ✛ | Airport: International/ Regional |
| 🚌 | Bus Station |
| ❶ | Tourist Information |
| ✉ | Post Office |
| ✝ ✝ ✝ | Church/Ruins |
| ✝ | Monastery |
| ☾ | Mosque |
| ✡ | Synagogue |
| 🏰 🏛 | Castle/Ruins |
| ∴ | Archaeological Site |
| ∩ | Cave |
| 🗿 | Statue/Monument |
| ★ | Place of Interest |

The main places of interest in the Places section are coordinated by number with a full-colour map (e.g. ❶), and a symbol at the top of every right-hand page tells you where to find the map.

# CONTENTS

Los Cristianos

## Insight on ...

## Information panels

## Places

## Travel Tips

# AN ELUSIVE ISLAND

*Part of Spain yet close to Africa, Tenerife is an island*
*with much to offer beyond its immediate attractions*

Tenerife and the other Canary Islands lie between Europe and Africa, small volcanic islands adrift in the Atlantic. Much of the harsh, awe-inspiring landscape resembles that of North Africa, and African cultural influences are evident. Yet the Canaries are part of Spain, the nation which conquered and Christianised them in the early 15th century – although since 1978 they have been an autonomous province with their own regional government, and many inhabitants insist that the island identity is quite different.

During the early part of the 20th century ladies and gentlemen of quality began travelling to Tenerife for a health cure in the winter. The climate was favourable, the waters were health-giving, and a select number of aristocratic visitors in the late 19th century had given the island social cachet. They were a bit uncertain about the food, however, and discreet guidebooks recommended "a discriminatory use of laxatives" to relieve the colic brought on by garlic and olive oil used in the cooking.

Tenerife continued to be visited by a well-heeled minority throughout the 1920s and 1930s. World War II put an end to foreign holidays, of course, and the poverty and international ostracisation of Spain in the years that followed also put it largely out of bounds. When Spain was received back into the fold, and airlines began direct flights to the island in 1959, things changed dramatically. At first it was winter sunshine that attracted holidaymakers; then Tenerife became popular as a place for cheap summer beach holidays

Today approximately 4½ million people visit every year, bringing new prosperity and many changes, some good, some bad. About 75 percent of tourists go to the beach resorts of the south, principally Playa de las Américas and Los Cristianos, but increasingly Tenerife and the smaller western islands of La Palma, La Gomera and El Hierro are becoming favourite destinations for people who enjoy walking amid spectacular scenery in a good climate.

This book takes the islands seriously, introducing readers to some of their history and their hidden delights, as well as detailing the best places to go if a restorative break based on sea, sand and guaranteed sunshine is what you have in mind. ❑

**PRECEDING PAGES:** age and youth take a view on the world; windsurfing at El Médano; the beach at Las Gaviotas; Tenerife's botanical gardens contain numerous rare species.
**LEFT:** dressing up for one of the many fiestas.

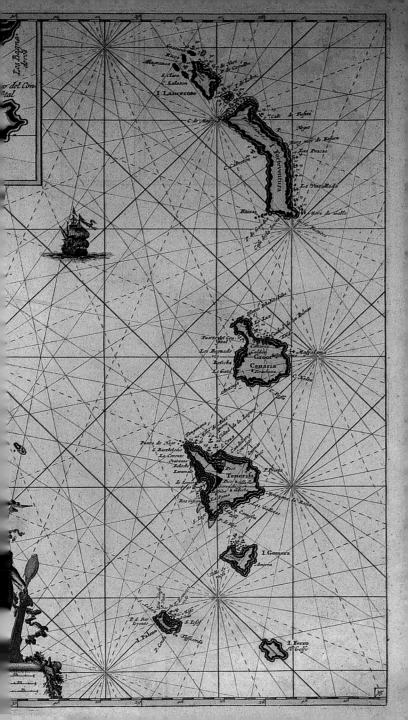

# Decisive Dates

## PREHISTORY

**c 3000 BC:** Settlement begins on the Canary Islands. Findings suggest that the earliest inhabitants were Berbers from the African mainland, in particular Morocco, where the indigenous people shared similar features.

**1st–2nd century BC:** according to the evidence of modern radio-carbon dating, the Guanches, who appear to have links with the Berbers, arrive on the islands – specifically Tenerife, although it is unclear how they got there.

## BEFORE THE CONQUEST (1ST–14TH CENTURIES)

**1st century AD:** Pliny the Elder (AD 23–79) writes of an expedition to the islands by King Juba II of Mauritania in North West Africa, which discovered numerous wild dogs. One theory is that the islands may have got their name from *cane*, the Latin word for dog.

**AD 150:** The Greek geographer Ptolemy shows the Canary Islands on his map of the world. The westernmost edge of the known world is shown running through El Hierro.

**1st–13th centuries:** The Guanches develop an ordered society, divided into tribes led by chiefs or *menceyes*. They grew cereals, kept domestic animals, and indulged in hunting and fishing. They made tools from bone, basalt and obsidian, and weapons from wood as they had no knowledge of metalworking.

**1375:** The Catalan Atlas depicts the Canaries, with Mount Teide prominently displayed.

## THE CONQUEST (15TH CENTURY)

**1402–5:** El Hierro is conquered by the Norman Jean de Béthencourt who brought 120 settlers, and two priests to convert the islanders. The larger islands resist his atacks.

**1440s:** Hernán Peraza, from an aristocratic Sevillian family for many years in dispute with de Béthencourt, attacks La Gomera and La Palma. His son, Guillén, is killed in the attack.

**1478:** Natives of La Gomera rebel against Peraza.

**1488–89:** Genoese merchants, who financed the conquest of Gran Canaria, invade the island. Peraza's son, Hernán, is killed by insurgents; in revenge many natives are killed, enslaved or exiled.

**1492:** Christopher Columbus stops at La Gomera on his voyage to the Americas. En route, he records seeing an eruption of Mount Teide.

**1494:** The conquest of Tenerife and La Palma is undertaken by a group of financiers and entrepreneurs, led by Alfonso Fernández de Lugo. Many of his troops are massacred near Acentejo (the place is now called La Matanza, The Massacre).

**1495:** De Lugo achieves a decisive victory on the same spot, in the Battle of Acentejo.

## THE TRADING BOOM

**Early 16th century:** Genoese merchants and bankers invest in sugar planations (the first sugar mills had been built by de Lugo). Many of the workers are Portuguese immigrants. The industry booms and brings great wealth.

**Late 16th century:** Competition from the New World brings the sugar boom to an end.

**17th century:** Tenerife grows rich on wine production and export, the archipelago becoming known as "the Isles of Wine".

**1656:** British Admiral Blake sinks 16 Spanish galleons carrying gold in Santa Cruz harbour.

**1665:** The Canary Island Company formed in London with exclusive rights to trade in Canarian wines in England.

**1685–87:** A plague of locusts descends on the islands and wrecks wine production.

**1701:** The Canaries' first university is founded in La Laguna.

**1703:** Signing of the Methuen Treaty, which granted

favourable trading terms to Britain's allies, the Portuguese, hastens the demise of the wine trade, as the leading role is taken over by Madeira wine.

**1701–14:** The War of the Spanish Succession brings the end of the wine boom.

**1706** Garachico is destroyed by a volcanic eruption on Mount Teide.

**18th-century:** a period of economic depression; the cochineal and silk industries bring only occasional relief.

**1797:** Admiral Nelson's attack on Santa Cruz is repelled.

## THE 19TH CENTURY

**1810:** The "Canarian Junta" makes the first appeal for an independent government.

**1822:** Santa Cruz de Tenerife becomes capital of the archipelago.

**1822:** The Spanish queen, Isabella II, makes the Canaries a free trade zone.

**Mid- to late 19th century:** numerous islanders emigrate, chiefly to the Caribbean island of Cuba and Venezuela in South America, in search of a better life.

**1881:** The development of Las Palmas as a harbour for steamships accelerates the battle between Tenerife and Gran Canaria for supremacy in the archipelago.

**1880s:** The British introduce the mass cultivation of bananas, bringing a new prosperity to Tenerife. In the following decade, the development of refrigerated shipping furthers the industry's fortunes.

## CHANGE AND DEVELOPMENT

**Post-Word War II:** Poverty and unemployment produce a great increase in emigration.

**1927:** The island is divided into two provinces, with Santa Cruz as the administrative centre for the four western islands, and Las Palmas de Gran Canaria capital of the eastern province.

**1931:** The Spanish Second Republic is proclaimed.

**1936:** From Tenerife, General Francisco Franco launches the campaign which marks the beginning of the bitter three-year Civil War and nearly 40 years of dictatorship.

**1940s:** Following the Civil War and World War II, the Canaries, along with the rest of Spain, suffer poverty and ostracism.

---

**LEFT:** a painting depicts the Guanches finding the image of Nuestra Señora de Candelaria.
**RIGHT:** the resort of Los Cristianos represents the modern face of Tenerife.

**1950:** Spain becomes part of the international community once more.

**1959:** With the introduction of the first direct flights to Tenerife, tourism on the island flourishes. Puerto de la Cruz becomes an internationally-known resort.

**1963:** MPAIAC, a militant separatist party, is founded.

**1975:** After the death of Franco and the end of the dictatorship MPAIAC initiates a campaign of violence, but new moderate parties prove more popular with the electorate.

**1978:** Under a devolved constitution, the Canaries become one of 14 autonomous provinces (there

are now 17) with extended regional powers. Also in this year the Reina Sofía airport on the Costa Silencio brings mass tourism to the south of Tenerife. Los Cristianos undergoes rapid development, and Playa de las Américas is created.

**1986:** Spain becomes part of the European community (now European Union) and negotiates a special status for the Canary Islands.

**1995:** The Canaries become full members of the EU but retain some import tax privileges.

**1990s:** Tourism spreads to the smaller western islands of La Gomera, La Palma and El Hierro, although it is far more low key.

**1999:** According to latest figures over 4½ million people a year visit Tenerife.  ❏

# LEGENDS OF THE ISLES

*It is the magical quality of small islands that invites the many myths and legends that surround the Canaries and their people*

Quite who Canarios were and how they lived before the arrival of conquering mainland Europeans is mainly a matter of supposition. But it is perhaps appropriate that the islanders should have an insubstantial quality, for the islands themselves have a strangely shadowy form, figuring in various mythologies over and over again.

## Atlantis

One of the best-known myths in which the Canary Islands feature is that of Atlantis, the sunken kingdom. As a rule of thumb, if you want to write a convincing history of a place that never existed, be sure to give it a good, long, dry bibliography. The story of Atlantis certainly has one, even though it is fundamentally fantasy and reality does not feature in any of its verbose and varied passages.

The "historical" evidence for Atlantis is to be found in two of Plato's dialogues, *Timaeus* and *Critias*, which describe the visit of Solon, an Athenian scholar, to Egypt, the cultural mecca of the time. Solon made his trip around the beginning of the 6th century BC and, from an aged holy man in Sais, a city in the Nile Delta, he heard what was supposed to be the true history of the Greeks.

Beyond the Pillars of Hercules, in the western ocean, had once lain Atlantis. Nine thousand years before Solon's time it had been the superpower of its day – wealthy, strong and ruled by the wisest of men. The capital of Atlantis was circular in plan, the centre being a huge pillar of gleaming bronze on which the laws were inscribed. Here, too, was the temple and palace of Poseidon, god of the sea. On one side lay the ocean and on the other the vast, well-ordered irrigated plain.

But power corrupts, and the rulers of Atlantis set out on a path of world domination. Only heroic little Athens stood up to it – and Athens won. But the victory was pyrrhic: a series of dreadful natural calamities destroyed Athens in 24 hours. Out in the west, Atlantis sank without trace to the bottom of Poseidon's ocean. Only Egypt survived the catastrophe, and became the guardian of this ancient lore.

The Atlantis myth may well be based on a dim memory of the destruction of the Minoan civilisation. The location given by Plato – beyond the Pillars of Hercules – is simply a literary convention, rather like modern writers placing imaginary societies in outer space. The Atlantis tale was the *Star Trek* of its day.

The fall of Minoan Crete was probably as cataclysmic as the submersion of Atlantis. Nine centuries before Solon's trip to Egypt the volcanic island of Thera, 112 km (70 miles) from Crete's northern coast, blew up. The Cretan civilisation ended with an horrendous bang.

Innumerable scholars have sought to locate Plato's Atlantis. Often the supposed location

---

**PRECEDING PAGES:** a 14th-century map shows the Canary Islands.
**LEFT:** a contemporary view of the Guanches.
**RIGHT:** athletic Guanches in Las Palmas.

coincides with an author's own country of origin: Swedish writer Olof Rudbeck placed its heartland in the Uppsala region, and there is a lengthy German work entitled *Atlantis, The Home of the Aryans.*

## Legends that defy logic

Less xenophobic scholars have looked to the Atlantic Ocean, beyond the Straits of Gibraltar, and have lighted on the Canary Islands as the surviving mountain peaks of Atlantis. One 19th-century Frenchman managed a reconstruction of the outline of the lost continent which took in the Azores, Madeira, the Canaries

The Atlantis myth has become entwined with Canarian prehistory at times, creating the "mystery of the Guanches", who have variously been portrayed as tall, blond shipwecked Vikings; primitive, club-swinging throwbacks; or the last survivors of an Atlantean master-race: pick your favourite theory. (*For more factually-based information about the Guanches, see pages 25–28.*)

## Racial myths

In the wake of Darwin's theory of evolution and a system used by Danish antiquarians to classify ancient finds, it was suggested that

and the Cape Verde islands. Such suggestions take little notice of minor inconveniences like geography and geology.

The Azores lie on the mid-Atlantic ridge, over 1,000 km (600 miles) from the Canaries, which are loosely attached to Africa. The Cape Verdes are located approximately 2,000 km (1,300 miles) south of the Canary Islands. Between the Azores and the Canaries are trenches reaching depths of 7 km (4 miles). By this reckoning, Tenerife's Mount Teide would have been higher than Everest. Moreover, the forces involved in removing a block of land the size of the present European Union would have destroyed the rest of the world as well.

mankind passed through a series of developmental stages, each of which could be equated with present-day peoples. These stages could be calculated by a system of classifying human skulls, which was worked out by measuring the breadth and length of the skull. On the basis of skull shape alone, a complex series of events was suggested; the more "primitive" inhabitants, it was believed, were driven further inland by invaders until they finally died out. This theory did not take into account the fact that the Canary Islands have very little inland area into which to be driven.

Towards the end of the 19th century the Canary Islands were seized on as a laboratory for the "proving" of racial theory. Physical anthropologists, like the Frenchman René Verneau, began working on the islands, measuring and sizing up the skulls of the living and the dead.

## The mystery of San Borondón

It is said that strange things happen at sea. Islands move around, and sometimes disappear completely. One such floating island is San Borondón, which is said to lie beyond La Palma, although how far beyond is open to question. According to some Portuguese sailors who passed it in 1525, San Borondón is 396 nautical km (220 nautical miles) north-west of La Palma; other 16th-century seamen put it some 30 km (18 miles) or so further off. One Renaissance geographer shifted it almost as far as the American coast.

Two La Palma sea captains, Hernando Troya and Hernando Alvares, could not find the island in 1525 (the year of the Portuguese sighting), and nor could their fellow islander, de Villalobos, who set out in search of it 45 years later.

Others apparently had had more luck: first the Carthaginians, then Spaniards fleeing the Moorish invaders. By the late 16th century, talk of the island was common among Portuguese, English and French pirates, who, it is said, hid there safe in the knowledge that the strong currents would keep pursuers at bay. The Italian military engineer Giovanni Torriani even went so far as to draw a map of the island, 422 km (264 miles) from north to south and 148 km (93 miles) from east to west, almost cut in two by major rivers. Torriani shows a total of seven cities on his map.

The Portuguese who landed in 1525 said it was full of tall trees. A Spanish nobleman turned pirate, Ceballos, confirmed that the forest came right down to the shore, and added that the woods were full of birds "so simple that they could be caught in the hand". There was a beautiful long sandy beach, but in the sand Ceballos had seen the footprints of a giant.

A French crew putting into La Palma after a storm, said they had left a wooden cross, a letter and some silver coins at the spot where they landed. Another ship-load of Portuguese saw oxen, goats, sheep and the footprints of more giants in the sand.

The power of the island currents was demonstrated in 1566 when Roque Nuñez, a Portuguese seaman, and Martín de Araña, a La Palma priest, set out for San Borondón. After only a day and a night they saw land, but as they argued over who should disembark first the current drove them off the shore again.

The elusive San Borondón has never been picked up on any satellite photo, but there are people who say you can see it, sometimes, from Tenerife and La Palma, its high peaks poking through the clouds. ❑

### MISUSE OF SCIENCE

The 19th-century scientists who believed that measurements of the skull gave important clues to the development of the human race were guided by genuine scientific interest, as were later phrenologists, who thought that mental faculties could be investigated by feeling bumps on the outside of the head.

Unfortunately, their theories were taken up by the Nazis in their search for racial purity during the 1930s. And during Franco's dictatorship, which had its own obsession with "purity of the blood", the isolation of the Canaries made the islands a favourite haunt of racial theorists and extremists.

**LEFT:** the sacred Garoë tree, which brought water to an arid land.
**RIGHT:** strong currents kept early ships at bay.

# THE GUANCHES

*It is uncertain how and when the Guanches, the islands' first inhabitants, arrived but their culture appears to have been well ordered and stable*

A major problem for archaeologists and pre-historians writing about the native inhabitants of the Canaries is to know what to call them. Each island had a different name and within each island there were also tribal names.

The name Guanche really only applied to the original inhabitants of Tenerife, but is often used generically for the pre-conquest island societies. This is useful shorthand, as long as we remember that each island had its own peculiarities within the culture.

## Origins of the species

The origins of the Guanche culture are unclear, but it was certainly related to the Berbers of North Africa. Many modern place names in the Canary Islands are also found in Morocco – the island of La Gomera and the Moroccan village of Ghomara have obvious similarities. Tenerife, too, is echoed in modern Berber place names – the element "Ten-" or "Tin-" is common in North Africa.

The native islanders lived in natural caves adapted for human habitation by levelling the floor with earth and stones and by building front walls of stone and timber. But unlike on Gran Canaria, where there are whole villages of man-made caves, only one purpose-built cave has been found in the province of Tenerife – Cueva de los Reyes, in Güimar.

It it interesting that this cave should be called *de los reyes* – "of the kings". On Gran Canaria man-made painted caves are traditionally thought to be the homes of kings, but in fact they were probably *harimaguadas* – a kind of semi-secular convent where young women were schooled in wifely and religious duties.

Gran Canaria's painted caves are rare (only half a dozen are known), and they fall into two types, either large artificial ones with geometric painted friezes, or small natural rock shelters decorated with human figures or wavy lines. The Güimar cave, therefore, was probably not a "cave of kings" at all, but a convent, as painting of any kind was almost exclusively a female activity.

Several European chronicles mention the important role played by women in pottery, basketry, religion, and harvesting. On Gran Canaria geometric art is linked with all these

activities, but on Tenerife and the western islands there is not such a clear connection.

## Pots, crops and gods

Some of the finest pottery vessels on Tenerife are bag-shaped pots with tubular spouts which are similar to the highly decorated spouted pitchers of Gran Canaria or the slab-mouthed *tofios* of Fuerteventura. The Gran Canarian and Fuerteventuran pots played an important part in religious ceremonies during which women poured libations of milk to the Guanche sky god, Alcoran. The spouted pots of Tenerife may well have had the same sacred purpose, although the god was known as Acguayaxerax.

---

**LEFT:** Guanche figures in Santa Cruz de Tenerife.
**RIGHT:** contemporary pots made in the ancient style.

On La Palma, bowls decorated with patterns of incised lines were probably used for libations to Abora, the sky god. Too little is known of the archaeology of El Hierro and La Gomera to suggest what form their libation vessels took, though Gomeran pottery seems very similar to that of Tenerife. Gomerans worshipped a sky god called Orahan. On El Hierro there were two deities – one male, Eroaranzan, who dealt with men and masculine affairs and the other, Moneiba, a goddess who concerned herself exclusively with women and female activities.

On Tenerife men did the ploughing but women were responsible for tending the crops and for harvesting and storing them. Unlike on Gran Canaria where grain was stored in sealed and marked pits, the women of Tenerife kept their food stocks in pots inside caves known as *auchones*, which were quite different from habitation caves.

The Guanches on all the islands lived in caves, although on Gran Canaria they also built villages of substantial houses. On Tenerife and the other western islands early stone buildings do exist, but they are little more than huts, often built against rock.

## Tribes and chiefdoms

Where the nobles lived on the western islands is not known; there are no recorded "palace" sites as there are on Gran Canaria and Lanzarote. However, we do know something of the political make-up of the islands at the time of the conquest. The nine chiefs or *menceyes* of Tenerife claimed descent from a single king, Betznuriia, and shared the broad, alpine plains of the Cañadas de Teide as common grazing land. The names of the *menceyatos* or chiefdoms survive as modern place names: Anaga, Tegueste, Tacaronte, Taoro, Icod, Daute, Adeje, Abona, and Güimar.

Gomera was divided into four tribal areas, although the royal families all claimed descent from a single king, Amalahuige. The four Gomeran tribes formed two exclusive zones – an alliance of the Orone and the Agana tribes lived in the west, the Hipalan and the Mulagana tribes in the east. This division was exploited to advantage by the Spanish conquistador, Fernán Peraza, who eventually took the island.

Twelve pre-conquest divisions are known on La Palma, though one of these areas – Acero – is the Caldera of Taburiente and may simply have been an area of common grazing. Another political unit was Tamanca, on the west coast, but the king of Tamanca was known as the "king of the three lordships". It is not known whether Tamanca was divided into three or controlled the adjacent bands of Tihuya and Ahenguarame. The island of El Hierro had just one king or chieftain.

Among the Guanches of Tenerife the office of *mencey* was hereditary, though the title had to be confirmed by the *tagoror* or council of elders. The title did not pass directly from father to son, but to the brothers of the former *mencey*. Only when the last brother died did

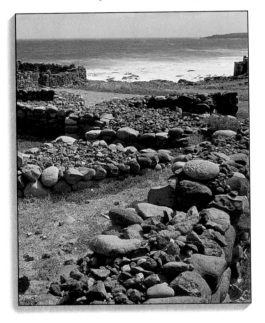

### SOPHISTICATED DWELLINGS

Guanche houses on El Hierro may have been grander structures than those on Tenerife. One European description (shortly after the conquest) reads: "Their dwelling was builded thus. First they maketh a circuit of dry stone walling, large and round, in which they leave but a sole entrance by which it is served; and then within this circle were placed beams against the wall, so that the beams remained clear of the earth, like a lean-to, and covered with ferns and branches; and within this circuit lived twenty or more adults with their off-spring." Despite this detailed account, no houses of this type have ever been found on the island.

the title finally go to the eldest son of the original *mencey*. As a gruesome part of the investiture ceremony each new chief had to kiss the bones of the first *mencey* of that lineage.

The *tagoror* was a place as well as a political body, a large circular space with rough-hewn, stone seats, the highest of which was for the *mencey* himself. Each tribe had its own *tagoror*, where justice was dispensed, war plans made and land allotted. Sites of these meeting places exist throughout the islands – a fine, though much altered, example survives at El Julán, on El Hierro, but unfortunately it is closed to the interested public and open to vandalism.

## Daily life

According to Thomas Nichols, the first Englishman to write about the Guanches in the 16th century, the inhabitants of Tenerife lived on "gelt dogs, goates and goates milke; their bread was made of barlie meale and goats milke, called *gofio*, which they use at his daie" (and modern Canary Islanders still do). *Gofio* is a finely ground, toasted flour, then made from barley but now of maize or wheat.

A variety of other crops were available, including local fruits and berries, roots and perhaps figs. Goats were the main domestic animals used for food, though the Guanches also kept

El Julán is perhaps the most remarkable site in the western Canaries. Some fine examples of Guanche writing have been found, pecked out laboriously in a pre-Roman Berber script, but they remain undeciphered. Elsewhere, rock-carvings are mainly simple geometric patterns incorporating spirals, crosses, circles and intersecting lines, though a few human and animal shapes have been recorded on El Hierro and La Palma. So far, very few rock-carvings have been found on Tenerife and La Gomera.

pigs and sheep. Fish bones have been found in excavations on La Palma and Tenerife but no deep-sea species have been recorded.

Hunting, like fishing, was apparently a high-status activity. Wild cats were hunted along with wild pig and birds like the Barbary partridge and quail. The peasantry, on the other hand, relied a lot on shellfish, and shell-middens are common, although the only ones to have been excavated (on La Gomera) are later, dating from the 17th century.

The land was apparently held in common and shared out by the tribal leaders every year. The peasantry had to pay a tax or tithe in produce to the *mencey*, or head man.

**LEFT:** remains of Guanche tombs and dwellings.
**ABOVE:** Guanche statues hold the commanding heights.

The Guanches had no knowledge of metal-working, and there are no ore deposits on the islands. Stone and bone were used instead. From bone they made needles, awls, punches and fish-hooks. Out of basalt they fashioned heavy knives, picks and chopping tools. Finer cutting tools were made from tiny pieces of obsidian, a black volcanic "glass", found in the Cañadas of Tenerife and on La Palma. Porous lava was shaped into circular mill-stones and into mortars for grinding grain. Containers were made from wood,

> **ANCIENT ARTEFACTS**
>
> Prehistoric Guanche tools and other objects are displayed in the Museo de la Naturaleza y El Hombre in Santa Cruz (*see page 138*).

leather, basketry and pottery. In cave sites such materials arepreserved in the dry atmosphere. Draw-string pouches of leather or basketry are relatively common finds.

The Guanches' main weapons were wooden spears and staves – the spears hardened with fire. As the Spanish conquerors discovered to their cost, these weapons were just as effective as the stone-tipped variety.

## Burial rites

The Guanche way of death was remarkably complex, for they mummified their dead – not as well as the ancient Egyptians but quite adequately. The body was washed in the sea by a specialist caste of undertakers, who lived a life apart from the rest of society (death and blood were taboo for Guanche nobles). Once the internal organs had been removed the body was dried in the sun; finally it was wrapped for burial in shrouds made of leather or basketry.

These mummies were then placed in caves on wooden litters or platforms of stones, or stood upright by themselves against the cave walls. Thomas Nichols visited some of these places: "I have seen caves of 300 of these corps together; the flesh being dried up, the bodye remained as light as parchment."

## Unanswered questions

Although it has been established, through their language, social customs and archaeological remains, that the Guanches had links with the ancient Berbers of North Africa, how and when they arrived on the islands remains more of a mystery.

Radio-carbon dating so far points to the 1st or 2nd century BC as the most likely time of arrival. There are a couple of earlier dates, around 500 BC, but these are not directly related to human activity – just a few fragments of charcoal and lizard bones, both of which occur naturally on volcanic islands. Even by these earliest dates the Cro-Magnon and Mediterranean populations, who have been suggested as early ancestors of the Guanches, had long been intermingled with early Berber tribes.

Even more interesting is how they got here. Apparently the Guanches had no boats when the Europeans arrived. So were they brought to the islands as prisoners by the Romans or the Carthaginians? Or had they simply "forgotten" their boatbuilding skills over the centuries? Only one European chronicler mentions a boat – a dug-out dragon-wood canoe with a matting sail – but he was writing his account a century after the conquest.

Unless further archaeological finds are made and the early writings deciphered, much of the islands' early history will remain the subject of supposition and guesswork based on the few materials available. ❑

**LEFT:** the indigenous tribes mummified their dead.
**RIGHT:** undeciphered script: Los Letreros on El Hierro.

# THE STRUGGLES OF CONQUEST

*The conquest of the islands began soon after they were mapped, and before long the*

*Guanches were subjugated by a combination of force, treachery and coercion*

It was not until the late 14th century that the western isles began to emerge from the mists of obscurity. Tenerife, Gomera and Hierro were roughly charted in 1367, and first really put on the map in 1375 when the *Catalan Atlas* was made. Probably drawn by the Aragonese royal cartographer Cresques Abraham, it is one of the most famous and beautiful medieval maps, a rich and intricate creation. Only La Palma is omitted, and Tenerife is unmistakably displayed with the gleaming, towering peak of Mount Teide conspicuously sketched.

The *Libro del Conoscimiento*, compiled from the legends of maps at about the same time, lists 11 islands of the Canaries and includes the name "Tenerife" – rendered as "tenerifiz" – for the first time. The roughly contemporary work of the Mallorcan mapmaker Guillem Soler improves on the *Catalan Atlas* and excels some later maps in placing the archipelago in its true position relative to the African coast.

## Early attempts at conquest

The western islands were coveted by European navigators but proved difficult to conquer. Between 1402 and 1405 the smallest, poorest and least populated, El Hierro, fell to the conqueror of the eastern islands, Jean de Béthencourt, who settled the island with 120 people from his native Normandy. He brought with him two priests, de Bontier and le Verrier, to convert and baptise the conquered people. Castilian colonisers also settled here in subsequent years, but their existence was poor and precarious, the history of the colony virtually undocumented, and its survival surprising.

Gomera, La Palma and Tenerife, by contrast, were all populous islands, whose natives saw off de Béthencourt's attacks. In the 70 years that followed his last efforts, the next largest island, Gomera, was the only one to fall.

The Las Casas-Peraza family of Seville, who had a long history of being slave masters in the

---

**LEFT:** tribal chiefs brought before the new rulers.

**RIGHT:** Jean de Béthencourt, the first conquistador.

Canaries and had been among de Béthencourt's backers, disputed the right of conquest of the western islands with numerous contenders: Béthencourt's heirs, fellow Sevillian merchant-aristocrats and the Portuguese prince, Henry the Navigator; it was not until the late 1440s that the head of the house, Hernán Peraza, felt secure enough in the possession of the islands of Lanzarote, Fuerteventura and Hierro to give undivided attention to the extension of the conquest. His campaigns were remembered by witnesses at a judicial enquiry some 30 years later and are celebrated in popular verses, sung in the islands to this day. His attacks on Gomera and La Palma were said to have cost him 10,000 ducats and the life of his son, Guillén.

## The subjugation of Gomera

On Gomera the native population was relatively numerous, and remained so until the 1480s. The traditional economy, yielding cheeses and hides, was not disturbed at first by the Perazas, who shut themselves up in their crude and comfortless keep of stone – which stands to this day, just outside the island's capital of San Sebastián – and sustained with their vassals a relationship of mutual fear.

The recurring tension between the Perazas and the islanders made the status quo untenable, and gave the Castilian monarchs a pretext for intervention. The natives rebelled in 1478, taking the opportunity of war between Castile and Portugal to "procure favours" from the enemy.

The Genoese merchants who financed the conquest of Gran Canaria in the early 1480s proved unwilling to leave fertile, exploitable

lands in the hands of native herders and gatherers, and in 1488 and 1489, royal forces from Gran Canaria made two brutal incursions. The young Hernán Peraza, who ruled the island as the resident lord was put to death by native insurgents. In revenge, the rebels were executed or enslaved in droves as "rebels against their natural lords", and the island was garrisoned from Gran Canaria.

The treatment of the natives touched tender consciences in Castile, where an inquiry was held to examine the proprieties of the case; the release of the enslaved and exiled Gomerans was recommended and many of them eventually returned to the archipelago. But their native

land was now ripe for transformation by European settlers. In the next decade, it became one among many colonial sugar-islands.

## Mercenary war

The conquests of Tenerife and La Palma, meanwhile, were proving elusive. The Peraza family made incursions in the 1460s and 1470s. The tomb of the head of the family, Diego de Herrera, bears an epitaph claiming he received the submission of all nine native chieftains of Tenerife. But the people were not subdued, and by the time the conquests of Gran Canaria and La Gomera were complete, the crown had no resources left with which to pursue attacks against the notoriously indomitable defenders.

The conquests of La Palma and Tenerife, therefore, were left to private entrepreneurs and mercenaries. The conquistadors were promised plots of conquered land, and booty, as yet uncollected, was pledged as the reward for those who could raise the necessary finance.

The organiser of the consortia of financiers and conquistadors, and captain of the hosts, was Alonso Fernández de Lugo, a ruthless and ambitious man who had held a subordinate command in the conquest of Gran Canaria. Most of his partners were Genoese merchants seeking investments in sugar-growing lands.

De Lugo's invasion of La Palma in 1492 was preceded by the missionary activities of the remarkable native convert, Francisca de Gazmira. That an episcopal licence should have been conferred on her, a lay preacher who suffered the double disadvantage of being a native and a woman, suggests extraordinary charismatic powers, which she seems to have used to

---

### TRICKED INTO SLAVERY

Leonardo Torriani, the Italian engineer who, in the 1590s, chronicled the European colonisation of the Canaries, describes the conquest of El Hierro: "The Christians began to disembark, and were received with great rejoicing and happiness. They seem'd to all the natives to be Gods and not mortal men… and with this illusion the heathens… began to board the lighters, as they wished to get out to the ships; and so many came on board that the ships were fully loaded. They were all taken to Lanzarote and dispatched from there to be sold in divers places." The people thought they were sailing off to the land of the gods, not being sold into slavery.

good effect among her people. It was perhaps thanks to her preparation that de Lugo encountered little opposition and some help when he landed on the western seaboard. Reinforced by Christian tribes of the west, he defeated tribes who had not united in resistance.

The interior was more difficult to subdue, for volcanic activity and erosion had combined to create a vast natural fortress, La Caldera, occupied by a single tribe under a leader known as Tanausú. According to a chronicle written a century later, de Lugo tricked him into attending a sham parley, at which he was overcome and his followers were all captured or killed.

his campaigns. In 1494, he barely escaped with his life after being lured into a trap at Acentejo near the mouth of the Orotava valley. The place name La Matanza (The Slaughter), remains to commemorate the massacre of his men.

## The fall of Tenerife

De Lugo returned the following year with larger forces, and won a decisive battle over the chief of Taoro, the richest of the nine chiefdoms, on a site near La Laguna. After overwintering, he found the natives depleted and debilitated by an unidentified disease – the first of a series of mysterious epidemics, presum-

It should be remembered that the late 16th century was a time when revisionists such as the Dominican writer, Fray Alonso de Espinosa, were challenging the received image of the conquest of the Canaries, praising the natural virtues of the natives, but nevertheless it sounds characteristic of everything that is documented about Alonso de Lugo.

De Lugo's operations were bedevilled by lack of finance and legal problems with his backers. He narrowly averted disaster in both

ably brought by the Europeans, which caused a demographic disaster comparable, on a smaller scale, to those which later devastated the New World. De Lugo resumed his march on Taoro, and at Acentejo avenged his former disaster in a definitive victory. The last chief of Taoro committed ritual suicide, his remaining followers submitted, and de Lugo was able to parade them before his monarchs, under the eyes of the Venetian ambassador.

## The fate of the natives

The fate of the captive natives was the subject of a furious debate. Clerical advocates – especially Franciscans – saw them as the epitome of

**LEFT:** many of the islands' native inhabitants were sold into slavery.
**ABOVE:** a depiction in tiles of the Battle of Acentejo.

all that was best in "natural" man: rude but educable, artless but susceptible to the friars' own arts, fully members of a human community.

Some early humanists came close in their image to the missionaries' view, sharing an appreciation of the primitive and emphasising the natural virtue of the natives. But most laymen rejected these images, many sharing the view of the German physician, Hieronymus Münzer, who saw some of the Guanche people in 1497, and described them as "beasts in human form".

Early colonial society was therefore an inauspicious milieu for the native. Survivors of the conquest were numbered in hundreds rather than thousands, even in Tenerife where they were most numerous, and those whom the slavers and conquerors spared, the newly introduced sicknesses depleted.

Spaniards of the period were more sensitive to differences of class than those of race, and some members of the native aristocracy found acceptance and cultural assimilation. Don Fernando Guanarteme, an Hispanophile Gran Canaria chief who was employed in the conquest of Tenerife, was able to marry his daughters to Spanish *hidalgos* (noblemen). The sons of the chiefs of Tenerife, although excluded from the most valuable portions of land, were treated as notables by society and given the dignifying title of "Don".

At a lower social level, surviving natives were mainly used as domestic slaves or followed their traditional solitary occupations of herdsmen and gatherers.

The early colonial administration did, however, recognise and record aspects of pre-conquest native life. Land grants on Tenerife refer to "land which had belonged to the King of Güimar", or "land on the Teno road… which the Guanches used to sow". The spot on which the last chief of Taoro committed suicide also became a celebrated landmark and is referred to in many early land grants to colonists.

Towards the end of the 16th century, when the islanders were threatened with extinction, antiquarians compiled information about them, probably in imitation of the compilations by missionaries in the New World, which were becoming known in Europe.

Writing in the 1590s, Alfonso de Espinosa was still fascinated by the debate on natural law. "They did not live altogether outside law," he claimed, "for in some things their actions were according to reason." Other literature of the time began to romanticise the islanders as noble savages. Félix Lope de Vega (1562–1635), the prolific Spanish dramatist, was one who created for them a bucolic idyll, one with which the Canary island natives would probably have found it hard to identify. ❏

**LEFT:** Alonso Fernández de Lugo raises his cross.

# Columbus on the Canaries

In 1415 the existence of Europe, North Africa, and the Near East were known; by 1550 world maps had been enlarged to incorporate North, Central and South America and the rest of Africa. Spearheaded by Cristobal Colón (Christopher Columbus), the Canaries played a key strategic role in the "discovery" of these new lands.

Although Latin America is now trying to disance itself from the man who paved the way for colonisation, many European countries claim a connection with Columbus. Mallorca claims to be the birthplace of the great man, and there are two supposed burial places in mainland Spain, one at Santo Domingo and one in Seville. In the Canaries there is hardly a town without a Calle Colón and the island of La Palma has a massive cement model of one of his ships, even though this is about the only island that does not claim a direct connection with the navigator.

In fact Columbus was the son of an Italian cloth-weaver in the city of Genoa, then one of the world's greatest maritime cities. However, it was the Spanish court which eventually sponsored his expeditions. The extent of his brief flirtation with the Canaries has for a long time been the subject of local discussion, fuelled by inter-island rivalry.

It was on his second voyage of 1492, a crucial journey that ended with the discovery of Cuba, that Columbus stopped at the Canaries, putting in at La Gomera. Quite why he chose the smallest island no one knows: some suggest he already knew and was attracted to Beatriz de Bobadilla, the countess of the island; others say it was because La Gomera, being the westernmost island, was the last stepping off point of the known world.

La Gomera was by no means the best port in the islands, and Columbus evidently knew that, because when one of his fleet of three ships, the *Pinta*, broke a rudder in heavy weather, he left it to divert for repairs in Las Palmas on Gran Canaria while he hastened on to La Gomera with the *Santa María* (his flagship) and the *Niña*.

Columbus himself described passing Tenerife (the last of the islands to be conquered, still in Guanche hands, and staunchly resisting Spanish attacks) at an opportune moment, as he noted in his logbook: "As we were passing...we observed an eruption of the volcano. The smoke and flames, the glowing masses of lava, the muffled roaring from the earth's interior caused panic among the crew. They believed that the volcano had erupted because we had undertaken this voyage." Unfortunately Columbus's logbook does not go on to detail his movements through the islands on this or further journeys. Certainly the *Pinta* remained in Las Palmas for some time, and it is thought that Columbus went in search of it, although some local historians are adamant that he did not touch ground on Gran Canaria. Nevertheless Las Palmas leads

the way in Colombiana, with a museum, a Casa Colón, a statue, and a church where he supposedly prayed before setting out for the New World. This claim is also made for the church in San Sebastián de la Gomera.

Publications about the Canaries are divided about the course of the navigator. Some maintain that the only time Columbus did not make landfall in Las Palmas was during the second journey, when they acknowledge that he was clearly in Gomera. For the first, third and fourth journeys they say his resting place was Las Palmas. Others say that Columbus also stopped in Maspalomas on Gran Canaria and on the island of El Hierro, and others still prefer not to commit themselves at all. ❑

**RIGHT:** Christopher Columbus: claimed by the Old World, rejected by the New.

# DAYS OF SUGAR AND WINE

*Sugar and wine made the western islands fabulously wealthy until competition and shifting fortunes put an end to the prosperous trade*

Alonso Fernández de Lugo, whose depredations we have heard about in the previous chapter, was the man responsible for the cultivation of sugar in the western Canary Islands. In the 1480s he had seen how readily canes sprouted in the soil of Gran Canaria, and he introduced the crop to Tenerife and La Palma as soon as he completed their conquests. He introduced it to Gomera later, when the island became his by marriage.

On Tenerife he built two refineries at El Realejos, a third at Daute and a fourth at Icod. He built another on La Palma at Río de los Sauces, which he mortgaged to an English sugar merchant, Thomas Mailliard, and a Genoese financier, Francesco Spinola.

De Lugo was indefatigable in promoting the crop, often making the land grants in his gift conditional on a promise to plant canes or erect a mill. By dint of his land grants, the Orotava Valley and the adjoining coast; Icod, Daute and Garachico in the north-west; and Güimar in the east turned to the cultivation and milling of sugar for export.

## Sugar kings

The industry was capital intensive. Neither the planting of canes nor the building of mills came cheaply. Huge expenditure was needed to stoke the fires of the "purging rooms" and to pay the specialised and heavy labour the work demanded. Mill owners charged up to 50 percent of revenue from produce brought to them for processing by small cultivators.

Thus the islands acquired a capitalist élite which owned the bulk of irrigable land and controlled the output of the sugar industry. Almost all of the really rich and successful businessmen were foreigners.

The Genoese Matteo Vigna, for instance, had been an indispensable source of finance for the conquest. "Without me," he declared, "the island would not be so well peopled as it is."

**LEFT:** a wine shop when trade was flourishing.
**RIGHT:** collecting orchilla, which was used as a dye.

Tomaso Giustiniani, his fellow-countryman, had interests in sugar, dye-stuffs and fish: an indication of his status is that in 1506 the visiting Inquisitors chose to lodge in his house in La Laguna.

Cristofforo Daponte had traded in dyes before the completion of the conquest and had

been a sugar-baron since 1497. He went on to marry a niece of Alonso Fernández de Lugo and lived to cheat the Inquisition of his soul: summoned to an interrogation, he was "unable to cross over, owing to great age and many infirmities".

All these, and others like them, served for long spells on the island council of Tenerife, exploiting their economic muscle for political advantage. Their presence was resented but unshakable. Accused by Castilian colonists of favouring foreigners, de Lugo admitted the charge, but claimed it was necessary. The islands, he said, needed the Portuguese for their hard work and the Italians for their money.

The presence of large numbers of Portuguese workers made the sugar industry viable, for they were employed to harvest the canes on a share-cropping basis. Thus the Canaries were spared the need to import black slaves on a large scale; the "plantation economies" created by the monocultures of the New World never afflicted the islands.

There were plenty of other sources of social tension, however. To the disputes between Castilian-born colonists and "foreigners" was added animosity between the owners of water-sources and the landholders desperate for irrigation for their canes.

The islands seem to have been better watered in the 16th century than they are today. A writer in the 1590s referred to "a large number" of springs, streams and waterfalls in northern Tenerife; but the deforestation that produced the pitch and stoked the sugar-mills in turn diminished the rainfall of the western islands, so that today a stream that does not run dry in summer is a rare find, despite the large numbers of valleys.

## Water problems

Surface water was never abundant, however, and exploitation brought problems of its own.

### FRONTIER SOCIETY

The early colonial society of the Canary Islands was lawless and litigious. As in other "frontier societies" there were numerous criminals and fugitives among the colonists, individualists who did not conform to social norms or configurations. Vendettas originating among the families of Seville were continued in the Canaries.

Prosecution of crime and exaction of justice were difficult because of the distances which separate the archipelago from mainland Spain, and punishment could be delayed or evaded by appeals to the Iberian peninsula.

Powerful local leaders could hire thugs for their own purposes, offering them protection and disregarding the law themselves. Alonso de Lugo, for instance, used his authority, backed by his henchmen, to declare that debts to himself and his wife should be discharged before all other outstanding debts on the island.

Matteo Vigna, to whom some 100 debtors owed a total of 450,000 *maravedis*, asked the Spanish monarchs to appoint "a good man from whom he might obtain his just due, for on the said island of Tenerife he could never obtain justice". Even with the foundation of a permanent Royal Tribunal in Gran Canaria in 1526, the western Canaries never acquired adequate judicial institutions for the relief of tension between neighbours in this often violent society.

Where the right to use local water was in private hands, it divided the colonists; where its use was communal, it brought them together in tense but narrow co-operation. Irrigation communities became a widespread and effective form of social organisation.

By the mid-16th century, a balance in the distribution of water-use rights had been achieved, with fortunate consequences for the islands' future. Small growers were protected by stable communities of *adulados*, people who shared by turns. They were equipped with powers of arbitration or jurisdiction sufficient to resolve day-to-day problems without recourse to the wasteful judicial structure of the realm and without the loss of local capital in expensive appeals to the courts of the Spanish peninsula.

At the same time the monarchs and their representatives firmly resisted any attempts to distribute water more equably or to wrest control of large-scale cultivators and millers. The murder of one of the most notorious water-monopolists in 1513, for instance, achieved nothing, for his heirs enjoyed redoubled protection. The justification for this favouristism was that the era of colonisation was a critical one for the economy of the Canary Islands: a radical experiment in an unpromising place. Success depended on investment by the wealthy and enterprising few, and the authorities intended to back them to the hilt.

## Cultural exchange

By the late 16th century the lure of the New World had brought immigration to the western Canaries virtually to an end; an era of demographic stagnancy was beginning. Yet enduring features of the three large islands of Tenerife, La Palma and Gomera were already taking shape. The primitive culture of the pre-conquest islanders had been overwhelmed by the civilisation of the invaders and replaced by a new society. Ultimately, the ancient Canarios were neither exterminated nor "acculturated" but simply assimilated. Caspar Frutuoso's description of La Palma at the end of the 16th century is an eloquent testimony: the three main populations of that island – Castilian, Portuguese and indigenous – were more or less

**LEFT:** an early representation of La Laguna.
**RIGHT:** it was an age of wine and music, according to a contemporary painting.

equally mixed, according to his impression, and already interbred to a great extent; those who conserved their ethnic identity coexisted as equals, and were indistinguishable in faith and habit. The colonial transformation was as thorough as anywhere in the Hispanic world.

Present-day islanders conserve traces of the pre-conquest past in a few areas of folklore, diet and dance. They find myths of Guanche survival comforting. But all save a tiny minority regard themselves as Spaniards. They do not think of the conquest as an alien triumph, like contemporary Mexicans or Peruvians do, but tend to identify with the conquerors.

## From sugar to wine

The sugar-based prosperity of the 16th century did not last. The development of sugar plantations in the Antilles and Brazil created a cheap and abundant source of supply which undercut Canarian production. Nevertheless, the growth of trade with the New World opened up the possibility of new economic strategies which the western islands, and Tenerife in particular, were able to exploit successfully.

The sugar market had been confined to the Old World, and to northern outlets in particular, such as England, Flanders and Germany; strong southern wine became the sought-after product to replace sugar, and it was also much in demand in the growing American colonies. The Malvasia grape, in particular, which had originated in the Aegean islands, and had been carried by Genoese planters to Sicily, and then to Madeira and the Canaries, proved highly adaptable, especially in Tenerife.

Malvasia was already established in the eastern Canaries by the late 15th century. It yielded specialist, sweet luxury wines, which were suited to long-distance trade, because they travelled well; commanded higher prices than drier, thinner local wines; and appealed particularly to northern tastes. Malmsey and Madeira are among its modern progeny. By the time Shake-

speare's Falstaff and Sir Toby Belch were draining "cups of Canary", wine was taking over as the islands' major export. To Bostonians of the late 17th century, the archipelago was known as "the Isles of Wine".

The fortunes of Canarian viticulture depended on access to trade. The most important trade routes were those to and from the New World, not only because of American markets for Canary wine but also because the New World trade needed Atlantic staging-posts which would attract shipping from all over Europe.

The Canaries were ideally placed – especially Tenerife, which had a range of fine oceanic harbours, and Gomera, which possessed the most westerly port on the route to the West Indies: the Atlantic wind-system made them ideal ports of call for shipping bound for the New World. But for almost the first three centuries of transatlantic navigation it was the policy of the Spanish crown to restrict the benefits of New World trade to Castilian subjects only, and the most effective way of excluding interlopers was to confine all traffic to one or two peninsular ports.

Thus the Canaries became the focal point for every kind of attempt to break into Spain's New World monopoly – smuggling, fraud, piracy were all most easily practised in the islands. In the 1560s, the Spanish monarchy introduced strict regulation and vigilance of the archipelago's trade with America, and native traders suffered along with the foreigners.

## Short-lived prosperity

No island benefited more than Tenerife from the relaxation of this system in 1610. One of her major ports, Santa Cruz, had recently been enlarged; her wine production exceeded that of other islands, and she had foreign connections and expatriate residents of long standing.

The consequent prosperity was reflected in rising fortunes that created an aristocracy of *bourgeois gentilhommes* in the island over the next 75 years.

Foreign capitalists converged on Tenerife to export the trade and cash in on New World routes. In the mid-century there were 1,500 English and Dutch residents in a total population of under 50,000. In 1665, the Canary Island Company was formed in London, with exclusive rights to trade in Canarian wines in England, and with the aim of cornering the

---

### STAIRWAY TO HEAVEN

Charles II's historiographer, James Howell, wrote that Canarian wines, "are accounted... the most desecated from all earthly grossness: it hath little or no sulphur at all in it, and leaves less dregs behind, though one drink it to excess. Of this wine... may be verified that merry induction that good wine makes good blood, good blood causeth good humours, good humours cause good thoughts, good thoughts bring forth good works, good works carry a man to heaven; ergo, good wine carrieth a man to heaven. If this be true, surely more English go to heaven than any other; for I think there is more Canary brought into England than to all the world besides."

market, but Francisco Tomás Alfaro, a Tenerife merchant, led the way in defying the monopoly.

The dispute came at a time of doubling prices in London, but hopes of great prosperity were short-lived. Tenerife's wines were easy to under-cut, and over-production and declining quality threatened their domination of the market. In July 1675 the island council banned the planting of new vines; and in 1685–87 famine and a plague of locusts wrecked production. But with the English imposing a ban on Canary wines in retaliation for the rejection of the Canary Island Company, there was no market in any case.

Eventually the War of the Spanish Succession (1701–14) wrecked the trade. Down to less than 2,500 pipes a year by the end of the war, import levels in England never recovered.

## Foreign dynasties

The fortunes of the Tenerife economy revived, and were sustained at a respectable level during the 18th century, thanks to the entrepreneurship of a number of merchant-dynasties in Tenerife, many of which were foreign. John Colgan Blanco, who was predominant among an influential Irish community which flourished in the mid-18th century, found the solution to the

Las Palmas. *Un lagar.*

The ruin of the English market was caused by a combination of events. The price of Malvasia made it vulnerable to competition: in 1670 it was twice the price of claret, and £4 dearer than Malaga wine, which was similar in character. Meanwhile, the slow but irresistible rise of Madeira wine was having an effect. It broke into the English market on a large scale in the 1680s, and aided by the Methuen Treaty of 1703, which granted favourable terms of trade to Britain's Portuguese allies, gradually came to displace Malvasia in English taste.

**LEFT:** wine is once more an important export.
**ABOVE:** a wine press, known as a *lagar*.

problem of Tenerife's failing viticulture. The island had always produced a cheaper wine from second-class grapes, known as Vidueño. Colgan turned these wines into an ersatz Madeira to undercut the Portuguese suppliers, ensured that it had the requisite body and colour, and offered it at competitive prices. From 1766 he exported it to British East India, at £10 for a pipe to Madeira's £24.

Market penetration was never very strong within Europe, but in Britain's American colonies it enjoyed enormous popularity, and in East India his "Madeira" established itself as a favourite sundowner's tipple, bringing a flavour of metropolitan life to distant colonies. ❑

# CHANGING FORTUNES

*Inter-island rivalry and the struggle for independence from Spain have helped to shape the past two centuries of Canarian history*

In the baroque-style streets of the wine-rich towns like Orotava in Tenerife and Los Llanos in La Palma, signs of Tenerife's fragile 18th-century prosperity are still visible. Even Santa Cruz de Tenerife, which was only a small port in the 18th century, has the sumptuous Casa de La Carta (also known as Casa de los Hamilton) with its intricately carved wooden cloister.

Tenerife is home to the richest architectural ensemble because it dominated the wine trade (*see pages 39–41*). Nearly 60 percent of Canarian wine came from this island in the 1770s, and it always enjoyed the lion's share of concessions to trade with the New World.

When uninhibited trade was allowed to selected ports in 1778, Santa Cruz de Tenerife was the only Canarian outlet included on the list. In the 1770s Tenerife was producing over four times as much wine as any of the other islands, over half as much corn and more than three times as many potatoes.

The population of the island was nearly 70,000 – an increase of almost 60 percent over 100 years. According to the census of 1768, Gran Canaria, Tenerife's rival to the east, had just over 40,000 inhabitants.

Tenerife's industry created wealth, while the other islands provided her with manpower. Prosperity also produced an intelligentsia: no other island had a comparable intellectual life. The Casa Nava Grimón in La Laguna was the setting of a lively *salón*, attended by figures who were held in high esteem in mainland Spain: Tomás de Iriarte, for instance, who was librarian to the king of Spain, and José de Viera y Clavijo, one of the few 18th-century Spanish historians, both dedicated their major work of research to the history of the Canaries.

In 1788 the Jardín Botánico (Botanical Garden) of Orotava was founded; and in La Laguna were concentrated efforts to found a university, although the initial plans eventually foundered.

But the golden age did not last, and Viera y Clavijo himself recorded the apogee and incipient decline of Tenerife's trade. "Her glories" he wrote in 1776, "are passing into oblivion." He bemoaned the lack of ideas and of enlightened spirits; the remoteness of the court and the rule of indifferent bureaucrats from the pe-

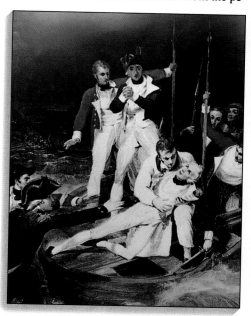

ninsula; the shortage of rain; the exposure to southern winds, which brought the locusts, and northern winds, which brought the pirates. Above all, he noted, the demand for Canarian wine was beginning to diminish.

## Looking for substitutes

For the rest of the century trade was in a state of crisis. Disrupted by the American war, and ironically damaged by the much-vaunted trade decree of 1778, which in effect increased competition from peninsular wines, the situation was only temporarily restored by the peculiar conditions of the French Revolutionary and Napoleonic Wars.

**LEFT:** a Spanish privateer protecting the islands.
**RIGHT:** Nelson falls during the attack of 1797.

In 1797, when Nelson's attack on Santa Cruz was beaten off, the citizens rowed out a present of wine to the defeated commander. It was a publicity gesture worthy of John Colgan Blanco, the earlier genius of the wine trade, himself. For a while the British navy consumed Tenerife's wine surplus during the blockade of the Atlantic against French shipping, but this unexpected reprieve was brought to an end by the peace of 1815.

By then, revolutions in Spain's American colonies posed an even more severe threat to the Canarian economy. Previously the islands' generally adverse balance of trade had been made

from Mexico in 1825 and exported on a large scale in the third quarter of the century, was concentrated in the eastern Canary Islands. The policy-makers in Tenerife claimed that they were not taken in by the "illusion of salvation" which cochineal represented. Even so, the arboriculturists of Orotava were aghast at the damage wrought in their native forests by the cochineal craze.

The cochineal grubs formed and fed on a peculiar species of cactus, which, in some areas, displaced native pines or defunct vines and canes. The ugly bulk of these plants, it was said, disfigured the landscape and threatened

up by remittances from Canarian workers in the American colonies, but the disruption of their payments home caused by the war reduced their families to irremediable misery.

There was no substitute to hand for the declining wine trade. La Palma was a little better off, as sugar production and trade had not been entirely eradicated there. Whereas the last sugar tithe in Gran Canaria was paid in 1648, and in Tenerife in 1718, La Palma still had a productive sugar mill in operation for most of the 19th century, although by then it had become a local industry.

The main new product of the mid-19th century, cochineal, which had been introduced

### TEMPORARY BENEFITS

In La Palma, silk made a contribution to the ailing economy. Mulberries had been introduced there as early as 1517 by Diego de Funes, a Tenerife physician. By the mid-1770s there were 3,000 weavers, but exports seem to have been directed to the same markets as wine, and production plummeted after the Napoleonic Wars.

La Palma and Gomera were also to reap the benefits of a well-run tobacco industry. Its leading figure was the creator of the Don Miguel brand, Don Miguel himself, who proudly showed foreign visitors round his factory in Tazacorte. But such successes were sporadic, and the structural problems of the economy remained unsolved.

the rainfall levels when planted in place of trees. When the cochineal boom was destroyed by the rapid rise of chemical dyes in the 1870s and 1880s, the intelligentsia of the western islands counted themselves fortunate that Tenerife, La Palma, La Gomera and El Hierro had largely escaped the scourge.

The "scourge" had been a profitable one while it lasted, however, and those islands which rejected it had few alternative crops with which to boost their flagging economies. A 19th-century English visitor to El Hierro reported, "there is no sign of the island having benefited by the sudden influx of wealth which cochineal brought generally to the archipelago. There are no public works half finished, and no large houses going to decay. All is poverty. The inhabitants are peasants, and the best of them are still but well-to-do peasants."

## Capital of the Canaries

Given this background, visitors to Santa Cruz de Tenerife today might be surprised by the appearance of prosperity. The Masonic eye that stares from the pediment of the temple in Calle San Lúcas seems to retain the glint of a bourgeois plutocracy. It is easy to imagine this same well-heeled class strolling by the ceramic-tiled fountains of the Parque Sanabria or making their homes in the elegant villas that surround it. And in the high Victorian splendour of the Teatro Guimerá, the ostentation of provincial parvenues is magnificently evoked.

Yet Santa Cruz is unrepresentative. In 1822 it was transformed from a modest port into the capital of the archipelago, where most of the institutions of government were concentrated. What is more, the town's monuments and opulent architecture date mostly from the very late 19th or early 20th centuries, when, thanks to steamship navigation, the fortunes of the archipelago had begun to revive.

Only a return to the free trade regime of the early and mid-16th century could have freed the islands of their dependence on vulnerable monocultures and structural trade deficits. The

dawn of the steamship age and the huge increase in European navigation to West Africa in the second half of the 19th century created the opportunity for such a revival of fortunes.

In 1852, following the examples of the Portuguese in their Atlantic islands, the government of the Spanish queen, Isabella II, decided to make the Canary Islands a free trade zone. Free-port status was granted to one port in each of the islands, except for Tenerife, which was allowed two – one at Santa Cruz

and one in what is now Puerto de la Cruz. In 1868 the entire archipelago was declared open to foreign shipping.

## Dispute between the islands

At first Tenerife was able to use its privileged status as the "capital" of the archipelago to channel new resources for her own benefit. Money was directed towards the painfully slow business of erecting an infrastructure for the internal development of the islands. In the 1860s Tenerife had the only first-class road in the archipelago, but even that extended only from Santa Cruz to Orotava . It was not until 1876 that the highway south reached as far as

---

**LEFT:** a bust of Nelson in Santa Cruz's Museo Militar; a cochineal colony on a cactus.
**RIGHT:** the Teatro Guimerá in Santa Cruz.

Güimar. Yet by the standards of the other islands this seemed absolutely spectacular. Gran Canaria, whose inhabitants felt starved of resources by what they perceived as the greed of the *tinerfeños* (as the Tenerife islanders are called), had barely 16 km (10 miles) of first-class road.

The resentment such disparities provoked helped to stimulate a political movement in Gran Canaria and, to a lesser extent, in the minor islands, aimed at increasing the autonomy of individual islands, or dividing the archipelago into two provinces with a capital in Las Palmas as well as Santa Cruz.

**CALLS FOR INDEPENDENCE**

In 1810 the Canarian Junta called for "a patriotic government, independent of that of the peninsula, to watch over all the Tribunals set up in the Province", and raised the Canarios' desire "to get rid of all the Spaniards now here and to put the people of this land in their place". In the late 19th century the voice calling most vociferously for independence was that of Secindino Delgado, who as a boy had taken advantage of a free passage to Cuba for anyone prepared to work there. He returned briefly to the Canaries in 1896 and the following year, in Venezuela, founded *El Guanche*, a newspaper promoting the cause of independence (*see page 69*).

Tenerife successfully resisted this initiative, but her economic supremacy was eroded by the development of Las Palmas as a harbour for steamships. In 1881 a harbour improvement scheme for Las Palmas was rushed through the Spanish government programme by Canarian politician, Fernando León y Castillo, whose power base was in Gran Canaria. The effect was swift and phenomenal.

By 1887, Las Palmas was carrying more traffic than Santa Cruz, and the huge foreign, particularly British, investment of the 1890s in coaling, fruit production, hotels and financial services tended to benefit Gran Canaria first and foremost. The western islands were not bypassed by the new prosperity, however, partly thanks to the continued importance of the port of Santa Cruz de Tenerife (even though it was in eclipse), but chiefly due to the beginnings of mass cultivation of bananas in the 1880s.

### Banana business

The commercially exploitable "Chinese" banana was introduced in 1855 by the French consul, Sabine Berthelot, who contributed so much to the study of the ethnology and natural history of the islands. The fruit had been known in other forms in the archipelago since the 16th century, when it was described by the English merchant Thomas Nichols as resembling a cucumber and "best eaten black, when it is sweeter than any confection". A *tinerfeño* trader of English origin, Pedro Reid, launched the first exports from 1880; the firm of Wolfson and Fyffe followed, laying the basis of what was to become a virtual monopoly.

In the 1890s the introduction of refrigerated shipping facilitated further growth in the banana industry, as it did in other areas of food production and transport. The Orotava Valley became carpeted with the thick fronds of banana plants that still cover much of the area. When the trade peaked in 1913, nearly 3.5 million hands of bananas were being exported from Tenerife, La Palma and Gran Canaria.

Yet the recurrent pattern of Canarian economic history could not be escaped. Just as the sugar trade had collapsed in the late 16th century, that of Malvasia wine in the early 18th century, and cochineal after only a generation's span of success, so banana exports were wrecked, after a scarcely longer supremacy, by World War I.

British control of seaways and the islands' internal economy made Canarian involvement in the war greater, and its effects more severe, than in mainland Spain. From 1913 to 1917, banana exports fell by over 80 percent and the unit value by nearly as much. Poverty and unemployment were endemic, and emigration became a flood. Such was the flow to the New World that the main post office of Santa Cruz had special letter-boxes for mail to Cuba and Venezuela. The process of recovery was slow and imperfect, impeded by global depressions and recessions. Indeed, Santa Cruz did not attain her pre-war levels of traffic until 1950.

The proclamation of the Spanish Second Republic in 1931 excited new aspirations. It was hoped that the Canaries, like other communities within the Spanish state, might obtain federal or, at least, quasi-federal autonomy, with Santa Cruz as the capital. An assembly, under the flamboyant Gil Roldán, convened in Santa Cruz insisting that the islands were "a unique natural region, endowed with a right to full autonomy, under the sovereign power of Spain". This status was not granted, and the programme was stultified by the advent of civil war in 1936, but the future of the islands had been foreshadowed. Under the devolved con-

Battered by economic ill fortune Tenerife seemed to lose heart in the struggle to retain political leadership over Gran Canaria. In 1927, the formal division of the archipelago into two provinces was meekly accepted. Santa Cruz became a provincial centre for the four western islands (Tenerife, La Palma, La Gomera and El Hierro), consoling itself with the fact that of the two provinces, its own was by far the bigger, richer and more populous, although Las Palmas excelled as a city in every way.

**LEFT:** harvest time on a banana plantation.
**ABOVE:** General Franco and friends, on one of his rare visits to Tenerife.

stitution of 1978, the Canaries became one of 14 autonomous regions of Spain (there are now 17), with extended powers given to each island's *cabildo*.

## Rejection and recovery

The outcome of the bitter Spanish Civil War was fortuitous for the Canaries. This was not because Franco had launched his campaign from Tenerife when he flew from his command post there on 18 July 1936 to rally his African troops to the rebel cause. Nor was it because the islanders had great sympathy for Franco's cause. It was far more prosaic than that: the Nationalists' victory in the war ensured that the free port privileges of the island became of even greater significance under a protectionist and autarchic regime, which allowed the islands to continue enjoying the economic benefits of free trade – although it took a while for these benefits to be felt. In the aftermath of World War II, Spain was ostracised by the USA and Europe, and her people suffered enormous hardships. But in the early 1950s US bases were established on the mainland, military aid was granted, and Spain became accepted as part of the international community.

The dictatorship ultimately brought long-deferred prosperity to the islands. The basis of

this recovery, in the western islands, was the continuing role of Santa Cruz as a staging-post for long-range shipping, with the growing diversity of the agrarian sector, based on bananas, tomatoes, potatoes and tobacco, large-scale fishing and the processing of foodstuffs.

## Island independence

Under Franco, the islanders were obliged to become loyal Spaniards. Banned by Franco and spurned by Republicans in exile, the Canarian independence movement which had been active in the late 19th century (*see page 69*), languished. But in 1963 MPAIAC (Movement for Self-Determination) was founded, its manifes-

to stating that Canarios were "a self-contained unity distinct from Spaniards".

In 1976–77, as Franco slipped into history, MPAIAC turned to terrorism, launching bomb attacks against peninsula-based companies and military targets. Its leader, Antonio Cubillo, was expelled; he returned to head the Canarian Nationalist Congress Party (CNC), but this had little electoral success. More moderate parties, the left-of-centre Coalición Canaria, and the right-of-centre Partido Popular, have split the vote between them in elections to the island's 60-member parliament.

One of the first tasks the coalition parties had to tackle was the wound of inter-island rivalry. A compromise was worked out whereby the status of capital is shared by Santa Cruz and Las Palmas. Government departments maintain offices in both capitals, and the presidency of the Autonomous Government alternates between the two every four years.

Autonomy for the Canaries means they defer to Madrid in matters of defence, foreign affairs and fiscal policy, but retain control over education, health, transport and culture. The Canarian parliament also has the power to vary taxation and thus raise additional funds. Although the Canaries are members of the European Union, they enjoy special status regarding import tax. Tobacco, alcohol, electronic goods and cameras are sold at duty-free prices, and VAT is only 4.5 percent compared with 16 percent on the mainland. The Canaries argue that low import duty is a quid pro quo for the high cost of importing goods; so far the EU has accepted this argument, but with pressure from Brussels for Europe-wide tax harmonisation it is unclear how long this will last.

The Canaries burgeoning tourism industry could probably survive increased taxation: the islands enjoy almost a monopoly as regards winter sunshine, and 80 percent of the GDP is tourism-related. But the wealth is unevenly spread, with smaller islands attracting fewer visitors, and relying more on agriculture, shipping and food processing. Some put the unemployment rate in the Canaries as high as 24 percent, and the average wage as the lowest in Europe – that is the problem that the Canarios face in the first decade of the 21st century. ❑

**LEFT:** the Monumento de los Caídos in Santa Cruz, a memorial to those who died in the Civil War.

# Franco's coup

The summer of 1936 was hot and sticky in the Canaries. Weather fronts from the Sahara brought a succession of scorching winds and choking dust. A paunchy little man called Francisco Franco Bahamonde, once Commander-in-Chief of the Spanish Army, must have found his Canarian posting gruelling. In March of that year Franco had been sent to Tenerife by the Republican government, fearful of his reputation as a soldier and of his right-wing sentiments – he was suspected of being involved in a series of plots aimed at setting up a dictatorship under a fellow officer, General Sanjurjo. While Sanjurjo was exiled to Portugal, Franco managed to wriggle out of charges of complicity.

In Sanjurjo's absence the plotters were headed by General Emilio Mola, who went to Germany seeking arms and ammunition. Franco agreed to back Sanjurjo, joining other discontented officers at their meetings in Tenerife or on Gran Canaria.

Franco refused to commit himself to any firm plan of action until he received the promise of command of Spain's best troops – tough Moroccan mercenaries and the ruthless Foreign Legion. Within 48 hours a plane had been chartered from Croydon aerodrome near London.

On 14 July 1936 the plane touched down at Gando airport (now Las Palmas). On board was a select party of English tourists, one of whom – Hugh Pollard, a retired army major – contacted one of Franco's officers and delivered his message – "*Galicia saluda a Francia*" (Galicia greets France).

On 16 July the ex-RAF pilot of the Dragon Rapide plane was warned to be ready. The same day, the commanding officer of the Las Palmas garrison, General Amadeo Balmes, conveniently died as he cleaned his pistol. By nightfall Franco had obtained permission to travel to his fellow-officer's funeral.

At midnight Franco and his wife and daughter boarded the Clyde-built steamer, the *Viera y Clavijo*. Shortly after docking in Las Palmas, he found that an arms search of the rebel HQ in Melilla on the Moroccan coastline had forced North African garrisons to start the uprising prematurely.

During that hot and hectic afternoon Franco left Las Palmas for the airport. Perhaps fearing an assassination attempt – he had survived three during his short spell on Tenerife – he commandeered "a

scruffy tugboat" to get him there. By the early hours of 18 July, Franco was in North Africa to broadcast his manifesto, promising "to make real in our homeland, for the first time and in this order, that trinity, Fraternity, Liberty and Equality".

The Canary Islands were in Franco's hands by 20 July. On the island of La Palma a false normality was maintained for a further eight sweltering days until the capital, Santa Cruz, was finally bombarded by a pro-Franco cruiser, and surrendered.

Within hours the repression began. Trade unionists, teachers, left-wing or democratic politicians, and writers and artists were imprisoned or murdered. Lieutenant Gonzalez Campos, the only offi-

cer in Tenerife to oppose the rising, was given a summary court-martial, along with the civil governor and his staff, and shot. The governor's crime had been to shout, "Long live libertarian communism", though he was neither a libertarian nor a communist, and independent witnesses heard only the words "Long live the Republic".

Republican prisoners in Tenerife were herded into Fyffes' warehouse, near the present football ground in Santa Cruz. There they sweated it out, waiting to be shot in batches in the appropriately named Barranco del Infierno (Hell's Ravine) until the sport grew tedious for their killers. The oil refinery now marks the spot, while street names still recall the days of Franco's rule. ❑

RIGHT: a somewhat romanticised portrayal of General Franco, painted by Enrique Segura.

# PIONEERS AND PUBLICISTS

*During the 19th century the Canary Islands proved irresistible to
a number of European scientists, writers and artists*

It was during the gloomiest era in the islands' economic history – the mid-19th century, when the wine trade had collapsed and only the short-lived cochineal industry offered any hope for the future – that foreign visitors were first attracted to the Canaries, and initiated what, in the long term, was to prove the most exploitable industry of all.

## Scholastic attraction

The first such visitors were scholars attracted by the islands' geology, climatology, botany and ethnography. They included German scientists Alexander von Humboldt and Leopold von Buch, who attempted to compile a systematic natural history of the islands from personal observations. The most influential of the early observers was Sabin Berthelot, a French diplomat who arrived in 1820, at the age of 26.

His main interest was in the acclimatisation of tropical plants and fauna. During a first stay of ten years, Berthelot became director of the Botanical Gardens, played a major role in the acclimatisation of cochineal and developed a passionate interest in all aspects of Canariana.

In 1839 he published a miscellany of Canarian life and landscape, enlivened by engravings which introduced the Parisian public to the romantic scenery and dress of the archipelago. In 1842 *L'Ethnographie et les Annales de la conquête* followed. Eight further volumes, written with the collaboration of the English botanist, F.B. Webb, completed his *Histoire naturelle des Iles Canaries*.

After an absence of some years, Berthelot returned to the islands as French Consul in Santa Cruz de Tenerife. "My friends," he declared on disembarking, "I have come to die among you". The prophecy was true, if long delayed. He died on Tenerife in November 1880, "an islander at heart", as he said.

---

**PRECEDING PAGES:** some 19th-century visitors were provided with transport.
**LEFT:** the islands had a romantic aura.
**RIGHT:** Sabin Berthelot, who loved Tenerife.

In the 1850s the islands had become more accessible via steamships from Cadiz to Las Palmas and Santa Cruz de Tenerife. Berthelot's tireless enthusiasm, and his friendships and collaboration with English scientists and artists extended the islands' appeal to England, and initiated a tradition of English interest.

## Elizabeth Murray

Notable among English visitors was a remarkable woman who arrived as the wife of a British Consul in 1850. Elizabeth Murray was the daughter of a reputable portraitist who had painted the Duke of Wellington and his staff in Spain in 1812, during the Peninsular Wars.

When her father died in 1835 she was able to exploit his connections to pursue a surprisingly independent way of life. Having, as she said, "neither master nor money", she travelled in the Mediterranean, completing her artistic education in a fashionable manner. Elizabeth first exhibited at the London Royal Academy in 1834, and a year later she was commissioned to paint views of Malta for Queen Adelaide. From there she went to Constantinople and developed a talent for exotic street scenes. Elizabeth found her ideal milieu in Morocco, where she spent nearly eight years. In 1846 she married the British Consul, and his posting to Santa Cruz took her, via Seville and Cadiz, to the islands, where she was received with enthusiasm by the local intellectuals and artists.

Murray was captivated by the scenery of the Canaries; she declared the view of the islands as she approached by ship "a spectacle which has nothing to match it in any other part of the world". She was indefatigable in seeking out subjects in the hinterland of Tenerife, accompanied only by a couple of servants.

Her sketches and observations formed the major part of *Sixteen Years of an Artist's Life in Morocco, Spain and the Canary Islands*, which appeared in 1859. Despite her lavish praise for the islands' topographical beauty, she declared Las Palmas "rather gloomy and uninteresting", and Santa Cruz containing nothing "of remarkable interest to the visitor". She found the religion distasteful, dress risible, architecture modest and mendicants offensive. The Canarian intelligentsia, who had welcomed her so heartily, now felt betrayed. They saw themselves depicted

as coarse, brutish, isolated and culturally impoverished – "speaking in dialect and living in caves" a Las Palmas newspaper complained. The press, which had begun by publishing extracts from her work, soon suppressed it and began printing shocked denunciations of the authoress. It was fortunate that her husband was recalled in 1860.

Outside the Canaries, however, Mrs Murray's book was a positive influence, one which showed an agreeable, and marketable, perception of the islands. What mattered were her attractive pictures, not her rather affected prose. The view of Orotova which forms the frontispiece of the second volume is enchanting. The steeply sloping

## ENGLISH ODDITIES

From the mid-16th century two categories of English residents had been well established in the Canaries: merchants and prisoners of the Inquisition: no less than 80 percent of the penitents who faced the tribunal of Las Palmas in the 18th century were English subjects. Few had felt much love for the islands. Notable exceptions were Thomas Nichols, a 16th-century sugar merchant, who published *A Pleasant Description of the Fortunate Islands*, containing the first description in English of eating a banana; and George Glas, who in 1764 produced a somewhat capricious translation of a history of the islands written by a late 16th-century Franciscan.

city with its baroque towers and cloisters, and the gleaming pyramid of El Teide beyond, remains an almost unspoilt view today.

Elizabeth Murray had a Victorian eye. She selected the romantic, the sentimental, the exotic and the picturesque in her genre scenes and landscapes; and she inclined to heavy-handed social comment in portraits of urchins, beggars and priests. The images which outraged the islanders appealed to public opinion abroad.

### Depictions of paradise

Elizabeth Murray never returned to the islands, but she influenced other image makers, including Marianne North, the well-connected daughter of an English MP. On a visit to Tenerife in 1875 she painted a large number of exotic plants, many sketched in the Botanical Gardens of Orotava. Her written recollections of Tenerife, in which the Canaries were depicted as a sort of paradise, where climate and views were perfect, reached a wide readership when it was published in 1892.

The last, most influential and the most formidable of the British Victorian viragos who travelled to the Canaries was Mrs Olivia Stone, who toured the islands in the winter and early spring of 1884. Mrs Stone was a professional travel writer whose aim was to facilitate travel and equip the tourist with a practical guide. In a letter to *The Times*, her husband declared her findings: that the Canaries "require only to be known, to be much resorted to by the English".

As her assistant, her husband made the first extensive photographic record of the islands, and her book was lavishly illustrated with his work. Her inspection of the archipelago was exceptionally thorough. She was the first English writer to visit every island and the first Englishwoman to set foot on El Hierro.

The notes Olivia Stone wrote up daily on donkey-back yielded an Arcadian image: the Canary Islands were a place where rainy mornings were so rare that people rose to look at them, and where poor health could be transformed by a salubrious climate. The first

**LEFT:** Santa Cruz harbour was transformed when steamships arrived.
**RIGHT:** the Marquess of Bute in fancy dress.

edition of *Tenerife and its Six Satellites* appeared in 1887, and Mrs Stone could be pardoned for congratulating herself, by the time the 1889 edition was published, that "visitors have poured into the islands" as a result.

### Fashion and culture

The most illustrious of these visitors was the distinguished 19th-century Scottish Catholic convert, the Marquess of Bute. In the 1870s he had devoted his wealth and dazzling linguistic skills to philanthropic works, and to

> **FOLLOWING A LEADER**
>
> The aim of travel writer, Mrs Olivia Stone, was to establish "the best way of going round the islands to see the scenery" – an example followed by Insight Guides.

travels in Italy and the Near East which produced an important series of academic translations. He went to Tenerife to improve his health, thereby establishing the fashionable credentials of the islands.

Bute became passionately interested in the Guanche culture, and while his contribution to the literature was modest, there is an interesting by-product. He acquired the entire records of the early Canarian Inquisition, hoping they might contain fragments of native speech. He subsequently presented the papers to the Museo Canario of Las Palmas, making the Canaries the only province of Spain to retain their early Inquisitorial archives *in situ*. ❑

# AN ARTISTIC ODYSSEY

*Marianne North, a remarkable artist, painted the flora and fauna of Tenerife*
*in the late 19th century. This is an extract from her autobiography*

*Marianne North spent much of her life roaming the world, recording natural history in a remarkable series of paintings now housed in the Marianne North Gallery in London's Kew Gardens. In 1875 she visited Tenerife, and recalled her impressions in her autobiography, "Recollections of a Happy Life", published in 1892. The following are extracts from that book.*

In the morning we landed at Santa Cruz. We drove on the same day to Villa de Orotava, creeping slowly up the long zigzags leading to Laguna, where everyone spends the hot summer months; in the New Year it was quite deserted, and looked as if every other house was a defunct convent. All had a most magnificent yellow stone-crop on their roofs, just then in full beauty; ferns too were on all the walls, with euphorbias and other prickly things.

After passing Laguna, we came on a richer country, and soon to the famous view of the Peak, described so exquisitely by [Alexander von] Humboldt; but, alas, the palms and other trees had been cleared away to make room for the ugly terraces of cacti, grown for the cochineal insect to feed on.

Some of the terraces were apparently yielding crops of white paper bun-bags. On investigating I found they were white rags, which had been first spread over the trays of cochineal eggs, when the newly-hatched insect had crawled out and adhered to them; they are pinned over the cactus leaves by means of the spines of another sort of cactus grown for the purpose. After a few days of sunshine the little insect gets hungry and fixes itself on the fleshy leaf; then the rags are pulled off, washed, and put over another set of trays. The real cochineal cactus had had its spines so constantly pulled off by angry natives who object to having their clothes torn, that it sees no use in growing them any longer, and has hardly any.

**LEFT:** one of Marianne North's realistic still lifes.
**RIGHT:** the artist at her easel.

The roads were very bare, and the much-talked-of Peak with its snow cap was spoiled for beauty by the ugly straight line of the Hog's Back on this southern side. Nevertheless the long slant down to the deep blue sea was exceedingly beautiful, and a certain number of date-palms and dragon-trees, as well as

the euphorbia and other fleshy plants, gave a peculiar character to the scene.

We found there was a hotel and we got possession of its huge ball-room, which was full of crockery and looking-glasses, and some hundred chairs all piled up on the top of one another. This room had glass doors, besides other rooms opening into it, but served to sleep in well enough; and I determined to stay and make the best of it, for the climate and views were quite perfect.

The people at Orotava were most friendly, the gardens lovely. The nobles who owned them were of the very bluest blood of old Spain; but not rich – they seldom went out of the island, and had kept all their old habits and fashions. The ladies walked about in mantillas, flirting their fans, and wore no other costume even at their evening receptions, merely adding some jewels, and flowers stuck most becomingly behind their ears. They had no education beyond what they got in some convent, but were thorough ladies. One old lady reigned supreme among them – the Marchesa de la Florida. When the good people found my hobby for painting strange plants, they sent me all kinds of beautiful specimens.

**THE DRAGON TREE**

"The Swiss manager of the Botanic Gardens [in Orotava], who also kept a grocer's shop, was very kind in taking me to see all the most lovely gardens. The famous Dragon Tree, which Alexander von Humboldt said was 4,000 years old, had tumbled into a mere dust-heap, nothing but a few bits of bark remaining; but it had some very fine successors about the island, and some of them had curious air roots hanging from the upper branches near the trunk, which spread themselves gradually round the surface, till they recoated the poor tree, which had been continually bled to procure the dye called Dragon's Blood."

## Travels on a donkey

My friend the gardener arranged with the farmer at the Barenca da Castro to take me in for three day; so I took some bread and a pillow, mounted my donkey, and rode thither through lovely lanes, mounting over the high cliffs till I came to my destination – an old manor-house on the edge of one of those curious lava cracks which run down to the edge of the sea, filled with large oaks, sweet bay-trees, and heath-trees thirty feet high. Half-way down was a stratum of limestone, from which a most delicious spring burst out.

The ground was covered with sweet violets. There were green beds of water-cresses all about the sweet clear pools on the little theatre of green at the mouth of the cave, and then some pretty falls to the lava rocks on the beach some thousand feet below.

People and animals were always coming and going, and were very picturesque. The men wore high top-boots, blankets gathered in round their necks, and huge Rubens hats. The women had bright-coloured shawls draped gracefully over their heads and shoulders, with red and black petticoats; sometimes hats on the top of their shawl-covered heads. They were all most friendly.

My quarters at the old house above were very primitive. A great barn-like room was given up to me, with heaps of potatoes and corn swept up into the corners of it. I had a stretcher-bed at one end, on which I got a very large allowance of good sleep. The cocks and hens roosted on the beams overhead and I heard my donkey and other beasts munching their food and snoring below. From the unglazed window I had a magnificent view of the Peak, which I could paint at my leisure at sunrise without disturbing any one. I returned [to Orotava] by a lower road, close to the edge of the sea, under cliffs covered with sedums, cinerarias, and other plants peculiar to the Canary Islands.

I stopped a while at the Rambla de Castra, on the sea-shore, standing almost in the sea, surrounded by palms, bamboos, and great *Caladium esculentum*. It was a lovely spot, but too glaring. After this little excursion I remained quietly working in or about Orotava till the 17th of February, when I moved down to Mr Smith's comfortable home at Puerto de Orotava. Mr

Smith when I stayed with him had a second wife, a most lovable Scotchwoman. He was 70 years old, and talked calmly of taking me up the Peak, not minding 15 hours on horseback; but the weather fortunately remained too cool for such an attempt. I believe he knew every stone on the way, and had shown it to Piazzi Smyth and all the travellers one after the other.

## A profusion of flowers

I had a room on the roof with a separate staircase down to the lovely garden, and learned to know every plant in that exquisite collection. There were myrtle-trees 10 or 12 feet high, bougainvilleas running up cypress-trees (Mrs S used to complain of their untidiness), great white lancifolium lilies (or something like them), growing high as myself. The ground was white with fallen orange and lemon petals; and the huge white cherokee roses covered a great arbour and tool-house with their magnificent flowers. I never smelt roses so sweet as those. Over all peeped the snowy point of the Peak, at sunrise and sunset most gorgeous, but even more dazzling in the moonlight. From the garden I could stroll up some wild hills of lava, where Mr S had allowed the natural vegetation of the island to have all its own way.

Magnificent aloes, cactus, euphorbias, arums, cinerarias, sedums, heaths, and other peculiar plants were to be seen in their fullest beauty. Eucalyptus trees had been planted on the top, and were doing well, with bark hanging in rags and tatters about them. I scarcely went out without finding some new wonder to paint, lived a life of most perfect peace and happiness, and got strength every day with my kind friends.

The town of Puerto was just below the house, and had once been a thriving place, some English merchants having settled there. Now only a few half-bred children remained, entirely Spanish in education and ways, though they talked their fathers' tongue after their fashion. I went off with a donkey-boy and a couple of donkeys for a week to Echod (Icod), all along the coast with fresh views of the Peak up every crack. At Echod there is the best view of all; and a few miles above that place are forests of the Canary pine.

**LEFT:** the painter's view of the Dragon Tree.
**RIGHT:** a botanically detailed painting which is part of the collection in London's Kew Gardens Gallery.

## Grandees and gardens

Echod is a lovely old place, full of fine big houses, with exquisite views up and down; but it rained most of the time. The Marchesa de la Florida had written to her cousin the Count of Santa Lucia, who took me to see some fine coast-views, and insisted on walking arm-in-arm over ploughed fields and slippery pavements at an angle of 45 degrees, much to my embarrassment.

Some other grandees, with terribly long strings of names, were most hospitable, showed me their beautiful villas and gardens at Corronel and Gorachico (Garachico), and even

pressed me to stay. The latter place is built on a glacier of black lava, and the next [volcanic] eruption will probably send the whole town crashing into the sea.

It was one of the most frightful bits of volcanic scenery I ever saw. The day I was there was wintry and dark with storm-clouds; the white waves ran in between the dark rocks, and sent up great jets of foam with an awful crashing and roaring.

Santa Cruz, to which I at first took a dislike, I found full of beauty. Its gardens were lovely, and its merchants most hospitable. I stayed there till the *Ethiopia* picked me up, on the 29th of April. ❑

# THE ADVENT OF TOURISM

*From a select few in the late 19th century to several million today,*
*visitors from cooler northern climates have favoured Tenerife's sun and scenery*

The first tourists to the Canary Islands were visitors who came to the "new health resort of Tenerife" on account of the climate alone. It had been eulogised in *The British Medical Journal* by its editor, Ernest Hart, who went on a "winter trip" to Tenerife in 1887 and wrote "the blue sky and all-pervading sun overhead, the delicious warmth but exquisite freshness of the air, all tell us that we have reached safely and happily the haven of our rest, and are safely lodged for this promising "winter holiday" in one of the choicest of the gardens of the earth – Puerto Orotava, the very pearl of the Fortunate Islands".

Those who followed in his footsteps were a well-heeled and elegant group. The Grand Hotel Taoro in Puerto de la Cruz, Tenerife, built in 1892 to cater for them, was the largest hotel in Spain for many years. It was founded on a mound of volcanic ash and rock called "the mount of misery", overlooking the little town.

Barren fields of lava were converted into gardens for strolling, lawns for croquet or bowls, and 4.5 hectares (11 acres) were transformed into a park planted with endemic and imported plants to please the international visitors. During almost four decades in which the hotel flourished, these visitors included members of the Spanish royal family, King Albert and King Leopold of Belgium, the Duke of York (later King George VI), the Duke and Duchess of Kent, and Umberto, Prince of Savoy who became the last king of Italy.

The Grand Hotel Taoro, which cost £20,000, mainly raised by British investors, complemented the Marquesa, Monopole and Martianez hotels in the town below. Santa Cruz, the island's capital, then had two first class hotels, the Quisiana and the Pino de Oro, which were chiefly used as staging posts for travellers arriving and leaving by sea.

**LEFT:** the early tourists couldn't expect luxury transport, but that didn't stop them exploring the islands.
**RIGHT:** visitors would be collected from the harbourside and delivered safely to their hotels.

Any brave soul who ventured into one of the smaller towns might find a simple inn but little more. Such was the popularity of the Grand Hotel Taoro that male guests who had not made reservations might find themselves accommodated either on or below the billiard tables, their rest disturbed by resounding dinner gongs, the

thwack of wicker carpet beaters, or the rhythms of an orchestra playing in the rococo bandstands in the gardens.

In 1929 half the hotel building was destroyed by fire. The conflagration proved disastrous; the damaged wing was not replaced and the hotel never recovered its former reputation. In 1975 it was reopened as the Casino Taoro and is today one of Spain's most successful gambling establishments.

## Early packages

Frequent sailings from Liverpool by fruit cargo ships of the Yeoward Line brought regular trippers or "Yeowardites" as they were rather disparagingly called by the resident British colony. The 16-day round-trip, calling at Lisbon, Madeira, Las Palmas and Tenerife, was widely advertised and very popular. Leisure wear was unknown: men with handkerchiefs knotted on their heads, accompanied by overdressed ladies, were amusing sights to the locals as they were taxied about in open Hudsons, Packards or Chryslers to see the places of interest.

The real crunch for development came towards the end of the 1950s. Until then, noth-

### GÜIMAR FOR HEALTH

In south-east Tenerife Güimar, said to have the island's best climate, was an early health resort. The Hotel El Buen Retiro had a resident doctor and was a great success.

sacrificed. The greatest and most insulting impact was the construction of the Belair tower block slap in the centre of Puerto de la Cruz, with an elastic permit to build eight floors, that somehow got stretched to 23.

During the 1960s, as agriculture continued to diversify and new land came under cultivation on an unprecedented scale, the tourist boom wrought a revolution on the economy and in the society of the islands. Although this mainly applied to the eastern islands, which have most of the sandy

ing had changed. Visitors were still arriving by sea, and air travel was long and tedious, involving a stop-over in Las Palmas.

When planes began to make direct, non-stop flights to Tenerife in 1959, everything changed. "All Inclusive Winter Sunshine Holidays" began in earnest, causing a major impact on the island, particularly Puerto de la Cruz. Extensions to hotels were built on the strength of advance payments by tour operators, banana plantations were developed into hotels and gardens. The Golden Age had arrived.

Like most golden ages, it had its casualties, and it was during this stage of rapid expansion that many old and atmospheric buildings were

beaches, Tenerife, with Puerto de la Cruz and Los Cristianos as centres, did not lag far behind.

In the subsequent decades the increase in tourism has been huge, as has the infrastructure to cater for it, including relatively sophisticated medical facilities set up for the ever increasing number of elderly people who came here on holiday in the early days.

## Southern centres

In Tenerife, the pressure on the Puerto de la Cruz area to build more tourist accommodation was partly responsible for the development of the south. Owners of banana plantations within the city limits were threatened with expropriation unless they made their land available for hotel building. Since many of them also owned land in the south of the island, their solution was to build terraces for plantations in the south and then transfer the earth and the stumps of banana plants to their new locations.

Water was a vital consideration, but the plantation owners were able to switch their supplies to the south by direct piping. Thus water was now available for the development of the south, first in the already settled communities of Los

### BRITISH INVASION

Tenerife alone now receives almost 4½ million visitors each year. Over a quarter of them are British, and some 75 percent go to the resorts in the south.

prepared to put up with the barest of comforts, and fleas, in the few local *fondas* (inns).

These islands had no tourist infrastructure until much later than Tenerife, but now that the joys of walking in these rugged volcanic landscapes have been discovered, they are attracting more visitors: independent travellers who like to get away from it all.

A range of accommodation, transport and restaurants have now been made available, but the islands still retain much of their old world atmosphere and tranquillity.

Cristianos, El Médano, Playa Santiago and Los Gigantes, and later in Playa de las Américas on the so-called Costa de Silencio, which was an apt name before the construction of the Reina Sofía airport, although less so today.

### The smaller islands

On La Gomera, La Palma and El Hierro there were no real tourists in the old days, only seasoned or adventurous travellers who either had letters of introduction to local residents or were

**LEFT:** Tenerife advertised its claim as the winter sunshine capital.
**ABOVE:** Los Rodeos Airport in the early 1960s.

### Sun and sand

Despite warnings about the dangers of sunbathing, people still flock to the Canaries to enjoy holidays that revolve around sun, sea and sand – even when the latter has been shipped here from the Sahara to make golden beaches (*see page 183*). The islands' reputation for reliable winter sunshine means that 80 percent of the gross domestic product is tourism-related, even though increased taxation means that life is not as cheap as it used to be. New visitor records are broken each year; soon the islands will reach 10 million visitors annually, each visitor spending an average of 10 days, and there is no sign that the bubble will burst.  ❑

# A BRIDGE BETWEEN CONTINENTS

*As stepping stones between three continents, the Canary Islands
have been strongly influenced by each of them in turn*

When the first autonomous government came to power in the Canaries in 1978, the slogan "A bridge between three continents" became part of a campaign to widen the islands' economic base. It's not a bad slogan: geographically, the islands are stepping-stones between Europe, Africa and the Americas, and they have been so ever since Columbus sailed across the pond in 1492.

## The European connection

This is the most obvious of the continental bridges. The islands form two provinces and one autonomous region of Spain, and are part of the European Union, although they enjoy a specially negotiated position within it, which guarantees cheap alcohol and no VAT on goods on the islands. It also guarantees excessively high prices for Canarian farm produce compared with countries like Morocco and Israel, which is not helping the survival of Canarian agriculture.

The connection with Spain is a very long-standing one: the Spanish maritime empire was born even before the late 15th-century conquest of the islands, and Columbus and those who followed in his wake used the Canary current to coast past the North African shore, through the islands and on westwards to the Americas.

The majority of the early European colonists were Spaniards from the harsh frontier regions of Extremadura and Andalucia. Portuguese, Italian and even English merchants soon followed as the islands' first industry – sugar – began to develop.

As shipping began to move more freely between continents, many Spaniards settled in the Canaries, while some of the descendants of the original islanders and the first European settlers moved on to the Americas. During the 16th and 17th centuries the Canary Islands were busy commercial centres through which passed much of Spain's American sea traffic. The ports of Las Palmas (Gran Canaria), Garachico (Tenerife) and Santa Cruz de La Palma (La Palma) flourished, until Garachico's harbour was destroyed overnight by a volcanic eruption in 1706.

The essential elements of Canarian society had been welded together by the time Garachico was buried by boiling lava, and Europeans and native islanders had intermarried and were inextricably mixed. However, the fortunes of the islands were so tied to the Spanish mainland that Las Palmas and the other ports stagnated along with the Spanish empire and economy during the 18th and early 19th centuries.

## African roots

The origins of the early Guanche inhabitants of the Canaries and their links with North African Berber tribes have been discussed earlier (*see page 25*). On the smaller islands

**PRECEDING PAGES:** the Charco de los Camarones in Puerto de la Cruz in the early 19th century.
**LEFT:** the influence of Africa lingers in tobacconists and, **RIGHT**, in entertainment provided for tourists.

and in the mountainous interiors of the larger ones, native islanders survived in enclaves and were able largely to ignore the conquerors and live almost as their Berber-speaking ancestors had done. But the power of the Inquisition – especially as the Spanish empire turned inwards during the 18th century – gradually imposed the trappings of Christianity on these African communities.

By 1800 the principal native pagan festivals had been taken over by the Catholic Church, and the heathen deities converted into various manifestations of the Virgin Mary. During the course of the 18th century the folk costume of the Canary Islands took on the form that it has today, as the gradual process of "civilising" the islanders went on.

Yet the North African roots of the islands' population never really died. They either went deeper underground or adapted to the changed circumstances in ways which kept everybody happy. Some examples of this are the native martial arts, *juego del palo* and *lucha canaria* (*see pages 85–87*) and certain fiestas. As in many other places, ostensibly Christian festivals still contain pagan elements today. Spanish became the accepted means of communication but it still contained a lot of Berberisms.

### RAPID ASSIMILATION

One example of rapid integration – whether willing or coerced – is that almost from the earliest days of conquest native islanders joined their European masters in attacks and invasions.

This happened first with attacks on the other Canarian islands, and later with the destruction of the Aztec and Inca empires in the Americas. Gran Canarians and Gomerans soon found themselves in the front line during the conquest of Tenerife at the end of the 15th century. And before the 16th century was out, Canarian wrestlers were putting on demonstrations of their prowess to amuse the Spanish viceroy of Peru.

## South American exodus

The bridge to the American continent, initially forged by the early explorers, was reinforced by the agricultural recessions of the 19th century which drove many islanders west to Argentina, Colombia, Venezuela and Cuba. And, like the Irish people who emigrated to the United States, these Canarian migrants took with them passionate, if ill-defined, ideas of liberty from foreign oppression and welded them into a coherent form in the Americas.

In 1810, as British and French forces decided the future of Europe on the battlefields of the Iberian peninsula, the Canarian junta raised for the first time the islanders' desire "to get rid of all the Spaniards now here and to put the people of this land in their place".

This view was echoed in Spain's American colonies. Simón Bolívar (1783–1830), the liberator of most of Spanish America, referred to "Spaniards and Canarios" as quite different peoples. In some of his decrees he included the Canaries in his list of Spanish colonies to be freed. In time, the vast Spanish American empire was whittled down to just Cuba and Puerto Rico, which many Canarios used as stepping-stones to continental America.

One of the most influential Canarian emigrants of the late 19th century, and one who

## Intimations of independence

In Havana, the Cuban capital, Delgado lived "in the greatest harmony" with the Cubans, whose character he found a pleasant contrast with the pretentiousness of the (Spanish) *peninsulares*. There he met left-wing emigrés from the Canaries and mainland Spain and got to know members of the Cuban independence movement. During a trip to the United States he met the father of Cuban independence, José Martí (whose mother was a Canario); shortly afterwards he began to work for the Cuban freedom movement, writing for an anarchist newspaper *El Esclavo* (*The Slave*).

learned a great deal from American revolutionary leaders, was Secindino Delgado (*see page 46*). At the age of 14, he had taken advantage of a Spanish government offer of a free passage to the island of Cuba for anyone prepared to work there for a year. This offer had been introduced in 1886, the same year that slavery was abolished by Spain (over 80 years after it was outlawed by Great Britain), and was designed to replace the cheap forced labour that had thereby been lost on the plantations.

**LEFT:** emigrants set off for the New World; Cuban José Martí influenced Canary separatism .
**ABOVE:** the folk costume evolved in the 18th century.

Forced to flee Cuba in 1896 Delgado returned for a short time to the Canaries where he further developed his ideas about the future independence of the islands. The following year, in Venezuela, he founded *El Guanche*, a newspaper devoted to promoting the cause of Canarian independence.

*El Guanche* seems to have been a short-lived venture, though it was re-established in 1924. Since then it has been used as the title of the journals of the Canarian Nationalist Party, the Free Canary Islands Movement, the Seven Green Stars Movement and most recently by the Canarian Nationalist Congress. Delgado's newspaper had sufficient impact to spur a three-day battle for the control of La Laguna during a Canarian insurrection in 1909.

Delgado's main aim was that the islands should gain a degree of autonomy from Madrid so that they could run their own affairs directly, although some of the successor parties that have used the *El Guanche* title have had more extreme aims.

### British interests

One slightly strange aspect of Canarian nationalism is the view, held with varying degrees of seriousness, that the Canaries would have been much better off if the Tenerife militia had

allowed Lord Nelson to take Santa Cruz in 1797. The reasoning behind this apparently curious notion is that the British, who invested heavily in bunkering facilities in the Canaries during Delgado's lifetime (1872–1912), were better administrators than the Spanish. This brings us to another bridge, that between Britain and the Canary Islands.

The British who, as mentioned earlier (*see pages 40–41*) had been heavily involved in the Canarian wine trade, later built most of the roads on the islands, set up the first public utility companies and created the Ciudad Jardín (Garden City), the most pleasant part of Las Palmas (Gran Canaria).

They also built up Canarian agriculture, growing bananas, tomatoes and early potato varieties, and they expanded the port of Las Palmas in the late 19th century, equipping it to accommodate steamships, at a time when Canarian farmers had just gone through their worst crisis.

Indeed, at one stage the possibility of annexation by Great Britain was taken so seriously that the Commander-in-Chief of the Spanish garrison in the islands informed Madrid, in 1873, that a separatist group "was proposing to take advantage of the right moment for England to annexe the islands".

### Other eyes on the islands

The British were not the only ones interested in the rump of Spain's overseas possessions as the Spanish empire eventually came to an end. The United States had its eye on the potential of the islands after it threw Spain out of the Philippines, Cuba and Puerto Rico in 1898, although nothing came of this interest. Nearly half a century later, Hitler had plans drawn up to take over the Canaries from France during World War II. British military intelligence had contacts with Canarian independence groups during that war, and it was probably the now infamous double-agent Kim Philby, former head of the Iberia section, who finally severed the connection.

The islands' strategic importance is well understood by NATO, as it was by the Warsaw Pact before its demise. The Canaries straddle the main shipping lanes from Europe to South America and the southern USA, as well as the routes from Europe to West and South Africa, and beyond.

All these historical links justify the description of the Canaries as a bridge between continents and cultures. Today, however, the islands are forging other links, chiefly through the growth of tourism. The opening up of air and sea communications – for a long time Iberia Airlines and the Trasmediterránea ferry company had a monopoly on these – as well as world-wide technological communications, mean that the bridges are much easier to cross in the early years of the 21st century. ❑

**LEFT:** showing solidarity with the Free Sahara movement.
**RIGHT:** a mingling of cultures at carnival time.

# THE VERDINO

*The verdino is the truly Canarian dog, whether or not they were the breed responsible for the islands' Latin name*

The most widely accepted theory of the naming of the islands is that some 2,000 years ago a galley loaded with explorers from Roman Mauritania reached Gran Canaria and found it teeming with dogs. *Canes* being Latin for dogs, the island gained its name. There are other theories: Thomas Nichols, the

first Englishman to describe the islands (in the 16th century), suggests that the islanders lived on dog flesh. Spanish historian Francisco Gomara says there were no dogs at all when the *conquistadors* arrived, and that the island was named after a red grape *uva canina*. Many archaeologists, however, believe the name of the island group derives from a North African tribe, the Canarii, from whom the islanders are descended.

## An awesome creature

Even if the accepted theory is correct, we do not know if the dogs the Mauritanians found here were antecedents of the Canary mastiff,

known as the Verdino because of its greenish shading (*verde* is Spanish for green), but the Verdino is championed as the true Canarian dog, unique to the islands, possibly because it is yet another symbol of the Canaries' independence from the mainland.

The Verdino is a smooth-haired, heavy guard-type dog with a broad jaw, usually brindled in stripes, or sometimes golden with white flashes on the chest. It weighs in at between 40–50 kilos (90–110 lbs). At its best it is an awesome creature of obvious strength and has all the characteristics of a dog which for centuries been assisting man in all manner of agricultural work; it is affectionate to known friends, extremely faithful, but also highly territorial.

Dr Luis Felipe Jurado, professor at the Veterinary Faculty of La Laguna University on Tenerife, has studied the Verdino for many years. He accepts the *canes* theory of the naming of the islands, and is convinced that the dogs preceeded men on the islands. He believes they arrived here on rafts from Africa: not man-made ones but great platforms of fallen trees and bushes that drifted here after rivers flooded on the African mainland.

## Dogs of prey

However and whenever it arrived, the Verdino is accepted as an integral part of the islands' past and a sad one at times. The *conquistadors* so feared these animals that they condemned most of them to death, allowing each shepherd just one to guard his flock.

This law, issued in May 1499, must have been blatantly ignored by the islanders, judging by the number of times it was made public and the fines that were imposed for disobedience. Offenders faced being scourged, but they continued to keep and protect their precious dogs. However, as many of the islanders had died as a result of the conquest, some of the Verdinos turned savage and attacked herds of goats. A price was put on their heads and they were termed "worse than wolves".

At one stage, during the early 16th century, a gold coin was paid to anyone who could produce the head of a Verdino, but a later Spanish ruler annulled the order, saying that the Verdino was "an honourable dog" and he didn't wish to judge it. But survival was difficult for the dogs during those harsh years. In Fuerteventura where for centuries they had guarded goats and sheep, a general "licence to kill" was issued against dogs of prey, as they were termed.

## Survival of the breed

Somehow the Verdino managed to survive, only to face a new threat in the 19th century when British and German dog-fighting enthusiasts settled in the islands, bringing with them the bull terrier. Cross-breeding to produce stronger, fiercer animals in this cruel sport threatened the purity of the breed.

Dog-fighting is officially outlawed now, and staged fights are rare. But lovers of the Verdino are still fighting to preserve the purity of the breed. Most are strongly opposed to selective breeding, but endeavour to choose mates that are not closely related, because of the dangers of interbreeding. Verdino owners and organisations such as Solidaridad Canario are stimulating public awareness and interest in the Canarian dog. It is presently an unregistered breed, although the Spanish Kennel Club has recognised it and is setting standards by which to judge a true specimen.

Lack of money is a continual problem, and Verdino enthusiasts, professional or otherwise, often disagree on all but the most basic issues. Efforts to breed the dog, to "follow through" on pups and to arouse government interest have been hampered by so many difficulties that today the Verdino banner is mostly flown by individuals, not groups.

But a brighter day is dawning for the Verdinos. These days they are guarded as zealously and lovingly as they once guarded their masters. Public interest in the dogs is flourishing and the price of a pure-bred Verdino pup has increased accordingly – assuming that an owner would part with one. Shepherds and goatherds in Fuerteventura, where the Verdino is still a working dog, are mindful of its value, and have replaced its basic diet of *gofio* (ground wheat or maize) and water with a higher-protein one. They are also more careful to remove ticks and other parasites which have always sapped the dogs' strength.

> ### CHANGE OF NAME
>
> The Verdino is sometimes called a Berdino, as the letters V and B are almost interchangeable in Spanish, particularly as spoken in South America and the Canaries.

In Tenerife the Club Español del Presa Canario (*presa* actually means bulldog) arranges regular meetings and holds competitions for Verdinos, which take place in the

main square of La Laguna, in Geneto, Tegueste and several other venues.

Perhaps the last word should be left to the 19th-century Spanish writer, historian and naturalist, Viera y Clavijo who describes the Verdino better than anyone else: "apart from its svelte figure, vivacity, courage and speed, it possesses that delicate and exquisite sentiment that allows it to enter society with man. The Verdino understands man's desires, fights for his security, obeys and helps him, defends and loves him, and... knows exactly how to gain the love of his owner." What more could anyone ask of an animal that has been described as man's best friend? ❑

**LEFT AND RIGHT:** one man and his dog: the breed has evolved, and fashions have changed, but the mutual loyalty remains the same.

# THE ISLANDERS

*Although visitors may see many similarities between Canarios and their*
*Spanish cousins, the islanders insist on their separate identity*

**C**anarian tourism was not a carefully planned industry, it just developed over the years. These days, the islanders are adapting to it very well, but there are many tourists who come here for a sun-and-fun package holiday, never venture outside the purpose-built resorts, and never meet a true Canario.

The multi-lingual hotel receptionist is more likely to be a *godo* – a so-called Goth, or peninsular Spaniard – than a Canario. Many of the chambermaids, waiters and gardeners in the tourist *aparthotels* are Andalusians and Galicians, attracted by comparitively high wages.

So how do you find a Canary Islander? And how do you know you have found the real thing? On Tenerife it is relatively easy; you can hire a car and head inland, or wander around the streets of Santa Cruz or Puerto de la Cruz, avoiding the tourist bars and souvenir shops. Or head west from Tenerife to one of the smaller islands, where you'll find plenty of real Canarios, among whom the German hippies on La Gomera and the British and Swedish astronomers on La Palma are easily identified birds of passage.

## Caricaturing the Canario

The well-known caricature of a countryman, once applied to all the islands, is Cho' Juáa, who made his first appearance in 1944 in the *Diario de Las Palmas*. His expansive belly rests on the waistband of his sagging trousers. Somewhere around what would once have been waist level is a broad cloth belt out of which pokes the handle of his *naife* or Canarian knife. On his feet is a pair of *closas*, over-sized down-at-heel boots, and on his head there is the black felt homburg that has seen better days – though when those days were is anybody's guess.

Over his well-filled shirt he wears a waistcoat, unfastened and unfastenable. And below

his *bandido* moustache, a cigarette stub adheres permanently to his lower lip – except on high days and holidays, when it is occasionally replaced by a cigar stub.

Cho' Juáa is no fool, though: like his literary counterpart, Pepe Monagas, who appears in several Canarian short stories by Pancho Guerra,

he has an eye for a bargain – and for a mug. In his business dealings he is aided and abetted by Camildita, his shrewd and shrewish wife. Not that Cho' Juáa is really mean, he is just canny. And there is nothing he loves more than an opportunity to show off his largesse. What appear to be the verbal preliminaries to physical violence break out when two Canarios attempt to pay the same bill.

## A new breed

Like caricatures anywhere, the Cho' Juáas and Camilditas were always an exaggeration and are now a dying breed. They can still be found on the smaller islands and in more remote vil-

---

**PRECEDING PAGES:** the solitary life of a shepherdess; bringing in the boats on the north coast.
**LEFT:** traditional dress is still worn for fiestas.
**RIGHT:** a local lady, head shielded from the sun.

lages, but there is no longer any place for their sharp negotiating skills in the cities.

Cho' Juáa is now increasingly dependent on his street-wise city successors. Better-educated, taller and less corpulent, the new Canarios grew up with the tourist boom. They have usually picked up a smattering of "beach English" (often rather rude), and maybe a bit of beach German as well.

From their Cho' Juáa predecessors they have inherited the ability to sell the same piece of useless *barranco* (ravine) slope twice over, and at varying market rates depending on who is buying, but they will insist on taking the buyer

capable of bellowing an order across a rowdy restaurant like a parade-ground sergeant, but he keeps your attention at the table by rattling off the menu in a low, almost inaudible, whisper. You must concentrate on him and him alone to find out what is on the menu today – and, of course, he would never insult you by referring to the price of an individual item.

### Party time

Like other Spaniards Canarios love a *fiesta* – anything from an *asadero* (a country barbecue) to a *verbena* (which could loosely be translated as an all-night street party, often on the eve of

out to a slap-up dinner to seal the bargain.

In this respect Canarios are really no different from other Spaniards. They love the chance to take the leading role – no matter how insignificant the play, nor how small the audience. Lines are never mumbled but projected across a crowded bar or bus, competing with all the other dramas being performed in the same small space.

Canarian restaurants at Sunday lunchtime are bedlam as three, or even four, generations compete for attention at the same table, and each table competes for the attention of the others. The waiters do deafening one-man shows in the midst of it all – the Canarian waiter is

a major saint's day); from a *trínqui* (drinks party) to a *mogollón* (a marathon street party that grows out of *Carnaval*). An invitation to *tomar una copa* (have a drink) really means to have several, so that tongues are loosened and conversation flows. Before the evening ends an *arranque* (one for the road) is often ordered.

To keep in top conversational form a Canario may pop into a bar for a rum at nine in the morning; for a *gin tónica* at eleven; and a bottle of *vino tinto* (red wine) with lunch. But to stave off the tongue-tying effects of too much alcohol, most drinks are taken with *tapas* or just a *bocata* – a *bocata* is literally a mouthful of food, a *tapa* slightly bigger.

Coffee, too, is an essential – small, strong and black (*café solo*); small and strong with a thick dollop of sickly condensed milk (*café cortado*); or a cup or glass of white coffee (*café con leche*). Coffee is invariably stiffened with liberal quantities of sugar. Even fresh orange juice, pressed out of sweet little oranges, is often heavily sugared – a tradition derived from the Canaries' first export industry, the growing of sugar cane.

## Old habits die hard

If the sugar industry, rum and *tapas* gave Cho' Juáa his sagging belly, it was one of the Canary

stop him showing an interest in any other female shape, size or colouring, and referring to them all as *guapa* (gorgeous). After all, he has his *machismo* to maintain.

While the average Canarian male is still ambivalent about the role of women, in his personal life and society in general, both sexes absolutely adore children. They are the future, and nothing is too much for them. There is private education and extra tuition for the completely uninterested, and piles of presents for every child's birthday, saint's day, Christmas, Epiphany, first communion or just for the sake of giving. In the Canaries there is no segrega-

Islands' other early staples – tobacco – that completed the caricature. Wherever Canarios congregate there is a fug of cigarette smoke – and the anti-smoking legislation passed by the Spanish parliament is treated with the disdain reserved for any Madrid initiative.

The Canarian male also tends to share old fashioned mainland Spanish attitudes to women, children and the Catholic Church. He likes his women "*morena, bajita y gordita*" (dark, short and plump) – although this preference doesn't

**LEFT:** a lifetime of hard work is reflected in the face of this countryman.
**ABOVE:** three generations share a day on the beach.

### INDIVIDUALISMO

A disregard for things they would rather ignore – like No Smoking signs, parking restrictions, red traffic lights, road signs and rubbish bins – is something that Canarios have in common with other Spaniards, although here it has been developed into something of an art form.

To many outsiders, particularly from northern Europe, it is amusing and irritating in roughly equal parts. In Spanish this quality is called *individualismo* (individuality) if referring to oneself, *insolidaridad* (lack of social responsibility) when referring to others in general, and *barbaridad* (barbarism) in the case of someone who has committed a personal affront.

tion of the generations – even the smallest of children accompany their parents to *fiestas*, *verbenas*, political demonstrations, classical concerts, the cinema, and that other social pillar, the Church.

Even the most irreligious Canario goes to church several times a year – for the baptisms, first communions, weddings and funerals of various members of their extensive families. But services are not so much an act of worship as an act in the on-going drama of life. The priest plays to a full house, but the congregation on the whole has little interest in his performance or his message.

The Canary Islands are further from Madrid than they are from Dakar. From Fuerteventura you can see the coast of Morocco, and feel its influences. For Canarios, geography outweighs all else. Even those with classic Latin features and Spanish surnames going as far back as anyone can trace them will swear blind that they are the direct descendants of pure-bred Guanches. Most have a deep-rooted distrust of *godos*, and some have an even deeper loathing of the *metrópoli* – Madrid.

The *metrópoli*, especially during the various agricultural recessions of the 19th century and during the years of the dictatorship, was seen as

## Lo nuestro

So what is it that makes Canarios so different from other Spaniards – at least in their own estimation? Perhaps it is best summed up by the words *lo nuestro* – "our own". *Lo nuestro* is *gofio* (finely ground toasted wheat) and milk for breakfast; it is a distaste for bull-fighting, *godos* (peninsular Spaniards), and Canarios from any island except their own; it is a secret affection for cock-fights and dog-fights (even if this is not always admitted to outsiders); it's a love of Canarian wrestling, the *lucha canaria*, of Canarian music no matter how grating, and of Canarian rum no matter how rasping; but above all it is distance and accent.

stifling Canarian enterprise and imposing unwanted officials on the islanders. Sending Franco to the Canaries as military governor in 1936 was one such metropolitan infliction. Today, even with autonomous government taking over some aspects of regional administration, there is still considerable disgruntlement about the number of *godos* in high places and the need to seek the permission of central government even for minor changes. Bureaucrats in Madrid are renowned for their relaxed approach, and some believe that they treat the Canaries as a colony.

It is difficult to define *lo nuestro*. It is a weird mix of the Spanish *picaresco*, or roguishness;

of South American "magic realism" – Canarios are always a little larger than life; and the distinctively Canarian sentiment that *Canarias no es Europa, somos Africanos* (the Canaries aren't Europe, we are African).

## Language barrier

Alienation from the mainland is most obvious in the language. Canarians do not pronounce the letter "z" as a lisped "th", like the *peninsulares*, but as an "s", like the people of Latin America. Islanders will refer to "Lah Palmah", "Santa Cru'" or "Ma'-

---

**LOST CONSONANTS**

Beware of confusions: lost consonants can make La Palma and Las Palmas sound almost exactly the same.

---

visiting tourists. On La Palma the accent is particularly soft and clear, but still more like South American Spanish. Addressed in peninsular Spanish, some islanders may react blankly, or else embark on a campaign of re-education, which will include differences in vocabulary as well as accent.

Words like *baifo*, a goat kid, is a Canarian peculiarity and comes from the native pre-Spanish language. Others, such as *naife*, *chóni* and *canbullonero* derive from the British commercial connection – *naife*, is a Canarian knife; *chóni*, a foreigner,

palomah" rather than Las Palmas, Santa Cruz or Maspalomas. In some places consonants are clipped so sharply they cease to exist: for example, the name Juan becomes Juáa. Words are slurred together into a torrent which can make comprehension impossible, even among Canarios themselves.

On La Gomera, some islanders dispensed with words entirely. Because of the difficult terrain, shepherds used a unique whistling language known as *siblo*, nowadays performed for

---

**LEFT:** children are much-loved, and included in all aspects of life.
**ABOVE:** young islanders on a park bench.

comes from the English "Johnny"; and a *canbullonero*, from the expression "can buy on", is a dock-side "fence" who buys stolen items of cargo from sailors in the port. The Canary Island word for a cake is a *queque*, and a *yora* is a passenger from a Yeoward Line ship.

Another idiom that Canarios share with speakers of Latin American Spanish is *Ustedes* as the accepted plural form of "you" instead of the peninsular *vosotros*. On the mainland, *Ustedes* is used when speaking to people you don't know well, or whose social status is higher than your own. In the Canaries, however, it is used among the closest of friends and family. *Vosotros* is looked upon almost as an insult. ❏

# CANARIAN COMBAT

*Wrestling is the islands' favourite form of combat, but stick-fighting
runs a close second and cock-fights still have many fans*

Among the native-born islanders, *lucha canaria* (Canary wrestling), is far and away the islands' most popular sport. The relevant governing body attempted to get recognition for the 1992 Olympic Games, arguing that *lucha canaria* is an international sport because Canarian emigrants introduced it throughout South and Central America as well as mainland Spain. The rejection of the proposal by the Olympic Committee was seen by Canarios as yet another slight by Madrid on *lo nuestro*, "our own".

*Lucha canaria* is believed to have Guanche origins. How uniquely Canarian it actually is may be debatable. It certainly preceded the conquest, but similar styles of wrestling can be seen in northern Spain, the Swiss Alps, northwest Britain and even in parts of Africa.

## Ancient and modern

Chroniclers record pre-conquest matches which generally took the form of personal duels or trials of combat, sometimes to settle disputes such as grazing rights. Wrestling was also a form of training for war and an entertainment at festivities – bouts usually formed part of the official merrymaking at a royal wedding.

According to early European writers, special places were set aside for native wrestling bouts. "They had public places outside the villages where they had their duels… a circle enclosed by a stone wall and a place made high where they might be seen," wrote one visitor.

The Spanish made some attempt to control the sport, but *lucha* was not easily put down. Indeed, in 1527 wrestling bouts were held in Tenerife as part of the festivities to mark the birth of the future Felipe II of Spain.

By the 19th century, however, the cultured section of society was of the opinion that "spectacles of this kind should figure only in the memory". But their views were not shared by

the majority, and until the outbreak of the Spanish Civil War in 1936, *lucha canaria* retained much of its original character.

A style of wrestling similar to that in Cumbria in the north-west of England was to be found in Tenerife, and stylistic differences occurred on each of the islands. The presence at

the matches of a *comisionado*, or second, harked back to the duels of pre-conquest days. In Gran Canaria the two opposing teams once known as North and South, preserving the former ancient division of the island into two separate Guanche kingdoms.

During the Franco era *lucha* was generally neglected but during the decades since democracy was re-established in 1976 far more public interest, and money, has been invested in the sport. Nowadays most of the main rings are modern sports halls or stadiums.

The rings – often built and run by the local town council – are known as *terreros*, a word of Portuguese origin, probably acquired during the

**LEFT:** *juego de palo* (stick-fighting) is skilful but potentially vicious.
**RIGHT:** *lucha canaria* is a sport with a long history.

various temporary alliances of native islanders and Portuguese against the Spanish.

In its modern form, *lucha canaria* is no longer an individual contest but a team sport. There are 12 *luchadores* (wrestlers) in each team, with only one man from each side fighting at any one time. The individual bouts, or *bregas,* are fought within a sand-covered ring between 9–10 metres (30–33 ft) in diameter.

At the start of a *brega* the wrestler takes his opponent's right hand in his and grasps the

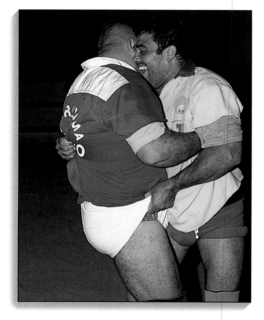

rolled hem of his opponent's shorts with his left. As the two wrestlers come together their right hands brush the sand-covered floor of the *terrero* and the *brega* is under way.

Using a combination of trips, lifts and sheer weight each contestant tries to unbalance his opponent. The *brega* is lost if any part of the wrestler's body – except, of course, his feet – touches the ground. If both wrestlers are toppled the man who hits the ground first is the loser. Each team member must grapple to win the best of three bouts to gain a point for his side. A winner is only declared by the judge after much debate. It sounds rough but the rules ensure that it is the most chivalrous of sports.

> ## WIELDING A BIG STICK
>
> Goat-herders were exempt from a post-conquest Spanish law forbidding islanders to carry weapons, as they needed suitable sticks to protect their flocks.

The *lucha canaria* is traditionally the sport of country people, practised in grain-threshing circles and performed on high days and holidays. These days threshing floors are few and far between, but an urban Canario will occasionally wrestle with a friend or relation during a Sunday barbecue in the country. *Lucha* has even been taken up by some foreign residents; two German brothers who were brought up in the islands have been members of the El Hierro team.

## Sticks and stones

Less common on the islands is *juego del palo* or stick-fighting (known as *banot* in Tenerife), but it is currently undergoing a revival. A controlling body for the sport has been established, and classes are now being given in branches of the Universidad Laboral throughout the Canary Islands.

In pre-conquest days stick-fighting formed part of a more dangerous game. When two Canarios challenged each other to a duel, they went to an agreed place, a raised arena with a flat stone, big enough for a man to stand upright at each end. Both competitors stood on their stone, armed with three stones each for throwing and three more which served for wounding, and carrying a stave called a *magodo* or *amodeghe*.

First they threw the stones, which they dodged with skill, weaving their bodies without moving their feet. After that they stepped down to the ground and faced each other with the *magodos*, each trying to smash the other's forearms and using the thin stones between their fingers as a kind of vicious knuckle-duster.

The staff is about 1.8 meters (6 ft) long and about 2.5 cm (1 inch) thick. Almost any wood can be used as long as it will provide a straight staff and will not shatter easily. Wood from the indigenous *membrillo* bush, or the introduced cherry tree are preferred.

A pole of appropriate length is cut green, stripped of its bark and left to season. The seasoned pole is then cured with pig fat to make it more resilient – linseed oil is sometimes used, though few practitioners of the sport would readily admit to using a manufactured product.

As with wrestling there are differences between the islands. Adherents of the Tenerife style go for speed, while the Fuerteventuran school prefers a defensive style, sacrificing speed for power. Even the name of the staff varies from island to island – on Tenerife it's often called a *banot*, as is the sport itself; in Gran Canaria it's a *garrote*, and in Fuerteventura it is known as a *lata*. Throughout the islands herdsmen still carry these staves.

*Juego del palo*, like wrestling, was a rural sport and the practitioners were mainly goatherders. In living memory groups of herdsmen have occasionally met to resolve disputes between individual herders. If agreement could not be reached by negotiation the matter was

North Africa as beasts of burden and for pulling a plough. For a while it became common to use a camel driver's crop, a stick of about 1 metre (3ft) long, as a weapon in stick-fighting. In 1860 the *palo camellero* was introduced to Tenerife and by the 1920s there was a thriving group of fighters on the island who used the short camel driver's stick. This style, however, did not survive the neglect of the Franco years.

Another form of combat popular in the islands is cock-fighting, which is still legal and draws excited crowds in some rural areas. It may seem barbaric to outsiders, but it is part of the culture. ❑

eventually determined by a stick-fight between the two men or their representatives.

The stone throwing and the knuckle-dusters went out of fashion years ago, but the stickfight has survived, although these days it is mostly staged as part of a fiesta or *romería*.

## Variations on a theme

A variant on the theme of stick-fighting was developed in the 19th century when camels were first introduced to Fuerteventura from

**LEFT:** tradtional wrestling bout in Puerto de la Cruz.
**ABOVE:** cock-fighting still retains a following in rural areas; *lucha canaria* is part of the islands' heritage.

### WHERE TO SEE THEM

*Lucha canaria* and *juego del palo* have become popular tourist attractions and there are demonstrations of both during most festivals. Local tourist offices should be able to tell you when and where they are on. Otherwise look out for advertising posters, or check the listings in local papers for details. Try the Hotel Tigaiga in Puerto de la Cruz, which holds regular Sunday morning bouts of *lucha canaria*.

Matches are frequently televised and if you watch one in a bar it's almost as good as being there in person, as an enthusiastic crowd of customers usually gets into the competitive spirit of the thing.

# WHAT PEOPLE ARE TALKING ABOUT

*Bar gossip and media comment tend to focus on the parochial,*
*from wrestling and carnival to island independence*

Visitors who do not speak much Spanish may wonder what is being discussed in the islands' bars and on the city benches where elderly people sit for hours. They may also wonder which topics fill the local papers or are debated so animatedly on the radio. The answer is, pretty much the same as in most

communities. Parochial interests outweigh national and international ones, and politics is not the average islander's favourite topic.

## Media and message

Literacy is not as high as in many parts of Europe, and only about 38 percent of the population regularly reads a newspaper. The vast majority gets information from television and radio. Island newspapers don't attempt to compete with the mainland press for international news. *El Pais*, a bulky daily flown in from Madrid, but costing less than local papers, caters for those interested in world affairs. Major international events are not ignored, but

appear in succinct form, usually on an inner page. More space is devoted to local sports – wrestling, basketball and, especially, soccer.

Festivals of every kind, simple village affairs, urban celebrations or the vitally important pre-Lent *Carnaval* are a favourite topic of conversation, and are covered extensively by the press. *Carnaval* exceeds all else in terms of column-inches, in daily reports and special supplements, before, during and after the event. The time, effort and money spent on *Carnaval* in these islands is enormous. If the same effort and enthusiasm was expended on business or industrial activity the Canaries would probably be at the top of the EU's economic league.

Newspapers carry occasional statistics on numbers of visitors to the islands – a continual breaking of records. Timeshare, which is considered to have had a negative effect on the tourist trade because all payments are made outside the islands, is a fairly frequent topic.

## Crime and punishment

Drugs, robberies and traffic accidents are frequent issues in the newspapers. Because of their free port status and their strategic position, these islands are naturally attractive to drug dealers. The large number of foreign visitors and Spain's lenient anti-drug laws are other attractions for the dealers – some think they almost amount to an invitation.

Theft is commonplace here, especially in residential areas with a lot of temporarily absent foreign residents. The police tend to get bored with catching the same delinquents at regular intervals. Car theft and pick-pocketing are pretty common, too, in the larger towns and resorts, but there's not much violent crime.

During the latter part of the 1990s newspapers reported a steep rise in the number of fatal traffic accidents, and in the number of vehicles on the road. Tenerife's roads themselves are quite good; it is speed or inexperience, drink or drugs that cause most fatal accidents, which usually occur at weekends, during the early hours of morning.

## Bar talk

The topics of conversation in bars depends, of course, on venue and location. In the *ventas* (wine shops) of the country districts the potato crop will probably be most discussed, as many excellent varieties of potatoes are grown and harvested up to four times a year. But the subject also comes up in conversations in the most unexpected places, such as women's hairdressing salons, elegant dinner tables and cocktail parties. In the latter places, *papas* (the local variant of the Spanish word, *patatas*) and their prices are discussed as ardently as stock prices in the City of London.

Tourism ought to be a frequent subject of conversation and press comment among the inhabitants of these tourist-dependent islands, but it crops up far less than one might think. Travel agents, hotel managers, or others in the business may discuss the topic, but the general public seldom bothers with it, unless it is to comment on the latest outburst of bad behaviour by lager louts in Playa de las Américas.

## Environmental issues

The subject of ecology comes up every time new residential enclaves or hotels are given the go ahead. It is also a hotly-debated topic when, with unwelcome regularity, forest fires break out each summer – often the result of discarded glass catching the sun. Hundreds of hectares of pine forest have been ravaged by fires in the last decade, though none as tragic as that in La Gomera in 1984 which claimed the lives of 21 people, including the newly appointed Civil Governor of Tenerife province.

The only positive outcome of these disastrous fires is that they increase membership of the environmental protection groups on the islands. Such groups are becoming more active, and the Canary Island parliament has passed a number of laws aimed at protecting the environment. The uncontrolled, unplanned and often unlicensed construction of cement-block houses on the fringes of towns and villages, and the thoughtless development of the coastal areas which went on for many years have been widely condemned, but lessons have been learned, albeit rather late in the day.

**Left:** setting the world to rights in a local bar.
**Right:** prices are high when sites for stalls at the annual carnival are auctioned.

## Independence

Independence – *Independencia* – is a word which often appears in newspapers and in graffiti sprayed on walls. Its meaning is twofold: there's a smallish group of radical separatists who want complete independence from Spain on ethnic grounds. They are represented by AWANAK – which translates roughly as the Canary Islands Popular Front in the ancient Guanche language (established in 1963, it used to be called MPAIC). The party symbol, a spiral labyrinth, can sometimes be seen accompanying a written invitation to *godos* (the nickname for peninsular Spaniards) to go home.

To most Canarios, however, independence means recognition of the islands' special status, protection of their interests, and separation from the main peninsula-based parties. They are represented by the more moderate Association of Independents of Tenerife (ATI), the Association of Canary Independents (ACI), and the Coalición Canaria, an eclectic grouping of disparate parties united in their desire to protect their island identities.

So if you are wondering what the talk is all about, it could be any of these things. Or it could, like anywhere else, be the lastest bit of local gossip, the price of bread, or the soap opera on television the night before. ❑

# ISLAND FESTIVALS

*From the mammoth Santa Cruz Carnaval to pious religious festivals and colourful village romerías, Tenerife knows how to celebrate*

There is nothing *tinerfeños* love quite so much as a fiesta, and people think nothing of travelling from one end of the island to the other to join in some of the best ones.

It's said that on just about every day of the year, there's a fiesta in full swing somewhere in the archipelago and this may well be true. Many of them are small local affairs which go unnoticed by the outside world, except when the strains of music and laughter float down the valley followed, much later, by the staccato report of fire-crackers and the sudden blossoming of fireworks in a clear night sky.

There are exceptions of course: the major events that everyone knows about, and the most important of these are *Carnaval* and the celebrations for Corpus Christi.

## Carnaval

*Carnaval* in Tenerife, particularly in Santa Cruz, is an all-consuming way of life, a kind of madness that gradually infiltrates and takes over people's lives, bringing the commercial and business sectors of the island to a near standstill as it moves into top gear.

The word *Carnaval* derives from the Latin carne vale, meaning "goodbye to meat", as Catholics were expected to exclude meat from their diet during the 40-days of Lent. Long before the Christian era, however, *Carnaval* was celebrated in much of southern Europe as a festival heralding spring, and the lean days of denial were times of genuine shortages, when the last of the meat salted for the winter had been finished up.

In mainland Spain, *Carnaval* was a fiesta protected first by Felipe IV (1621–65) then by Carlos III (1759–83), who introduced masked balls in imitation of the Venetian celebrations.

In 1802, Puerto de la Cruz (then known as Puerto de La Orotava) was already fully dedi-

cated to enjoying itself at *Carnaval* time, a fact supported by the diaries of the Viscount of Buen Paso, Juan Primo de Guerra, whose entry for 12 February states: "My sister says... that she would be happy, if I am in agreement, to take a house in Puerto de la Orotava for a few days to enjoy the diversions of the *Carnaval*..."

Much later, during Franco's dictatorship, carnivals were banned throughout Spain as it was feared that fancy dress parades would create the ideal climate in which crime and dissent could flourish undetected. Never ones to give in easily, the *tinerfeños* were quick to rename their carnivals Las Fiestas de Invierno (Winter Festivals), thereby side-stepping the unwelcome prohibition.

Being familiar with Tenerife and knowing there was little crime or subversion on the islands, Franco turned a blind eye on the continuing revelries, but he did draw the line at individuals masquerading as religious or military figures. Since his death (in 1975), anything

---

**PRECEDING PAGES:** putting on the glitter for *Carnaval*.
**LEFT:** fantasies can be indulged once a year, at least.
**RIGHT:** a *Carnaval* participant in the guise of Fidel Castro: aping political figures is part of the fun.

goes, with domestic and international public figures pitilessly lampooned at *Carnaval* time.

## Carnaval today

The Santa Cruz de Tenerife *Carnaval* is widely accepted as being the best in Europe and among the best in the world, probably surpassed only by those of Rio de Janeiro and New Orleans. Puerto de la Cruz does not lag far behind. Organisers in Las Palmas de Gran Canaria make similar claims for their fiesta, but let's not take sides.

### BREAKING RECORDS

Santa Cruz earned a place in the *Guinness Book of Records* in 1987 when 240,000 people crammed into the main square for the biggest carnival ball ever held.

the doors in their entrance ways, due to an ancient law requiring house-owners to provide such facilities to the general (male) public.

*Carnaval* is both thirsty and hungry work. A *cubata* (rum and Coke) is the traditional drink, and *churros* (deep-fried doughnuts) and *pinchitos* (spicy pork kebabs) are among the snacks on sale in the numerous kiosks, sites for which are at a premium and are auctioned off well in advance for thousands of pounds sterling. For more on *Carnaval, see pages 96–97.*

*Carnaval* lasts for about 10 days, but the highest of its high points is on Shrove Tuesday, when the *Coso*, the Grand Parade, takes place. Each year there is a different theme and the floats and costumes are astonishing. There is always a strong Latin American influence and, increasingly, a strong gay element. Dancers are often accompanied by *murgas*, groups of people singing satirical and topical songs.

Events on such a scale naturally call for careful forward planning, with extra police drafted into the area and the recent introduction of *pipís moviles* (mobile lavatories), to try to prevent the city's gutters from overflowing. Many of the older houses still have a discreet urinal behind

## Corpus Christi

The second major event of the year, and the most widely celebrated of the religious fiestas (after Christmas and Easter) is the *Octavo* (Eight Days) *de Corpus Christi*, held at the end of May or beginning of June. Corpus Christi is revered in all Catholic countries, and in Tenerife it is celebrated principally in La Laguna and La Orotava, two ancient towns whose deep-rooted rivalry is reflected in the extravagantly-designed and painstakingly fashioned carpets of flower petals and coloured volcanic sands with which the streets and squares are strewn, as each town attempts to outdo the other in its acts of devotion.

Works of art comparable to religious paintings and tapestries, these carpets of flowers take months of intricate preparation and planning, and are destroyed in a few short moments by the feet of the devout taking part in the solemn procession. The smell of crushed petals and leaves, however, lingers on till nightfall.

Traditionally, the religious festival of Corpus Christi was followed closely by the *romería*, a colourful fiesta where food, wine, music and dancing are the order of the day. So popular have these rustic celebrations become – with flower-decked oxen pulling carts laden with Canarios in national costume, tempting the

## More reasons to celebrate

There are plenty of events later in the year, as well. Mid-July in Puerto de la Cruz sees the *Fiesta de la Virgen del Carmen*, with nautical high jinks around the old harbour. At the end of August Los Cristianos hosts the *Nuestra Señora del Carmen* festival, with processions, fireworks and loads of atmosphere. In mid-September, La Laguna celebrates *Santísimo Cristo* with fireworks, veteran car rallies and bouts of *lucha canaria*; and the whole island makes a big day of 12 October, *Día de la Hispanidad* commemorating Columbus' discovery of the Americas (*see page 275 for a list of events*).  ❏

crowds with choice morsels washed down with local wine – that in recent years, towns and villages have co-operated with each other so that instead of clashing, *romerías* are held at intervals over a period of several weeks. Two of the biggest are the *Romería de San Isidro* in mid-June in La Orotava, and the *Romería de San Benito* in La Laguna, about two weeks later. Smaller celebrations are held in Icod, Güímar, Arico and Granadilla throughout June: tourist offices will supply exact dates.

**LEFT:** Corpus Christi flower carpets in La Laguna.
**ABOVE:** ready for bed after a hard day's celebrating; it's an honour to carry the statue of the Virgin.

### NUESTRA SEÑORA DE LA CANDELARIA

On 15 August, people come from all over the Canary Islands on a pilgrimage to the Basilica of Nuestra Señora de la Candelaria (*see page 173*) for the fiesta of the patron saint of the archipelago. It is said that the image of the Virgin was discovered by Guanche shepherds in 1392 and was venerated by the islanders as "Chaxiraxi" before the Spanish brought Christianity to the Canaries and was instrumental in the conversion of the people. Candelaria, on the east coast, is the islands' major holy site and the square outside the basilica is thronged with thousands of people. The date coincides with *Asunción* (the Day of the Assumption) which is a national holiday.

# TENERIFE GOES WILD AT CARNIVAL TIME

*Carnaval is a time of excess and exuberant behaviour, but it's not a spontaneous outburst of energy – it takes most of the year to organise*

Just before Lent, Tenerife explodes into the party mood. The giant fiesta held in the island's capital is now a world-famous event – even earning itself a place in the *Guinness Book of Records* for many years. Serious party-goers, if they aren't in Rio da Janeiro or New Orleans, may well be somewhere in Tenerife. Santa Cruz hosts the biggest jamboree, but the northern resort of Puerto de la Cruz is no slouch when it comes to fancy dress and fire-crackers. To outsiders, Carnaval may have an air of spontaneity, but fiestas on this scale take plenty of organising, and as soon as the coke cans and doughnut wrappers have been swept up for one year, preparations begin for the next. The effort and expense put in to this ephemeral merry-making may seem extraordinary, perhaps wasteful, to sober-sided north Europeans, but to anyone with a hint of Latin blood, its worth every peseta.

## BACCANALIA

This baccanalia (including the hangovers) now stretches for the best part of two weeks, beginning with the election of a Carnival Queen, followed by spectacular street processions of elaborate floats and costumed revellers, which climax on Shrove Tuesday. Besides the parades, there are all kinds of concerts, dance displays, street entertainments and amusements for children. For hours on end, the streets of the old town resound to the strains of salsa and steel bands.

Each year, the Mardi Gras celebrations revolve around a different theme, offering an unmissable opportunity to let off steam. In the Franco era, carnival time was regarded (not without reason) as a potential source of subversion and dissidence. Today, no sacred cows are out of bounds and any shade of sexual or political opinion can be voiced.

▷ **MOMENT OF GLORY**
Fantastic costumes like this one can take all year and huge sums of money, to make, but are considered well worth it, even though their glory is short-lived.

△ **GETTING AHEAD**
The bigger the better seems to be the rule where headdresses are concerned, but wearing them while retaining balance, and a smile, is no easy feat.

▷ **LATIN LEANINGS**
Many of the Carnaval costumes and tableaux have a distinctly Latin American flavour, and would look just as much at home at Rio de Janeiro's Shrovetide celebrations.

## THE BURIAL OF THE SARDINE

The strange ritual known as El Entierro de la Sardina (Burial of the Sardine) takes place on Ash Wednesday. Strictly, it's more of a cremation than a burial, culminating in a spectacular bonfire when the giant effigy of a fish is set alight in the square near the port. At the head of the funeral procession, a beautifully detailed papier-maché "sardine", with jewelled fins and gorgeous mournful eyelashes, sways gently from its moorings on a huge float of winking lights. To the accompaniment of drums and whistles, the bier trundles majestically through the cobbled streets of Santa Cruz. Bands hammer out a repetitive, insistent dirge, and costumed mourners scream and beat their breasts in mock anguish. Their outfits are utterly extravagant – and sometimes unspeakably lewd. As the wake approaches the port, the fish is lifted from its dais and set alight, erupting skywards in a cacophonous shower of sparks.

△ **BANDING TOGETHER**
Music is an essential ingredient, although some bands are as notable for their costumes as for their rhythm.

▷ **CLOWNING AROUND**
Complete strangers suddenly become the best of friends at Carnaval time, even if nobody remembers which clown they kissed the next morning.

◁ **YOUNG REVELLERS**
Children have their own processions and enjoy Carnaval every bit as much as their elders.

# EXPATRIATE LIFE

*From descendants of 19th-century diplomats and entrepreneurs to retired*
*winter sunseekers and lotus-eaters, the expatriate population is booming*

According to a Police Headquarters survey there are more than 23,000 foreigners officially resident in the province of Tenerife. This is a significant number considering that the region's total population amounts only to some 700,000 – especially if you take into account the numerous foreigners who are not legally registered. The figures also exclude large numbers of semi-expatriates, those who flock, like migrating birds, to the Canary Islands between November and April to benefit from the superb winter climate. Some stay in their own villas, others come here on extended and inexpensive package deals.

The largest group of foreign nationals in the province of Tenerife is the British – there are 11,000 officially registered with the British Consul, plus, he estimates, a similar number who are not registered – either because they are here for less than six months, or because their papers are not in order.

The second expatriate group is the Germans, with about 6,000 officially registered with their Consul (again, the true number is reckoned to be much higher). They are followed by the Indian community, whose members are prominent in the commercial sector, owning many bazaars specialising in electrical goods and gifts. The Belgians make up the fourth largest community, followed by Scandinavians, while the Honorary French Consul has around 1,000 nationals on his books.

By far the greatest number of these expatriates live on Tenerife itself, generally in or close to Puerto de la Cruz, La Orotava, Santa Ursula, El Sauzal, Tacoronte, Mesa del Mar and Bajamar in the north. Some live in Santa Cruz and nearby Radazul and Tabaiba; and in the south they concentrate around Los Cristianos, Playa de las Américas, the Costa del Silencio, Médano, Callao Salvaje, Marazul and Puerto Santiago-Los Gigantes. Additionally, there are small pioneering groups living on the lesser islands of La Palma, La Gomera and El Hierro, most notably at Los Llanos de Aridane in La Palma, a town known for its wines, which is becoming increasingly popular among the British and the Germans.

## Better health and lower tax

Of the legally-documented residents, irrespective of nationality, some 70 percent are retired. Most of them choose to live here because of the mild climate, said to be particularly beneficial to those suffering from cardiac disease or respiratory conditions such as asthma.

There are others who came here when the Canaries were a tax haven, and stayed, or kept coming back, when this changed. Generally, income tax is still lower than in the UK and many other European countries, but in recent years the islands have shown no reticence in introducing a wide range of taxes where once there were none.

**PRECEDING PAGES:** guaranteed sunshine is the major attraction for most new residents.
**LEFT:** golf is big business among expatriates.
**RIGHT:** taking it easy in the shade.

Like any region known for its low taxes, the region also attracts its share of tax avoiders and evaders, bankrupts and those who prefer to keep a low fiscal profile, but fortunately these are in a minority.

There are also significant numbers of foreign residents working in the province and in possession of work permits of *cuenta propia* (self-employed) or *cuenta ajena* (employee) status. The range of occupations is wide, principally embracing the tourist and related catering industries and the booming property market, but also including the teaching profession and import and export sectors. There are also Ger-

being allowed to play tennis on a Sunday afternoon, "although croquet parties on their own private lawns were given regularly…"

Falklands-born Baillon first came to Tenerife in 1906 to take on the daunting task of managing Fyffes vast banana plantations near Adeje, and several members of the Baillon family still live on the island. Among other eminent expatriate families were the Reids, whose members served as vice-consuls in Puerto de la Cruz from 1878 to 1973; and the Ahlers family, now in its fourth generation on Tenerife, who were the founding partners of one of the island's major import companies.

man and French *pâtisseries*; a certain amount of foreign-language publishing; even a British-owned donkey sanctuary. There's a sprinkling of German and British doctors, too, and a few British dentists are beginning to arrive.

## Distinguished expatriates

It's all a far cry from the early expatriate days of the late 19th and early 20th centuries. The days when long-term British resident Alexander Baillon reported in his memoirs: "It was the custom for ladies to go about in hammocks", so pot-holed and muddy were the streets; and when members of the British Games Club (founded in 1903) objected to fellow members

### LASTING MEMORIALS

Wandering around the towns of Puerto de la Cruz and Santa Cruz de Tenerife you may notice street names which pay tribute to various distinguished European families who have contributed so richly to the island over the years. Some of them have been Hispanicised so may not be immediately apparent.

Names include Valois (Walsh), Cologán (Colgan), Dr Ingram (a popular Edinburgh doctor who lived and practised here in the 1920s), Blanco (White), Enrique Talg (whose family own the Hotel Tigaiga), Richard J Yeoward (of shipping line fame), Carlos J. R. Hamilton (shipping agents), Buenaventura Bonet, and many more.

## Join the club

As in other places that attract large numbers of expatriates, many of the foreign communities on the island run their own clubs and organisations and hold their own social events. In Puerto de la Cruz the British Games Club offers a choice of bowls, tennis, croquet and badminton, as well as many less energetic pastimes, but its appeal may be dwindling, as it counts few younger residents among its membership of just 220, a quarter of whom are not British at all.

### READ ALL ABOUT IT

English-language newspapers, such as the fortnightly *Tenerife News*, bring local and national events to those who have not mastered a great deal of Spanish.

number of British residents who have still to gain a fluent grasp of Spanish.

There are Lions Clubs and Rotary Clubs in Puerto de la Cruz and Playa de las Américas, both with multinational membership. In Santa Cruz, there is the island's own, largely British, masonic lodge – masons were banned for many years in Spain, but are now legal once more. In the south of the island, there's the Children's Centre at Guaza, and during winter months the Swallows Group meets twice weekly in Los

The Wednesday Group of English-speaking people meets once a month for lunch and organises various activities, while ESTA (the English-Speaking Theatre Association) usually puts on two shows a year, the proceeds of both going to charity.

The English Library in the pleasant Parque Taoro area of Puerto de la Cruz, holds more than 3,000 books, and a British video library has opened in nearby Santa Ursula, providing a much-needed service to the considerable

**LEFT:** employees of Fyffes banana company at a reception in Tenerife.
**ABOVE:** expats often run a bar or restaurant.

Cristianos, where children and young people exchange books and arrange activities.

German-speaking expatriates are catered for by the Santa Cruz branch of the Altavista Club whose membership is also open to Spaniards. For French-speakers, social life revolves around the Alianza Francesa Club and the sociable Union Française des Etrangers, which also operates a French-language video club.

## Church and school

Expatriates also stick to their own form of worship and education. In Santa Cruz, St George's Anglican Church has a regular congregation, and in Puerto de la Cruz All Saints' Anglican

Church, built in 1890, has a resident chaplain who holds services every Sunday and Wednesday; the church is loaned frequently to the German, Swedish and Finnish communities. For German residents there are also regular church services weekly in Puerto de la Cruz and monthly in Santa Cruz.

Children's needs are not forgotten either: in Puerto de la Cruz the British Yeoward School, founded in 1969, offers a British curriculum to children from the kindergarten stage to the age of 18. In the south of the island, there is the British Council-recognised British Wingate School at Cabo Blanco.

### BUYER BEWARE

If you have fallen in love with Tenerife and are seriously considering buying a property on the island, there are a few basic guidelines to follow:

● Timeshare salespeople can be a nuisance and should be firmly ignored unless you are genuinely interested in what they have to offer.

● Before doing anything, always consult a solicitor.

● Choose an estate agent with a credible track record.

● Consult the Instituto de Propietarios Extranjeros (Institute of Foreign Property Owners) before you sign anything. They can be contacted at Apartado de Correos 418, 3590 Altea, Alicante, Spain.

Santa Cruz has a state-sponsored German school providing education up to the age of 18, and a private German school has been set up on the outskirts of Playa de las Américas.

## Paradise lost?

Life in Tenerife isn't quite the utopia that many resident expatriates thought it would be. The climate, of course, is the reason most people came to live here, and that hasn't changed, but the cost of living – once cheap by northern European standards – is rising all the time, and realists accept that it will continue to do so. Strangely, while eating out needn't cost the earth, the food on sale in shops and markets is a major expense. However, tobacco, wines, spirits, petrol and diesel are all cheaper than in the UK, as are *contribuciones urbanas* (rates). Electricity and water tariffs are on the increase, but central heating bills are minimal.

Services aren't all some people expect: patience and fortitude are needed when faced with the shortcomings of such utilities as Telefónica (the telephone company) and UNELCO (the electricity generating board), both of which fail to meet customer demand.

People thinking of taking the plunge and moving to Tenerife also need to consider carefully all the things they may miss. Couples should make sure they're both equally committed: many a marriage has foundered when one partner has found it impossible to adapt.

Think of the future, too, as there is no safety net to provide long-term hospitalisation or residential care. It is inadvisable for anyone to put themselves in a situation where they could not afford to return home if necessary.

Having stressed the negative, it should be said that many foreigners are extremely happy here. Once settled, their main concerns include environmental issues and conservation, about which they are sometimes more vocal than the local authorities would like. But local politicians have recently become more aware of their considerable voting clout, and realise that the expat strength could be sufficient, in some areas, to upset the municipal apple-cart. The role may have changed, but foreigners are still a force to be reckoned with on Tenerife. ❏

**LEFT:** many retired people have found that it's a good life on the islands.
**RIGHT:** fresh fish is just one of the advantages.

# FOOD

*The food of Tenerife has much in common with that on the Spanish mainland,*
*but you will find quite a few island specialities*

While some tourists seem content to stick to safe and familiar routines of pizza and hamburgers in the large resorts, there is no shortage of restaurants all over Tenerife ready to offer you a taste of real Canarian cooking. Essentially, of course, the style is Spanish, featuring many of the classic dishes found on the mainland – *paella, gazpacho*, a wide variety of *tapas* and so forth, which many visitors will recognise from previous holidays in Spain.

Like mainland Spaniards, Canarians generally prefer to eat their main meal of the day at lunchtime, and favour later meal times than most Europeans are used to – lunch at around 2pm, supper rarely before 9pm and often later. In tourist areas, however, most restaurants adapt opening hours to suit their predominant clientele. Restaurants described as *tipico* often serve regional cooking in attractive, rustic surroundings. Few Canarian recipes scale gastronomic heights, but fresh ingredients and homely specialities give local cuisine plenty of distinctive flavour.

## Fresh from the sea

As you would expect on Atlantic islands, fish (*pescado*) is a staple but immensely varied element in the Canarian repertoire. All around the archipelago lie some of the world's richest fishing grounds, although exploitation by many trawler fleets is taking its toll on some varieties, and much now has to be imported.

Canarian menus still offer an amazing range of species, however, many of which defy precise translations. Look out for delicious local fish like *vieja, cherne, sargo* and *sama*, besides the more generally familiar *bacalao* (cod), *merluza* (hake), *atun* (tuna) and *mero* (perch). Fish is generally served either simply grilled or made into a soupy stew with vegetables and potatoes (*sancocho* or *cazuela*). The classic

Spanish seafood dishes *calamares a la plancha* (fried squid rings) and *gambas al ajillo* (prawns in garlic) are never difficult to find.

Look carefully at the menu when you order, because fish is sometimes priced by the kilo rather than by the portion, which can make the bill a nasty shock.

## Catering for carnivores

Tourist restaurants offer plenty of pork, lamb and veal for visitors, but beef herds have declined greatly in recent years and steaks are mostly imported from South America. The most typical Canarian meat dishes include chicken or rabbit – *conejo en salmorejo* consists of rabbit pieces marinaded in a sauce made of oil, vinegar and herbs. You may even find goats' meat (*cabrito*) on more adventurous menus. Cooked properly, it is very tasty.

A *puchero canario* is a typical hotpot with meat and vegetables, sometimes flavoured with saffron. *Potaje de berros* is a classic rib-sticking soup made with watercress, pork ribs, beans

**LEFT:** there's a wide variety of enticing *tapas*.
**RIGHT:** fish is just one of many food products on sale in the La Laguna market.

and a mixture of whatever vegetables happen to be in season.

As the local market stalls show, there's a terrific choice of fresh vegetables in Tenerife – expect plenty of tomatoes which come in all shapes and sizes and usually have a lot more flavour than those you get in supermarkets at home. If you order a salad, it is generally served as a starter, rather than an accompaniment to a main course.

One indispensible item on any Canarian menu is *papas arrugadas* – small wrinkled potatoes cooked in their jackets in brine to concentrate the flavour. Not good if you're on a

used to thicken stews or soups, and is the basis of a few puddings. *Escaldon* is a tasty seasoned broth with wheat *gofio*.

## Sweet things

Desserts tend to be very sweet, and often contain almonds or honey. The best honey comes from the national park, Las Cañadas del Teide, and is mainly made from the nectar of the Teide broom, or *retama*. A honey museum, La Casa de la Miel, in El Sauzal promotes the island's honey producers.

A classic favourite dessert is *bienmesabe*, a rich, creamy mixture of eggs, cinnamon and

low-sodium diet because the salt crystallises in a visible white crust after cooking, but absolutely delicious.

*Mojo* is a spicy sauce which comes in two varieties: *rojo* (red) made with chilli and red peppers, and *verde* (green), a less fiery type containing parsley, coriander and other herbs. Another curiosity is *gofio*, or toasted cereal flour (generally made from maize, but sometimes barley or wheat, or even ground chickpeas), which dates back to Guanche times. Once a staple food, it still forms part of the diet of many islanders. To be honest, this worthy but stodgy stuff is a dubious virtue made of what was once a necessity, but it is sometimes

nuts. *Turrones de melaza* (almond cakes) and *frangollo* which uses sweetened *gofio* with milk, may be on more imaginative menus. The ubiquitous Spanish flan (*crème caramel*) is always available, along with fresh fruit and ice cream (*helado*).

## Exotic fruit

Lots of exotic fruits are grown locally these days, including mangoes, papaya, kiwi fruit and guava. In winter, sample the delicately flavoured chirimoya or custard apple, whose soft creamy flesh conceals shiny black seeds. At least once in a lifetime, try a prickly pear – these orange cactus fruits are surprisingly sweet. The stubby local bananas often find their way into Canarian cooking, perhaps flambéd with rum, or fried in batter. The banana was introduced to the islands from the West Indies several centuries ago, but it only took off commercially in the late 19th century.

The type that grows best in Tenerife is a small curved variety called the Dwarf Cavendish which originates from Indochina. The flavour is intense and sweet, but it is not as popular as the larger varieties which grow in the Caribbean or Central and South America, and has been difficult to market for export in Europe. Spain formerly guaranteed to offload

Canarian wines can be very good, although production is limited and they are expensive compared with mainland Spanish wines. Viniculture on the islands dates back many years. In the 16th century, Tenerife wines were made with sweet Malvasia grapes (Canary Sack was Falstaff's favourite tipple), but now they are more in line with the drier tastes of modern palates. Good reds come from the Tacoronte region in northeast Tenerife; white wines from around Icod. Tenerife's wines are divided into five "denominations of origin" or appellations, and quality control has improved greatly in recent years. ¡Salud! ❑

the lion's share of Canarian production at subsidised rates, but is now running into difficulties with EU trading regulations.

## Cheese and wine

Most island cheeses are made from goat's or sheep's milk. They vary greatly in consistency and flavour, depending chiefly on the time of year they are made, but they are often fairly strong and salty. Arico, near the west coast of Tenerife, is a noted cheese-making centre.

---

**LEFT:** appetising local dishes on La Gomera.
**ABOVE:** roasted red peppers are a popular dish; with chillis, they make *mojo rojo* sauce.

### LOCAL LIQUOR

Rum (*ron*) is distilled in the Canaries, and often mixed with ice and Coca-Cola to make the classic Spanish drink called a *Cuba Libre* (Free Cuba – a name with obvious political connotations). Be wary of it on a hot day, as the taste is innocuous and the ice-cold Coke can conceal dangerously large measures of rum.

Also on offer are a variety of sticky liqueurs, like *ronmiel*, an orangey concoction made from palm sap, and *cobana*, which is made from bananas.

*Sangria* – that ubiquitous mixture of red wine, brandy, lemonade and chunks of citrus fruits is prepared almost exclusively for tourists – locals seldom touch it.

# VOLCANIC ISLANDS

*If you are exploring the area around Tenerife's El Teide or the south of La Palma,*
*you will rapidly recognise the awesome power of the islands' volcanoes*

The world's surface is made up of a number of thick slabs or plates of rock, which are constantly moving, very slowly, in relation to one another. These movements are caused by currents of heat that are generated within the molten core of the Earth. Over hundreds of millions of years the plates on which Africa and South America sit drifted apart, forming the Atlantic Ocean. As Africa rubbed along the southern edge of Europe, enormous pressure built up and created the Atlas Mountains in North Africa. As the Atlas chain folded, huge blocks of rock in the Atlantic were shoved upwards. Local releases of pressure around these blocks let liquid rock flow upwards through cracks. Volcanoes formed where the cracks reached the surface.

Outcrops of these original basement rocks have been exposed at the bottom of La Palma's Caldera de Taburiente and in the cliffs of northern Gomera. On these western isles these rocks are relatively recent, going back a mere 20 million years or so, but on the eastern island of Fuerteventura they date back 37 million years.

Tenerife, the three smaller islands in the western province, and Gran Canaria are purely volcanic. They are separated from each other by deep-water trenches and almost certainly were never linked to Africa.

The chances of seeing an eruption are fairly remote. The last one was on the island of La Palma in 1971. El Teide still oozes sulphurous trails of smoke and Timanfaya on Lanzarote burns away just beneath your feet. It is just a matter of time, of course, but whereas that could mean next week, it might not be for another million years or so.

Whether people would be warned of an impending eruption is a bit uncertain. Despite the large resident and tourist populations the Canaries have a scanty network of seismo-

graphs to record geological movements. Contingency planning is almost non-existent, though estimations have been made of the ash falls that El Teide might produce.

So far the historic eruptions have occurred in sparsely inhabited areas and have not been too calamitously sudden. But no one knows

where the next one might be. A visit to one of these awesome volcanic areas demonstrates the mighty power of nature.

## Tenerife

Tenerife was built up by the two most violent types of volcanic eruptions known – Plinian and Peléan. A Plinian eruption is a stupendous uprush of boiling gas several miles high. Peléan eruptions are equally explosive, but in this type the boiling lava and gases roll out from the volcano in a glowing incendiary avalanche. A normal avalanche is propelled by gravity alone, but these *nuées ardentes* (burning clouds) have internal sources of energy which make them

---

**PRECEDING PAGES:** a vast volcanic crater in the National Park near El Teide.
**LEFT:** succulents bloom on a blanket of lava.
**RIGHT:** the 1971 eruption on La Palma.

move faster, further and more devastatingly than any simple landslip or normal lava flow.

It was the work of such eruptions which constructed a huge volcano much higher than the present Mount Teide, which dominates Tenerife, and is the highest mountain in Spain at 3,718 metres (12,197 ft). These cataclysmic eruptions emptied the magma chamber under the volcano and the upper part collapsed under its own weight. The base of the walls of this original vast volcano are all that remain, defining a sheer-walled *caldera*.

The flat white expanse between these walls and the peak of El Teide itself are known as

*cañadas*. They are formed of fine sands and gravels eroded from the *caldera* walls. In a wetter era many centuries ago Las Cañadas was covered with lakes.

## Parque Nacional del Teide

The area of the Las Cañadas is now a National Park which includes the peak of El Teide within its limits. It is not one but two *calderas*. The separating wall is Los Roques de García, a distinctive barrier of dark mauve and pink rocks protruding from the white *cañadas*.

Volcanic activity on Tenerife is today centred around El Teide and its several parasitic cones which have sprouted on the northern

edge of the *caldera*. The most recent eruptions have been explosive, forming a small *caldera* at the very summit of El Teide in which a new cone is growing.

The most recent eruption of El Teide was in 1909, and there were three eruptions in the 18th century. Christopher Columbus saw smoke and ash emanating from Pico Viejo as he sailed for the New World in 1492. Las Narices de Teide (Teide's Nostrils) on the south flank of the mountain blew in 1798. The road to Chio now cuts through its dark grey lava flows and clinker. Little or no vegetation grows among the scattered volcanic bombs, and its jagged surface is a malevolent landscape for walkers. The drab, fresh lava flows here contrast with the older lava flows in the park, which are altogether smoother and surprisingly colourful.

El Teide is classed as a strato-volcano; it is made up of different lavas and ashes which have spilled out in a series of eruptions from several craters at different times, which explains why the rocks around it are so varied in texture and colour. It is the colours that impress the most. Solid rivers of chocolate and russet browns run alongside frozen oranges and burgundies. Here and there streaks of jet-black obsidian (a natural glass) glint in the sunlight, and huge spheres of lava that broke away from the main lava flows lie stranded on the buff-white back-drop of the Las Cañadas.

Las Cañadas and the peak of El Teide are easy to reach. In the Visitor Centre the National Park authorities screen a film about all the parks on the islands, and there is a display of rock specimens and a model showing the geological development of El Teide. Information

### LAVA TYPES

The Canary Islands have a wide range of lava types. Around El Teide there are flows of pahoehoe lava – lava fields on which you can walk barefoot. This is smooth and satiny, sometimes formed into coiled strands like rope. Pahoehoe lava cools slowly and remains viscous for some time, allowing the gases to ooze out through the steadily solidifying "plastic" skin.

Ahah lava is a complete contrast. This type cools quickly, the gases being spat out, ripping the surface into jagged blocks. Walking across it even in hiking boots is not to be done for pleasure – at best it means wrecking a good pair of boots.

on points of natural and archaeological inter- est in the area is also available in the centre.

Here you can find out about plants like the tiny Teide violet or the bizarre Tajinaste, which are found only here. The Tajinaste grows around the Parador – the only place to stay unless you fancy overnighting at the refuge as you hike up to the peak itself, and a good stop for coffee. From here there are sweeping views up to the top of Teide and nearby is the picnic site at Roques de García, the ancient remnants of the wall which divides the *caldera* into two. Erosion has carved Las Roques into weird and wonderful shapes.

days the summit seems as busy as Puerto de la Cruz, and thousands of pairs of feet have worn tracks across it. And such is the desire of visitors to take home a souvenir rock that the park authorities are seriously worried about the survival of the peak itself – tons of rock are removed by souvenir hunters each year.

Tenerife's recent volcanic history is not con- fined to the National Park. The coastal town of Garachico was destroyed by lava flows in the spring of 1706. The peninsula of black lava which can be seen today jutting out to sea covers the former harbour, once of major importance on the Spanish route to the West Indies. The

town was rebuilt on this lava and some of the older houses are made of the black pumice pro- duced in the eruption.

## La Palma

In 1949 La Palma suffered two fearsome explo- sions causing the southern quarter of the island to be completely cut off by lava. Contemporary observers shared the sentiments of Italian engineer, Leonardo Torriani, who chronicled the conquest of the islands in the late 16th cen- tury, and was almost lost for words when he witnessed the eruption of Tegueso in 1585. "I believe, indeed, that not even the most ingen- ious spirit is capable of describing such horror,

Between the Visitor Centre and the Parador is El Teide's main attraction – the cable car which runs up to near the summit. The cold and the thin sulphur-laden air make a trip to the top unsuitable for people with heart complaints, and even the very fit may find the scramble from cable car to summit exhausting. But hun- dreds of visitors make the trip daily, if the cables aren't iced up or the wind too fierce.

El Teide's very popularity and accessibility are threatening its special character. On some

**LEFT:** a floor of broken lava is hard on the feet.
**RIGHT:** thick ropey strands of lava, known as *pahoehoe*, cover parts of El Teide.

fear and calamity." He soon regained enough composure to devote a full chapter to the event. "Tegueso... burned each day and more fiercely with resplendent flames and many coloured plumes of smoke. This smoke changed from golden black, to golden white, yellow, sky-blue and red..."

Captain Andrés de Valcáred, a military man, who saw his aunt's La Palma farm buried by lava in 1646, was more impressed by the noise of eruptions than the colour. "There was such a noise and terrible rumble as if there was a great number of artillery pieces being fired off, and with such loudness that it was heard in all the islands. And there were thrown out stones in such numbers that they seemed like flocks of birds and... were seen everywhere on the island. By night they were seen the more clearly for it seemed each stone was a living streak of fire."

## Teneguia's eruption

In all the descriptions there is a common pattern of events. Before the eruption proper comes a series of earthquakes which steadily increase in frequency and violence. The quakes eventually rip open the earth and molten rock emerges to form a series of small cones which are built up by more molten rock and ash.

### THE POWER OF NATURE

The awesome power of a volcanic eruption on the island of La Palma was brought home to the rest of Spain by Radio Tenerife in 1949: "The human mind simply cannot imagine the power of soulless nature. Out of the mountain came a slow, oh so slow river of fire, growing by the minute, until it stood over 3 metres high and nearly 200 metres across. Its edges turned black as it cooled; the top too was black – scaly and scarred like the hide of some antediluvian monster. On it came. No-one could hold it back. No-one could turn it aside. Everything in its path was obliterated. Everything. Houses, farms, orchards..."

Teneguia, south of the town of Fuencaliente on La Palma erupted in 1971, the most recent volcanic eruption on the Canary Islands. It is estimated to have produced the equivalent of 2 million lorry loads of lava, even though the eruption was a relatively small one, lasting from 26 October to 18 November. The lava flow actually increased the length of the island by a few metres.

During both of the 1646 and 1971 eruptions, volcanic "bombs" were spewed out of the volcano's mouth. Once living streaks of fire, they litter the surface of the lava flows. These bombs are formed as solid chunks of rock that are hurled through liquid lava in the throat of he volcano. Their crusts are usually crazed, revealing an inner core of solidified frothy lava.

The lava from Teneguia's most recent eruption is solid but still warm under foot, and the cracks in its surface still emit scorching gases. The whole of La Palma's southern tip is a wasteland of black cinders, rubble and what appear to be streams of hardened tarmac. The area looks like the scene of an immense industrial disaster.

## The boiling kettle

Volcanoes and lava flows are to be found throughout La Palma and the word caldera, which is now used by geologists to describe large basin-shaped hollows in a volcano, comes from La Palma's Caldera de Taburiente, now a National Park. Caldera is Spanish for a boiling-pan or kettle and when you stand beside the Roque de los Muchachos Observatory and look down into it, you can understand how apt the word is. The enormous basin below is full of cloud which bubbles and heaves like boiling porridge.

The 19th-century German geologist, Leopold von Buch (who compiled a natural history of the islands), first applied the term caldera to volcanic features, but, despite its sheer walls and their rainbow-coloured lavas and ashes, the Caldera de Taburiente is not a vast volcanic crater. For what nature can build up, nature can tear down again. The Taburiente caldera is the product of the inexorable process of erosion. As La Palma has gradually risen from the Atlantic, streams have cut into the soft ashes of the island mass. Large chunks of the caldera's walls have slumped into the 8-km (5-mile) basin, to be broken down and carried seaward by the constant flow of water.

Below the clouds, the Caldera de Taburiente is a wooded Shangri-la, accessible only on foot. At its centre is a knife-sharp slab of rock, Idafe, which was sacred to the native islanders before the conquest, and whose last act was played out in the natural fortress of the caldera.

## La Gomera

La Gomera has no signs of recent volcanic activity, yet it does possess spectacular volcanic scenery. The most impressive example is the cliff of basalt columns, resembling a giant church organ and called Los Organos (the Organ Pipes), which are best seen from the sea just west of Vallehermoso's beach.

When the lava from a long ago eruption cooled, it slowly shrank and cracked into six-sided columns which have weathered to different heights to produce this remarkable feature – approximately 20 metres (65 ft) wide and 80 metres (260 ft) high.

Volcanic domes of thick viscous lava and dykes of resistant rock which stand out as natural walls in the deeply cut ravines may also

be seen in the centre of the island in the Parque Nacional de Garajonay (*see pages 206–8*).

## El Hierro

The smallest island of the Canaries, El Hierro has seen no eruptions in recorded history, although geologists know that it has suffered volcanic activity more recently than La Gomera. El Golfo, on the western side of the island, is the semi-circular remnant of a former crater dissected by the sea to reveal several hundred metres of lava flows lying one above the other. What is more, most of the island's surviving basalt core is pock-marked by hundreds of small craters. ❏

**LEFT:** only massive underground energy could produce formations such as this.
**RIGHT:** the volcanic gravel surface of El Teide.

# THE SOURCE OF LIFE

*Although they are blessed with more water than their eastern neighbours,*
*the supply and control of water is still a problem for the western islands*

Tenerife and the smaller western Canary Islands are more fortunate than their eastern neighbours in that they receive triple the amount of natural water. There are three sources: rain, snow – which covers the slopes of El Teide on Tenerife for about five months a year – and moisture from the clouds collected by the vegetation on the upper regions of all four western islands.

Water from these three sources soaks through into underground natural deposits, although about 80 percent is lost by run-offs to the sea or by evaporation. And in contrast to the eastern group there are no water desalination plants, as yet, on the western islands.

## Extracting the water

Water is extracted by two methods. First, by blasting *galerias* or tunnels horizontally into the mountain-sides, aimed at the underground deposits. This method began in 1860 and today there are about 940 *galerias* on Tenerife alone, measuring a total of 2,000 kms (1,300 miles). Mounds of excavated rock can be seen at the mouths of the *galerias*, which are usually about 1.5 metres (5 feet) in diameter and are commonly accompanied by a small square building housing a simple water distribution device. The second method, begun in 1925, was the drilling of vertical wells, aimed at the same underground deposits.

Nature has also provided a few springs, which are found at various levels on the islands where water encounters an impermeable layer of rock. The volume of water from these springs decreases in summer and they are seldom visible from the roads.

## Controlling the flow

At present all water on the Canary Islands is produced and owned by private enterprise. Municipalities contract to buy their requirements from owners and then distribute it to

individual consumers who are charged on a metered basis. Irrigation water is also sold by water companies or individual owners and is distributed via standard-sized pipes or open channels, for an agreed number of hours per day, week or month. It is measured in *pipas*, each *pipa* being the equivalent of 480 litres

(105 gallons). Each hour's worth of water flowing down one of these channels equals 100 *pipas* (48,000 litre/10,500 gallons).

Water for irrigation is stored in open tanks, visible all over the islands, and filled from wells or *galerias*. The agreed amounts must be released from the holding tank on the given time and day, in order to avoid overflow, even if it is raining.

## The power of water

The private ownership and production of water became a hot political issue in 1985 when the Spanish Parliament in Madrid promulgated a new water law, replacing that of 1879. In spite

---

**LEFT:** water deposits remain in an old well.
**RIGHT:** most properties have their own water supply.

of general local opposition to this law in the Canaries, where many water owners are small farmers, the Canary Islands Autonomous Government, dominated at that time by the Socialist Party, approved the new law. In direct consequence of this, the party was voted out of office in the general election of 1987. The newly elected centre-right government promptly suspended the new law, and proposed new water legislation.

Apart from political fortunes and the high cost of water, a more immediate problem con-

cerns quality rather than quantity. In Tenerife's Orotava Valley, one of the areas of heaviest usage, an excess of natural fluoride in the water has caused dental problems, especially in young children, and some areas in the south have brackish water with a disagreeable taste. The authorities apply strict health controls on domestic water, but even so it remains a wise precaution to stick to bottled water for drinking.

The fast development of tourism in the south of Tenerife, however, will require sea water desalination plants, if only to distil brackish water and keep the golf courses green, although agriculture will survive on natural water for years to come.

## *Galerias* and Garoë trees

La Palma has the greatest rainfall in the Canaries with an average of 64 cm (25 inches) a year, which has earned it the sobriquet "Isla Verde" – Green Island. Water on La Palma comes mostly from *galerias* with a few supplementary wells. Exceptional features are the various streams in the great Caldera de Taburiente.

La Gomera, from where water was taken by Columbus to bless America, still obtains its water from wells – there are only three *galerias*. An important contribution comes from the forests in the upper regions of the island where the long-needled Canary pines and giant briar shrubs condense astonishing amounts of water from the clouds all year.

El Hierro, the most westerly and least developed of the islands has the most complicated and the quaintest sources of water. Because of the extreme porosity of the terrain, water can only be recovered from wells at sea level, from where it is pumped up to high towns and villages. Accordingly water cisterns, some quite ancient, are to be found all over the island. Most have wooden lids with a hole just large enough to admit a bottle on a string, and custom allows passers-by to fill one bottle.

El Hierro also has an ancient medicinal spring, the Pozo de la Salud, or Well of Health at Sabinosa, whose waters are believed to produce cures for a variety of ailments. And the Garoë Tree of El Hierro is famous for its water-producing qualities. George Glas, writing in 1764, tells how "its leaves constantly distil such a quantity of water as is sufficient to furnish drink to every living creature in Hierro, nature having provided this remedy for the drought of the island".

Today, nature is assisted by the Spanish Institute for the Conservation of Nature (ICONA) and continues to provide a "remedy for the living creatures of Hierro". Basins of stone have been placed by ICONA near the roadside at Los Aljibes de Binto, where trees in the cloud belt distil quantities of fresh, clear water – as much as 1,000 litres (220 gallons) in a night.  ❑

**LEFT:** Tenerife's rivers are rarely more than desolate trickles, especially in summer.
**RIGHT:** wooded areas of La Gomera are rich in water.

# PLACES

*A detailed guide to the western islands, with principal sites clearly cross-referenced by number to the maps*

The western province of the autonomous region of the Canary Islands comprises the islands of Tenerife, La Gomera, La Palma, and El Hierro. Tenerife, shaped like a ham, is the most populous island, the cultural centre of the archipelago. Its major city, Santa Cruz, shares with Las Palmas on Gran Canaria the role of capital of the Canaries: government offices are maintained in both cities and the presidency of the autonomous government alternates between them. Mount Teide, which made a great impression on 19th-century scientists Charles Darwin and Alexander von Humboldt, was once regarded as the Everest of Europe, and helped put the island on the map. It was to Tenerife that the first tourists came.

Life in the Anaga hills of the north and the Teno massif in the southwest has not changed greatly in the past few centuries, although electricity has now come to even the most remote villages. Elsewhere, the arrival of tourism has had an impact on the landscape and economy: residential developments (*urbanisaciones*) around Puerto de la Cruz, the first of the tourist towns, has devoured most of the banana plantations of the northern shore. In the south, big, brash develop-

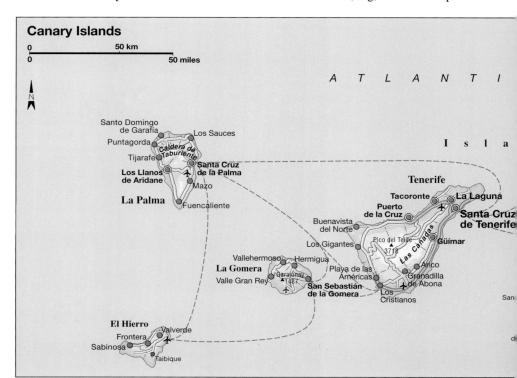

### Canary Islands

ments like Los Cristianos crowd a once-deserted shoreline, harbours are thronged with yachts, and modern villas creep up the hills.

About 32 km (20 miles) to the west of Tenerife is the round island of La Gomera. Rising steeply to a point at Mount Garajonay, the island's centre is covered by the Parque Nacional Garajonay forest, laced with excellent walking tracks. The six major valleys of La Gomera are steep and heavily terraced, although much of the terracing is now abandoned following the island's depopulation. Tourism is far more low-key but keen walkers are attracted to it, and a number of restaurants and hotels have sprung up to cater to their needs.

La Palma, shaped like a canine tooth, is the greenest of the islands. It is a mountainous place and on its highest point, the Roque de los Muchachos, stands a splendid observatory, staffed and visited by astronomers from all over the world. Santa Cruz de la Palma, the port and capital, is one of the prettiest towns in the archipelago, with elegant balconies and squares. Around the southern shores are beaches of black sand, and in the north is the Caldera de Taburiente, a vast and forested volcanic cavity with the status of a national park.

El Hierro, the smallest and most remote of the western islands, is the one that produces the best local wine. The tablelands at its centre are reminiscent of northern European pastures; the massive bay of El Golfo is part of the largest volcanic crater in the world.

Away from the beaches which most people associate with the Canary Islands, these are the landscapes of the independent traveller, undiscovered, diverse and intriguing.  ❏

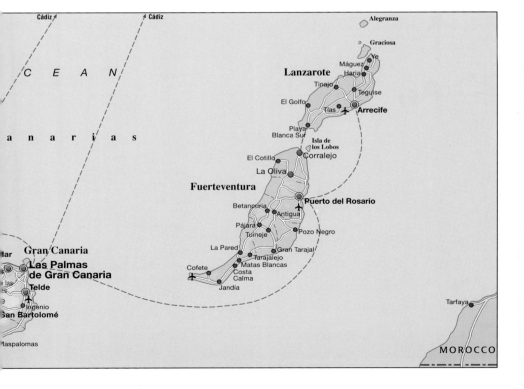

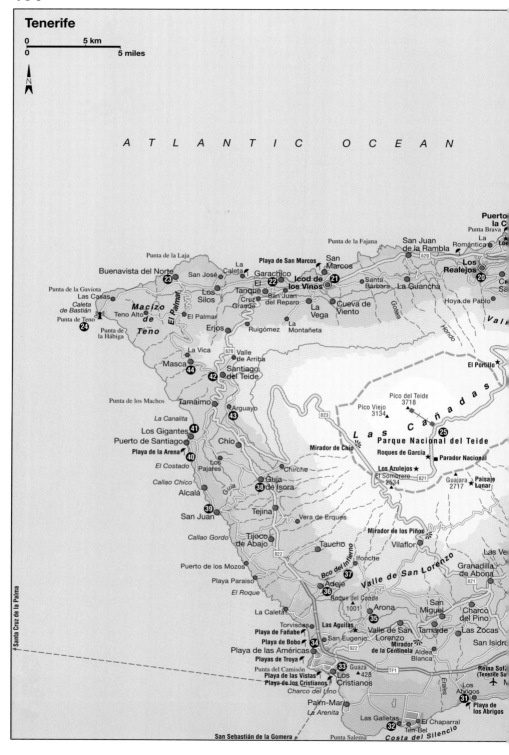

# Tenerife

0 — 5 km
0 — 5 miles

N

**ATLANTIC OCEAN**

Puerto
la C
Punta Brava
Punta de la Fajana    San Juan    La
de la Rambla    Romántica    Lo
820
Punta de la Laja    Playa de San Marcos    San    Los
La    Marcos    Realejos
Buenavista del Norte    Caleta    San José    Garachico    Icod de    San Juan    Santa    La Guancha    20
23    22    los Vinos    21    Bárbara    C
Punta de la Gaviota    El    Hoya de Pablo    Sa
Las Casas    Los    Tanque    San Juan
Caleta    Silos    Cruz    del Reparo    Cueva de    Val
de Bastián    Macizo    Grande    La    Viento
Punta de Teno    de    Teno Alto    El Palmar    Vega
24    Teno    Erjos    Ruigómez    La    Hondo
Punta de    Montañeta
la Hábiga    La Vica    820    Valle    El Portillo
Masca    de Arriba
44    La Canalita    Santiago    Las Cañadas
42    del Teide
Punta de los Machos    Tamáimo    Pico del Teide
Arguayo    3718
La Canalita    43    Pico Viejo    25
Los Gigantes    41    3134    Parque Nacional del Teide
Puerto de Santiago    Chío    823    Roques de García    Parador Nacional
Playa de la Arena    40    Mirador de Chío    Los Azulejos    Guajara    Paisaje
El Costado    Los    El Sombrero    821    2717    Lunar
Callao Chico    Pajares    Chirche    2534
Alcalá    Guía    Guía    38    de Isora
39    Tejina
San Juan    Vera de Erques
Callao Gordo    Tijoco    Mirador de los Piños
de Abajo    Taucho    Vilaflor
822    Ifonche    Las Ve
Puerto de los Mozos    Bco. del Infierno    37    Granadilla
Playa Paraiso    Adeje    Valle de San Lorenzo    de Abona
El Roque    36    821
Roque del Conde    Arona    San
La Caleta    1001    35    Miguel    Charco
Torviscas    Las Aguilas    del Pino
Playa de Fañabe    Valle de San    Tamaide    Las Zocas
Playa de Bobo    34    San Eugenio    Lorenzo    San Isidro
Playa de las Américas    822    Mirador
Playas de Troya    de la Centinela    Aldea
Punta del Camisón    33    Guaza    428    Blanca
Playa de las Vistas    Los    TF1    Reina Sof
Playa de los Cristianos    Cristianos    (Tenerife
Charco del Lino    Erales    Los
Palm-Mar    31    Abrigos
La Arenita    Las Galletas    Playa de
32    El Chaparral    los Abrigos
San Sebastián de la Gomera    Punta Salema    Ten-Bel    Costa del Silencio

Santa Cruz de la Palma

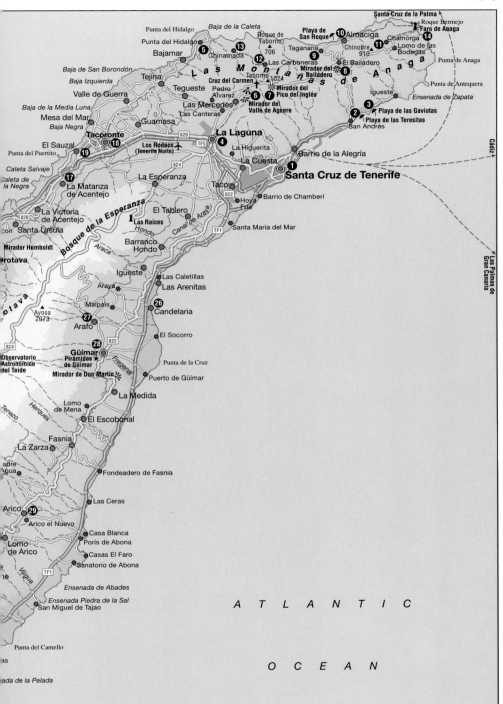

Santa Cruz de la Palma

Punta del Hidalgo    Baja de la Caleta

Roque Bermejo
Faro de Anaga ⑭

Punta del Hidalgo    Playa de
San Roque  ⑩ Almáciga  Chamorga

Bajamar  ⑤          Roque de       Taganana    Chinobre  ⑪  Lomo de las
        Chinamada  Taborno         ⑨         910    Bodegas
                   ⑬      706              Las Carboneras        Punta de Anaga
Baja de San Borondón                Mirador del  ⑧
                    Las Montañas de Anaga    El Bailadero
Baja Izquierda      Tejina                Mirador del    Punta de Antequera
                              ⑫  Taborno   Bailadero
Valle de Guerra   Tegueste   Cruz del Carmen  1024
                   Pedro    Mirador del  ⑥ ⑦  Iguste    Ensenada de Zapata
Baja de la Media Luna    Álvarez   Pico del Inglés
Mesa del Mar        Las Mercedes  Mirador del    ③  Playa de las Gaviotas
Baja Negra         Las Canteras  Valle de Aguere   ②  Playa de las Teresitas
          Guamasa                      San Andrés
El Sauzal  Tacoronte ⑱   820    La Laguna
          Los Rodeos    TF5  ④
⑲     (Tenerife Norte)    La Higuerita    Barrio de la Alegría
Punta del Puertito         824    La Cuesta
Caleta Salvaje            La Esperanza        ① Santa Cruz de Tenerife
Caleta de  ⑰                    Taco
la Negra  La Matanza         822  Hoya    Barrio de Chamberí
          de Acentejo       El Tablero  Fría
La Victoria           Las Raíces      Santa María del Mar
de Acentejo  820        Hondo    TF1
Santa Úrsula       Barranco
Mirador Humboldt        Hondo   Araca
rotava           Araca
             Iguste       Las Caletillas
             Araya        Las Arenitas
             Malpaís  ㉖  Candelaria
         Ayosa ㉗
         2073  Arafo    El Socorro
         824  ㉘  822
Observatorio   Güímar
Astronómico  Pirámides ★   Punta de la Cruz
del Teide   de Güímar
      Mirador de Don Martín    Puerto de Güímar
      Lomo   La Medida
      de Mena
Fasnia  ⑲ El Escobonal
La Zarza
adre
gua    Fondeadero de Fasnia
          Las Ceras
Arico ㉙
   Arico el Nuevo
Lomo    Casa Blanca
de Arico   Porís de Abona
      Casas El Faro
      Sanatorio de Abona
   Ensenada de Abades
   Ensenada Piedra de la Sal    A T L A N T I C
San Miguel de Tajao
Punta del Camello
as
ada de la Pelada            O C E A N

# TENERIFE: INTRODUCTION

*Tenerife, the most populous of the Canary Islands, has far more to offer than many holiday brochures suggest*

In more than simple landmass terms, Tenerife is the largest of the Canaries. It is also the cultural and academic centre of the archipelago, and has the widest range of attractions for visitors. Its neighbour and administrative rival, Gran Canaria, may outstrip it in some fields, but Tenerife has a head start in terms of natural grandeur. On the down side, much of its coastline is rather drab, with smallish grey or black beaches (sometimes bottle-blonded with imported Saharan sand), and arid treeless hinterland dominates the southern and eastern sides. Despite this, those who believed perhaps a decade ago that the island was nearing the end of its developmental potential for tourism have been confounded. New waves of speculative investment revenue pour in to keep the cement mixers churning, and the most unpromising terrain erupts into holiday settlements.

The jaded imagery of holiday brochures paints Tenerife in brash colours. After riffling through pages of azure swimming pools garnished with improbably brilliant vegetation, it's all too easy to dismiss it as yet another doomed monument to mass tourism. While some of its larger, more raucous resorts display the worst excesses of the package holiday industry, they are just one facet of a complex and varied island. To get the best out of it you need to stir from the poolside. Just an hour or two's drive inland takes you through mysterious primeval forests, Wild West valleys of cactus and weather-shattered rock, flourishing banana plantations and precipitous mountains. Most striking of all is the crater scenery of Tenerife's dominant physical feature – Mount Teide, the colossal central volcano which casts the world's biggest sea shadow and rears above cloud level to split the island into two climatic zones. It has remained dormant for just over 200 years, but its sulphurous wheezings have never entirely ceased, and recent seismographic warnings show the folly of taking this geological monster for granted.

Most visitors stay in one or other of the main resorts. To the north lies Puerto de la Cruz, favoured by a more traditional clientele which finds compensations for cloudier skies and dark, gritty beaches in the greener scenery and the core of quaint old buildings. On the sunny southern shores is the vast conglomerate known as Playa de las Américas, which extends its amorphous tentacles beyond its original confines to encompass the older port of Los Cristianos. Even newer satellites stud its northern bays, villa complexes pepper the barren hinterland hills with rashes of ready-mixed concrete, and on the northwest of the island, the upmarket developments of Los Gigantes cling tightly to the steep terrain of the Teno massif. ❑

**PRECEDING PAGES:** banana plantations nestle in the hills of Tenerife; the Casa de los Balcones in La Orotava; the rooftops of La Laguna.
**LEFT:** the North Coast of Tenerife, with El Teide in the background.

# SANTA CRUZ

*Tenerife's capital is an easy city to explore on foot. You could visit a few museums, dawdle in shady squares, do some serious shopping, then head for a couple of nearby beaches*

Tenerife's capital on the north-eastern side of the island is a bustling commercial and administrative centre, with one of Spain's busiest ports. Framed between azure sea and the jagged backdrop of the Anaga hills which shield it from the moisture-laden trade winds, **Santa Cruz ❶** has an enviable setting. Its industrialised outskirts, often hazy with air pollution and strangled by traffic congestion, give new arrivals less favourable first impressions, but visitors who spend any time here will soon develop an affection for this friendly, easy-going Spanish town. One way *not* to enjoy Santa Cruz is by trying to find a parking place in the height of the holiday season. During major fiestas, especially its astonishing Shrovetide carnival (February), many thousands of extra visitors invade from all over the world to enjoy the party.

European associations with Santa Cruz date back to the 15th century, when the Spaniards Sancho de Herrera and Alonso Fernández de Lugo arrived to wrest the island from its aboriginal Guanche inhabitants using their usual mixture of ruthlessness and perfidy. The strategically placed deep-water port quickly developed as a major trading link between Europe, Africa and the Americas, but its economic success made it a regular target for seaborne raiders.

In 1822 Santa Cruz was named capital of the Canary Islands, and that title was maintained until 1927 when the islands were split into the twin provinces of Santa Cruz de Tenerife and Las Palmas de Gran Canaria.

**LEFT:** an overview of Santa Cruz.
**BELOW:** the Plaza de España.

## Town centre

Santa Cruz has no particularly outstanding sights, but a short wander through its older quarters and shady squares of handsome colonial architecture is a good way to enjoy the place away from most of the traffic. The area most visitors want to explore on foot is easily contained within the drawn bow shape formed by the seafront highways and the tree-lined boulevards known as the Ramblas, which slice through the western sectors of the town. Santa Cruz's main traffic hub, The **Plaza de España ②** makes a good starting point, easily distinguished by its tall Cabildo Insular buildings which incorporate the island's administrative headquarters, main post office and tourist information centre. The centrepiece of the square is a towering monument to the dead of the Spanish Civil War, one of several haunting reminders of the Franco era in Santa Cruz.

Adjoining the Plaza de España is the **Plaza de la Candelaria ⑥**, a pedestrian precinct and public meeting place. At one end a statue made from white Carrara marble, dating from 1778, depicts the local legend of the *Triunfo de la Candelaria* (Triumph of the Virgin of Candelaria, *see page 173*), The Virgin,

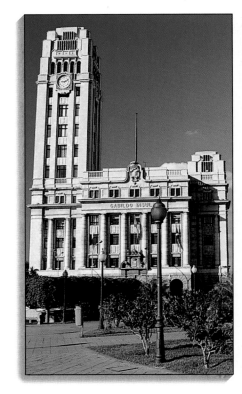

*The Calle del
Castillo is the
city's principal
shopping street.*

poised on top of a four-sided column, makes her appearance before the fou Guanche chiefs who stand around the base.

## City shopping

The principal shopping thoroughfare, **Calle del Castillo** **Ⓒ**, leads out of th Plaza de la Candelaria. While the *centros comerciales* (shopping centres) i any of the main resorts can satisfy holidaymakers' basic needs, only the capita has much in the way of big-town shopping. Many coach tour companies includ half-day shopping trips to Santa Cruz in their brochures, and there are regula bus services from all parts of the island. In Calle del Castillo and Plaza de l Candelaria, department stores, craft shops and bazaars (many of these Asian-run specialise in the goods encouraged by Tenerife's historic free port status, espe cially cameras, computers and other electrical products, cheap alcohol, tobacc and perfume. Unfortunately, all that glitters is not gold. Despite the cajolin signs announcing "tax-free" or "duty-free" goods, things may not be quite a cheap as you expect. Beware counterfeit or fake "brand names" (Rolex watches Lacoste clothing, etc.), pirated music, books and videos, and duff guarantee which can turn amazing electronic bargains into instant scrap. And don't forge that island export regulations differ from those in the rest of the EU, so you duty-free allowances are restricted to one litre of spirits or 200 cigarettes.

Maya is the granddaddy of Tenerife's department stores, a traditional multi storey emporium on Plaza de la Candelaria which stocks a wide range of fashio items, luxury goods and local specialities like leatherware, Nearby, severa handicraft shops sell local lace, palm-woven baskets, pottery and woodwork. Tr Artespaña or the Casa de los Balcones on Plaza de la Candelaria.

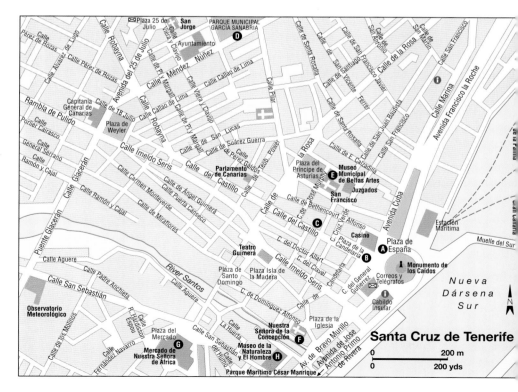

## Museums and markets

At the top end of Calle de Castillo lies the **Plaza de Weyler**, flanked by a stern phalanx of military buildings, including the Capitania General, where the island's former governors (including Franco) lived. Striking a more peaceful note, the square's lawned gardens contain the white Fountain of Love, made from Genoa marble. Several other green oases lie north of Calle Castillo. Furthest afield, bordering the Ramblas, is the **Parque Municipal García Sanabria D**, laid out in the 1920s with flame trees and many other sub-tropical specimens. Later additions include some fine pieces of modern sculpture.

From the park the Calle Pilar takes you back to the Plaza del Príncipe de Asturias, an idyllic enclave of ancient laurels – a former friary garden flanked by the **Museo Municipal de Bellas Artes** (Fine Arts Museum) **E** (open Mon–Fri 10am–1.30pm, 2.30–6.30pm; admission free) in which a section is devoted to Canarian art; and the baroque church of **San Francisco**. A street or two away stands the modest but attractive **Parliament Building**.

Best-known of Santa Cruz's churches is the **Iglesia de Nuestra Señora de la Concepción F** (open during daylight hours, like most of Tenerife's churches), a short distance south of the Plaza de España. Its six-tower belfry has long been a city landmark. Originally constructed in 1502, it was ravaged by fire in 1642 and had to undergo extensive rebuilding work.

The brightly illuminated nave is flanked by twin aisles and a series of side altars, while a statue of the Virgin Mary by the 18th-century sculptor José Luján Pérez adorns the high altar. Recently, the church has undergone years of restoration work and has become something of a museum as well as a place of worship. It is once again a repository for British flags seized during Nelson's

Map on page 136

*A statue washed by a fountain in the Parque Municipal García.*

**BELOW:** Nuestra Señora de la Concepción.

*Fresh flowers are always on sale in the Mercado de Nuestra Señora de Africa.*

attack and the great silver Cross of the Conquest which gave the town its nam (Santa Cruz means "holy cross"), and which Lugo was said to have planted disembarking here.

Just beyond the church the (usually dry) valley known as the Barranco Santos needs negotiating via one of its bridges. There are two main landmar on its banks: first, the arcaded market building of **Mercado de Nuestra Señor de Africa** where exotic fruits, flowers and spices lie heaped in a blaze of fr grant, photogenic splendour. On Sunday mornings, a lively *rastro* (flea marke takes place in the neighbouring streets.

The second landmark is an old hospital which provides handsome premis for one of Tenerife's best museums, the reorganised **Museo de la Naturale: y El Hombre** (Museum of Nature and Man) (open Tues–Sun 10am–8p entrance charge). This incorporates the island's anthropological and archae logical collections (trepanned skulls and mummies, pottery and artefacts belon ing to the aboriginal Guanches), along with excellent displays of marine a shore-based wildlife, fossils, minerals, etc. Several of Tenerife's state-r museums, including this one, are free of charge on Sunday.

## The port

The port of Santa Cruz is well worth a look. Its huge harbours are capable dealing simultaneously with a vast tonnage of varied shipping; port activi stretches several kilometres up the coast from the Plaza de España. State cruise liners mingle with battered Middle Eastern oil tankers and Russi; trawlers, state-of-the-art refrigerated cargo vessels load up with bananas a tomatoes, and agile hydrofoils buzz back and forth to Gran Canaria. Whi

**BELOW:** embroidered linen for sale in the city.

## OFFICERS AND GENTLEMEN

Admiral Nelson chanced his arm in an attack on Sar Cruz in 1797, and lost it when grapeshot shatter his right elbow. The cannon alleged to have inflicted tl injury on Britain's foremost naval hero is called El Tig (The Tiger), now proudly displayed (along with sor tattered flags from Nelson's ship) in the **Museo Milit** (Military Museum) (open Tues–Sun 10am–2pm; entran charge) housed in the 19th-century military headquarte of the Cuartel de Almeida.

By all accounts it was a gentlemanly battle. Admiri the courage of the reckless English raiders, the reside Spanish Governor behaved with great generosity towar them, sending each captured man back to his ship witl pint of wine and a loaf of bread.

Despite his horrific amputation injuries, anaesthetis only by stiff tots of grog, Nelson courteously thanked t Governor and presented him in return with cheese an cask of English beer. The museum displays a copy of t letter in which the Admiral writes: "I beg Your Excellen will honour me with your acceptance of a cask of Engl; beer and cheese." This traditional exchange of gi between Spanish and British fleets is still re-enacted fr time to time today.

ssing by, Tenerife's tour guides regale British coach parties with a new anec-
te: the disgraced publishing tycoon Robert Maxwell met his unresolved fate
ile sailing from this port of call.

To the south of the port, a previously desolate zone of under-used seafront has
cently been transformed into the **Parque Marítimo César Manrique**, con-
ning a lido of landscaped pools and leisure areas.

**Maps:
Area 130
City 136**

## pital beaches

ie capital is a good base for exploring the nearby beaches. Take the route
rtheast, a serpentine road to the coastal town of **San Andrés**, whose houses
pear to be clambering over each other up the sheer hillside. Alongside this
wn is the artificial beach of **Las Teresitas ❷**, built in 1975 by Santa Cruz
inicipal council. A total of four million sacks of sand were shipped from
e Spanish Sahara to create one of the biggest man-made beaches in the world.
s now a favourite bathing spot for Santa Cruceros. Much controversy rages
garding the future development of the hillside behind Las Teresitas beach. En-
·preneurs wish to use this prime location to construct hotels and apartments,
iile the local people and the ecologically aware lobby for the area to remain
tural and unspoilt, and for the tourists to go elsewhere.

If you want to get away from crowds of sun-worshippers, continue around the
xt headland where a steep track leads down to the secluded beach of **Las
aviotas ❸**. This curve of brown sand, appropriately named after the seagulls
it circle its high cliffs, has a couple of bars and remains quiet enough to attract
ieumatic nudists. At one end the **Punta de los Organos** is a strange cliff with
cks shaped like organ pipes, similar to that on La Gomera (*see page 205*). ❏

**BELOW:** the busy
port of Santa Cruz.

# LA LAGUNA AND THE ANAGA HILLS

*xplore the attractive university town of La Laguna before heading for the hills and rocky coast of the island's northern tip*

Maps:
Area 130
City 144

ith a population of around 122,000, **La Laguna** ❹ is Tenerife's second most important town. Situated in the middle of the **Valle de Aguerre**, where semi-tropical crops are cultivated, it lies just 8 km (5 miles) from ₂ centre of the capital, with the outskirts of the two towns merging along the ₌ Cuesta highway. Because of the altitude (550 metres/1,805 ft), La Laguna joys a cooler climate than the coastal areas, which contributes to the attrac-ns of living here.

La Laguna means "the pond" or small lake and it was probably because of this ₌ture that the conquistador, Alonso Fernández de Lugo, founded the settlement d made it capital of the Canaries in 1496. The archipelago's only university s opened here in 1701 and during term time the presence of so many students bues shops, bars and restaurants with a youthful, exuberant air.

In the historic quarter the original layout of rectangular blocks remains, so ₌re are narrow streets running between ancient mansions that enclose plant-decked patios. Because it has managed to retain its essentially Spanish ₌aracter, La Laguna reveals how towns on the island looked before modern velopers moved in.

**PRECEDING PAGES:**
villages cling to
the hillsides.
**LEFT:** the beach
at Taganana.
**BELOW:** Santuario
del Cristo.

## ₌uring the old quarter

₌u could start your tour of the old town at the **Plaza** **₌ Adelantado** (Governor's Square) ❹, where the **₌untamiento** (Town Hall) is situated. This hand-₌me example of neo-classical architecture contains ₌ flag which de Lugo planted on Tenerife to claim ₌ island for Spain.

From the Ayuntamiento, walk down the **Calle** **₌va y Grimón** to the **Santuario del Cristo** ❸, ₌me of the Canaries' most revered statue of Jesus, ₌ich was brought to Tenerife by de Lugo. Every ₌ptember this becomes the object of devotion for ₌usands of pilgrims from all over Spain. Retrace ₌ur steps a short way and take a right turn into the ₌lle San Agustín. Near the Palacio Episcopal, a ₌th-century mansion called the Casa Lercaro houses ₌ **Museo de Historia de Tenerife** ❹ (open Tues–Sun ₌am–8pm; entrance charge) with exhibits tracing ₌ island's history from the Spanish conquest to the ₌th century. Some of the earliest maps of the Canary ₌ands are on display here.

Turn left along Calle Sol y Ortega then left again to ₌ pink-painted cathedral, **Santa Iglesia** ❹, which ₌s founded in 1515 although the present edifice, ₌wned with a dome and twin towers, was erected ₌tween 1904 and 1915 after the previous one had ₌len into ruin. Inside, the arched nave is illuminated

SAN FRANCISCO
REAL SANTUARIO
DEL
SANTISIMO CRISTO
DE
LA LAGUNA

**TIP**

A good outing on a
wet day would be to
the Museo de la
Ciencia y el Cosmos
(open Tues–Sun
10am–8pm; entrance
charge) in the new
University quarter on
the outskirts of town.
There's a planetarium
and lots of interactive
science apparatus.

by beautiful stained-glass windows, while in one corner the gilt-encruste
**Capilla de la Virgen de los Remedios** (Chapel of Our Lady of Mercy) offe
a message of hope for a steady stream of supplicants. Behind the high altar lie
the simple tomb of de Lugo, "Conquistador de Tenerife y La Palma, fundad
de La Laguna" (Conqueror of Tenerife and La Palma, founder of La Laguna

From the cathedral, the **Calle Obispo Rey Redondo** leads past the **Teatr
Leal**, where plays and concerts are performed in a triple-tiered hall; to th
town's oldest church, the **Iglesia de Nuestra Señora de la Concepción C**
This was constructed in 1502 although the tower, the third on the site, date
from 1701, and major renovation work was carried out in 1974. Its interior
noteworthy for the deftly carved wood of the ceiling, pulpit and choir stalls, ar
a 15th-century font, which was used to baptise converted Guanche leaders.

## The Anaga Hills

La Laguna is the gateway to the **Montañas de Anaga** (Anaga Hills), a swee
of volcanic peaks that fills the northeast corner of Tenerife. The principal rou
into this thinly populated area runs northwards out of town along the spin
cord of the Anaga, punctuated by a succession of stunning viewpoints.

Soon after La Laguna, the tree-lined carriageway reaches the village of L
Canteras where a side road turns off the ridge route to **Punta del Hidalgo**
(16 km/10 miles). This quiet town rests in the shadow of the twin peaks
**Dos Hermanos** (Two Brothers) which rise up to 344 metres (1,128 ft) a
308 metres (1,010 ft). Popular with German tourists, the resort area has tw
sea-water bathing pools. Local people maintain that sunsets here are the mc
spectacular on Tenerife, fit to ravish the most jaundiced retina.

**BELOW:** the Palacio
de Nava y Grimón
in La Laguna.

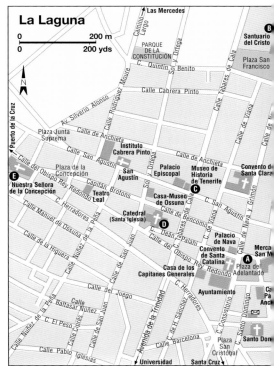

Maps:
Area 130
City 144

Beyond Las Canteras, the Anaga road elbows its way into the **Monte de las ercedes**, a dense forest of laurel trees, regarded as the most beautiful on the and. In reality it is a remnant of the primitive woodlands which during the rth's Tertiary era stretched up and around the Mediterranean as far as Asia. The first opportunity to escape the forest comes after 8 km (5 miles) at the **irador del Valle de Aguere ⑥** which overlooks La Laguna. Beyond the vn haughty El Teide lords over the skyline. A few minutes' drive further is **uz del Carmen**, with a chapel and statue of Nuestra Señora de las Mercedes. At a height of 920 metres (3,018 ft), this *mirador*, surrounded by verdant oodland, is a popular area for picnics and barbecues.

It's a short walk to **Taborno**, the highest peak in the Anaga Hills. Members the public aren't allowed on the actual summit (1,024 metres/3,360 ft) because rcraft navigation beacons have been installed there. Nevertheless there are zzying views of the surrounding countryside.

The next stop on the road is the **Mirador del Pico del Inglés ⑦**, a truly ectacular balcony, 960 metres (3,150 ft) up in the air, from which to gaze in ve at the island below. From here the road follows the Anaga's spine for 10 km miles) to the **Mirador del Bailadero ⑧**; its name is a corruption of *ladero*, or bleating place. This indicated a spot where, in the event of severe ought or shortage of grazing land for animals, the Guanches would separate eep and goats from their young so the mothers' bleating would appease the ods and make them send rain. Possibly as a result of this belief, El Bailadero s long been regarded as a meeting place for witches, although nowadays its ost frequent visitors are thirsty families who drive up to the two bars that ing grimly to the precipices.

*Admiring the view spreading out below the Mirador del Pico del Inglés.*

**BELOW:** fishing at Punta del Hidalgo.

After El Bailadero there are two routes available for vehicles: one is a head
ear-popping descent to the picturesque white village of **Taganana** ❾ and on
**Almaciga** ❿ 6 km (4 miles) away on the northern coast. This route entails pas
ing through a black tunnel that burrows from one side of the summit ridge to th
other, with El Bailadero's bars perched high above. At Almaciga there are a co
ple of restful beaches with magnificent views of Mount Teide.

The second route crawls uneasily along a knife-edge of rocks to **Chinobr**
another superb viewpoint encompassing the whole of the north of the island.
due course (10 km/6 miles) the road arrives at the safe haven of **Chamorga**
a scattering of white farmhouses among steep hillsides etched with terraces b
what seems a giant's hand. In the village centre a pretty little chapel is dedicat
to a local man who died in the mountains.

## Walking the hills

The ridgeway through the hills is the key to a superb network of *senderos turísı*
*cos* (tourist paths) that lead through dense woods and deep gorges to hidden vi
lages, lost valleys and secret beaches – the Anaga that few people ever see. Th
choice of walks ranges from gentle strolls to demanding expeditions that can la
from dawn to dusk. If you are thinking of doing any serious walking you shou
ask the tourist office in Santa Cruz for advice, and obtain a detailed map show
ing the mountain trails (*see box below*).

An easy 2-km (1-mile) walk begins in **Las Carboneras** ⓬, a village reache
by a spiralling road down from the ridgeway between Cruz del Carmen ar
Pico del Inglés. The road ends at the pretty little Plaza de San Isidro and a se
pentine path leads beneath towering cliffs and above yawning chasms. At fir

**BELOW:**
a steep path in
an Anaga village.

## GUIDELINES FOR WALKERS

**M**ost basic safety precautions for walkers are ju
common sense and most serious walkers dor
need reminding. But just in case, remember to:
● wear sensible shoes or boots and warm layers
clothing and take waterproofs.
● take supplies of food and water.
● get a reliable map of the *senderos turísticos* from th
tourist office in Santa Cruz or from Canarias Trekking, Ca
Quevedo No. 1, Edificio Gran Via, Oficina 2, Santa Cruz
Tenerife, tel: (922) 20 10 51. You could also ask the
where you can obtain an Army Ordnance Suvey ma
(Servicio Geográfico del Ejército). For advance informatio
you can visit the Canarias Trekking website at http
www.canariastrekking.com
● take a compass: finding your way when visibility is go
is not a problem, but cloud cover can sometimes make i
lot more difficult.
● keep strictly to signposted routes. If a path has be
washed away by heavy rain or blocked by a landslide do
try to continue.
● let somebody (a friend or the reception desk at yo
hotel) know your proposed route.
● if possible, always walk with a companion.

e terraces zig-zagging down the hillsides appear well tended but further on ey have become neglected and overgrown.

The path skirts a rock face and brings you to **Chinamada** ⑬. At first the hite houses look like the other farms in the Anaga; only when you get closer you see that the doors and windows are set in the rock wall with the living uarters extending into caves in the mountainside. Everything the community quires has to be carried in from Las Carboneras but nearly all daily needs are et by the fertile land. Along with staple foods of potatoes, wheat and maize, ttuces, peppers, cauliflowers, figs, tomatoes, lemons, oranges, apples, pears, ocados, apricots and cherries are grown. The villagers also make their own tent wine and aromatic goats' cheese and hunt rabbits and partridges.

A longer and more difficult walk leads to the **Faro de Anaga** (Anaga Lighthouse) ⑭ in the far northeast, which warns away ships sailing around this wild rner of the island. It stands 200 metres (656 ft) above sea level and is manned three keepers who live there with their families. All their necessities have to carried in from the village of Chamorga, 2 km (1½ miles) away. The children so have to make the steep climb up there to school. The starting point of the alk comes at the end of the road that plummets from El Bailadero, through ganana and Almaciga, to the slumbering coastal village of Benijo. From here ke the dirt track snaking around the cliffs, with superb views of the twin naga Rocks: the **Roque de Dentro** (Inner Rock) rears out of the waves like a ant tooth to a height of 178 metres (584 ft) whereas the flatter **Roque de Fuera** )uter Rock) reaches just 64 metres (210 ft). Looking back, the vista extends most to Punta del Hidalgo while the skyline is pierced by the pyramidal **Roque** Taborno, 706 metres (2,315 ft) high. ❑

Map on pages 130–31

*Colourful flowers brighten the hillsides in spring.*

**BELOW:** Taganana women look cheerful, despite their burdens.

# THE NORTH COAST

*e north coast offers many treats, from Puerto's urban architecture*
*nd state-of-the-art lido to colonial La Orotava, and the dramatic*
*rocky coast towards Punta de Teno*

Maps:
Area 130
City 152

■ or hundreds of thousands of tourists **Puerto de la Cruz** ⓯ is the sophisticated holiday town that introduced them to the delights of Tenerife. It's
true that a brash newcomer, Playa de las Américas, has thrust ahead in the
pularity stakes, but Puerto knows its market, and is quite glad to see south-
 Tenerife siphoning off younger, more raucous holidaymakers.
As the principal town on the northern coast of the island, with a population
 approximately 40,000 people, Puerto de la Cruz occupies a favoured situa-
·n where the fertile Orotava Valley runs down to the rocky shore of the
lantic. Visitors who prefer to stay in traditional, established resorts enjoy the
tinctive Canarian architecture of Puerto and the greener scenery of the north
ast. The lush vegetation so evident around the town is the result of a damper
mate, so be prepared for cloudier skies in the north. You may have to top up
ur tan elsewhere, but with fast motorway connections to Santa Cruz and the
uth of the island, it makes a convenient touring base. And if you're planning
 do any island-hopping, the domestic airport of Los Rodeos near La Laguna
an easy drive.
Puerto's beaches are very different from those in the south: the shores are
turally rugged, often lashed by heavy surf, sheltering only small handker-
iefs of dark volcanic sand. The rocky setting is an
rinsic part of the resort's appeal. A walk along the
destrianised Paseo San Telmo after a mid-Atlantic
rm gives unforgettable views of foaming breakers.

**PRECEDING PAGES:**
Puerto de la Cruz.
**LEFT:** fishing boats
in the harbour.
**BELOW:** Puerto's
promenade.

## erto's past

e town's importance as a commercial and trading
ntre extends way back. In 1706 the volcanic erup-
n of El Teide, 26 km (16 miles) west of the town
vastated Tenerife's main port, Garachico, and Puerto
 la Cruz (then called Puerto de la Orotava) became,
ernight, the principal outlet for local produce, par-
ularly the island's wine.
Two other developments which had profound re-
rcussions were the arrival of well-heeled Victorian
urists from England in the last decades of the 19th
ntury; and the fact that Puerto's mild climate made
an ideal rest and recuperation centre for British
pire builders on their long voyage home from Af-
a and Asia.
Since that first influx of visitors, who stayed in such
tels as the Monopol or the Taoro (which is now the
sino), the total number of people visiting Puerto has
creased steadily. Today, over 100,000 arrive each
ar, with the Spanish, British and Germans leading
 throng. February's spectacular *Carnaval* brings in
tra visitors and August attracts Spaniards fleeing
m the mainland's summer oven.

*Ornate religious processions never seem out of place in Puerto de la Cruz.*

## The best of old Puerto

The town's main square and focus of its social life is **Plaza del Charco de l** **Camarones** (Square of the Shrimp Pool) **Ⓐ**, so called because local peop used to catch shrimps there in a tidal pond. Shaded by graceful palms and glos laurel trees, which were brought from Cuba in 1852, it contains an animate children's play area and a stage on which bands perform occasionally in t open air. Chess is sometimes played with giant pieces on the pavement in o corner, watched by a thoughtful, knowledgeable audience. The square is also t site of Puerto's biggest and busiest taxi rank.

From the plaza you could make a short detour down Calle Blanco and turn le to **Casa Iriarte Ⓑ**, one of the town's best-preserved 18th-century buildings, wi carved Canarian balconies and a verdant patio, situated on the corner of Iriarte a San Juan. The writer Tomás de Iriarte y Nieves-Ravelo was born here in 1750 b now the house contains shops selling craftwork. Upstairs there's a naval museu and display of old photos and posters, including one advertising sailings fro Liverpool to Santa Cruz de Tenerife for the sum of six guineas.

Alternatively, a short distance from the northeast corner of the plaza along **M** Marina is the **Puerto Pesquero Ⓒ** fishing port, a tiny, stony beach which in t 18th century offered the island's main outlet for exports. Nowadays local fis ermen berth their boats here. At its eastern side is a black and white buildi with a wooden cross on the wall, the **Casa de la Real Aduana Ⓓ** (Royal Cu toms House), the oldest building in Puerto, which dates back to 1620 and w occupied by Customs officers until 1833. In recent years the upper floors we turned into a gracious private residence, while the lower floors and patios we filled with antique furniture and craft products for sale to the public (op

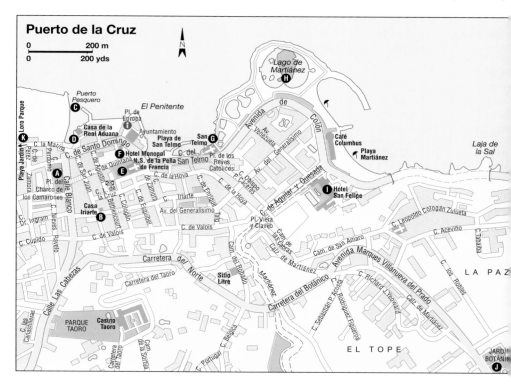

Puerto de la Cruz

Mon–Sat). The local *cabildo* has purchased the old building, which is to become handicraft museum and architectural heritage site. The entrance to the Customs House lies in the cobble-stoned Calle de las Lonjas.

Map on page 152

Beyond, on the Plaza de Europa, are the local tourist information centre, the **Ayuntamiento** (Town Hall), built in 1973, and the headquarters of the municipal police. Across the road the traditional 18th-century **Casa de Miranda** belonged to the family of Francisco Miranda, a hero of Venezuelan independence. Part of Casa de Miranda is **Bodiquita**, a wine bar and restaurant. It drips with suspended hams and green ferns among old brandy casks; a cool place for some refreshment. From here, the steps of the Calle Punto Fijo lead to the **Iglesia de Nuestra Señora de la Peña de Francia** (Church of Our Lady of the Rock of France) **E**, Puerto's main church, which was built between 1684 and 1697, although the tower was a later addition in 1898. The dark interior acts as a gloomy frame for the magnificent high altar, while the organ was brought from London in 1814 by Bernardo de Cologán, an islander of Irish descent. In a room at the back there's a fleet of massive carts which are pulled through the streets during religious processions.

*The Plaza de Europa features a statue of Puerto-born engineer, Agustín de Betancourt (1758–1824), who had an illustrious career as a builder of roads and canals for Tsar Alexander I.*

In the Calle de Quintana beside the square, the **Monopol** **F** is one of Puerto's oldest hotels, with a beautiful *patio* and Canarian balconies. At the end of this street is **Punta del Viento** (Windy Point), a terrace overlooking the rocky shore and Lago de Martiánez complex of swimming pools. Beneath is a restaurant on an open balcony in the cliff face.

The promenade, Calle de San Telmo, runs from the Punta, alongside foaming Atlantic breakers to the brilliant white **Iglesia de San Telmo** **G**, looking for all the world as if it's been carved out of icing sugar. This chapel is dedicated to the

**BELOW:** the Casa de la Real Aduana.

patron saint of sailors, invoked on countless occasions by seafarers negotiatin
Puerto's perilous coast. Mass is celebrated in German here and buried under th
floor are victims of a flood caused by a great storm in 1826.

Beyond San Telmo, the **Plaza de los Reyes Católicos** (Square of the Catho
lic Monarchs) is adorned with a bust of Francisco Miranda, the Venezuela
hero whose family home was mentioned earlier.

## Pools and plants

*The Botanical Garden is also home to the Palo Borracho (Drunken Log), a bloated, swaying tree that appears to have been watered with the island's Guajiro rum.*

A little further on you come to one of the recent efforts to expand Puerto's na
ural assets: a magnificent lido zone landscaped with fountains, palm trees an
sculpture designed by the Lanzarote architect and artist, César Manrique. **Lag**
**de Martiánez**  (sometimes known as the Lido San Telmo) is a series of larg
freeform pools meandering over an apron of lava jutting towards the sea, whe
bathers can enjoy seawater in perfect safety, within earshot of natural wave
crashing on the rocks just beyond. A modest admission charge allows you to sta
all day. Adjoining the lido, the rocky shores of **Playa Martiánez** to the ea
have been combed and expanded into an acceptable bathing beach.

To the west of the harbour, near the **Castillo San Felipe** (a small 17th-centu
fort which stages exhibitions from time to time), yet another ambitious coast
development project has recently been completed, promising a new and saf
bathing beach: **Playa Jardín** is fringed by traffic-free promenades and beaut
fully landscaped sub-tropical gardens. These too are dedicated to the memo
of environmental guru Manrique.

**BELOW:** the Lago de Martiánez.

Curving westwards from the Plaza de los Reyes Católicos is the Avenida
Colón, a pleasant boulevard lined with stalls displaying jewellery, clothes ar
souvenirs. Seated at their easels, artists vie with eac
other to do high-speed portraits, either represent
tional or comical, of willing sitters. At the end of th
avenue is the **Hotel San Felipe** ❶, worth notir
because it is from here that coaches leave for vario
tourist attractions.

From here, too, it's a very short taxi ride to th
famous **Jardín Botánico** (Botanical Garden)
(open daily 9am–6pm; entrance charge). You wi
appreciate it most if you choose one of the hotte
days to go, because this explosion of tropical veget
tion forms a refreshing, relaxing haven. The garde
was founded in 1788 by King Carlos III of Spain as
half-way house for exotic plants from America, Afric
and Asia en route for Spain, hence the official nam
the Jardín de Aclimatación (Acclimatisation Garde
de la Orotava.

Unfortunately the transfer of many new species
Spain didn't prove a success but this botanical treasu
house of 4,000 trees, bushes and plants, remains as
living legacy of glorious failure. Among the enormo
variety of trees is the colossal *Coussapoa dealbata*,
Gothic horror from the South American jungles whi
hasn't even been blessed with an English name. Th
200-year-old tangle of trunks and roots, branches a
bark, seems to be biding its time until nightfall. The
so they whisper, it snakes out those wooden tentacl
to gorge on tourists locked inside the garden.

## Only a bus ride away

A free bus from the bus stop near the Hotel San Felipe will take you to the **Loro Parque** (Parrot Park) **K** (open daily 8.30am–5pm; entrance charge) in the Punta Brava district. On view here in cages are more than 200 species of these iridescent birds in what is said to be the biggest collection in the world – although Miami's Parrot Park does cover a wider area. Visitors can see some 1,500 birds on display but behind the scenes there are at least 2,500 more.

As well as an outdoor display by performing parrots, there's an flying demonstration by trained birds who delight in rearranging the hair partings of members of the audience. Lorovision, an 180-degree cinema, gives a stomach-churning idea of what it's like to be able to fly – and also to drive a fire engine or sports car at breakneck speed. Another of the park's attractions, and one that is worth the entire entrance fee, is Europe's largest dolphinarium.

From the San Felipe stop a free bus also serves the **Bananera el Guanche** (Guanche Banana Plantation), a privately owned garden where you can watch a video about the banana plant – despite the size, it's not a tree – and then stroll along marked paths admiring a wide variety of exotic fruit. Here are papaya, mango, pineapple, lychee, pomegranate, kiwi, grapefruit, custard apple and the medlar, similar to a crab-apple, which can only be eaten when decaying. In addition, there are plants that yield coffee, peanuts, sugar cane, tobacco, ginseng and sapodilla (chicle), whose milky sap is used to make chewing gum.

Towards the eastern zones of the town, known as La Paz and Botanico, a couple of interesting older houses are open to the public. **Abaco** (open daily 10.30am–1.30pm, 3–5.30pm; entrance charge; tel: 922 37 01 07) is a well-restored Canarian mansion dating from the 17th century. Guided tours point

Map on page 152

*The little yellow train takes visitors around Loro Parque.*

**BELOW:** residents of Loro Parque exchange gossip.

## PUERTO BY NIGHT

Even if you're not at all interested in gambling, Puerto's **Casino Taoro**, once the biggest hotel in Spain, can be a riveting experience – particularly when a Spanish croupier attempts to explain in English the rules of French roulette to an ecstatic Italian tourist who believes he's just hit the biggest jackpot this side of Las Vegas.

Prospective punters will need their passports to get into the casino because reception runs a computer check on everyone who enters, making sure their credentials and credit are acceptable. Gamblers here run the gamut from wide-eyed innocents abroad to battle-hardened high-rollers who've spent far too many sleepless nights in joints similar to this one.

As a backcloth to all the wheeling and dealing, through the curtained windows there is a view of the coast spread out below, and the Orotava Valley above, with house lights looking like so many diamonds scattered across a cloak of black velvet.

If you feel like visiting a club, try the **Andromeda** in the Lago de Martiánez complex, which has been constructed below sea-level. A swish black and silver amphitheatre, topped off with a restaurant, provides the setting for a good floor show.

*The original Church of Nuestra Señora de la Concepción was destroyed by earthquakes.*

**BELOW:** Corpus Christi flower carpet in La Orotava.

out the main features and historical associations of the house and its fine gardens. It's a popular venue for folklore shows with cocktails.

**Sitio Litre** (open daily 9.30am–6pm; entrance charge; tel 922 38 24 17) is another dignified private mansion, with one of the oldest gardens in Tenerife, containing a splendid collection of orchids and a venerable dragon tree. It was once the home of the Victorian botanical artist and traveller Marianne North (*see page 57*), and is alleged to have played a role in one of Agatha Christie's thrillers. The shady café specialises in freshly squeezed fruit juices.

## Exploring the region

Within easy reach of Puerto by car or bus are a number of historic and beautiful towns. Top of the list comes **La Orotava** ⓰, situated 335 metres (1,100 ft) up in the fecund valley of the same name, some 4 km (2½ miles) east. Before the Spanish conquest the town formed part of Taoro, the richest of the nine Guanche kingdoms, and in 1594 Fray Alonso de Espinosa enthused: "Around La Orotava is the finest, most fertile land in these islands, and even in the whole of Spain, because on it can be grown and bred everything you may desire."

The township developed around the **Iglesia de Nuestra Señora de la Concepción**, built in the 16th century and destroyed by earthquakes in 1704 and 1705. Many of the town's narrow, cobbled streets and fine stone mansions have been preserved. The present church is an outstanding example of baroque architecture and was declared a national monument in 1948. It dates from the late 18th century although the marble high altar was rescued from the remains of the first church. Above the dark interior a halo of blue hovers around the dome, irradiating the finely carved choir stalls and a beautiful statue of Saint John.

The neo-classical style **Palacio Municipal** overlooks the **Plaza de Franco**. At Corpus Christi in June, ephemeral religious pictures of quite staggering beauty are created on the paving stones, using volcanic cinders, sand and earth from the Parque National del Teide. If you can't be around for the actual festival, look out for shops selling postcards of these extraordinary works.

From the plaza, go around the corner to the **Calle San Francisco**, site of the Casas de los Balcones (Houses of the Balconies), 17th-century mansions with two tiers of exquisitely carved pine wood balconies. A craft shop occupies one of the houses and allows visitors to view the palm-shaded patio within.

Further up the street is the **Hospital de la Santísima Trinidad** (Hospital of the Holy Trinity) with a revolving drum in its main door which was used as a receptacle for abandoned babies. The terrace outside provides a glorious vantage point from which to gaze at the luscious **Valle de la Orotava**.

East of Puerto de la Cruz, the Autopista del Norte sweeps past the twin towns of **La Victoria de Acentejo** (The Victory of Acentejo) and **La Matanza de Acentejo** (The Massacre of Acentejo) . The latter gets its name from the site in a gorge where in 1494 Guanche warriors inflicted a disastrous defeat on the Spanish invaders, who were led by Alonso Fernández de Lugo. Legend has it that he was only able to escape by giving his red cloak to a soldier, whom the Guanches killed, believing he was de Lugo. The Spanish leader was able to resume his campaign the following year, when, after five hours of bloody battle on open land nearby, the Guanches were defeated – they were said to have lost nearly 2,000 men, the Spanish just 64.

Beyond La Matanza, the town of **Tacoronte** ⑱, 19 km (12 miles) from Puerto de la Cruz, is the centre of an area which produces some of the most distinguished Canarian wines. Because of this, the town has a selection of fine restaurants. Nearby, just off the Autopista del Norte at **El Sauzal** ⑲, well-marked signs take visitors to a fine old house called **La Casa del Vino La Baranda** (open Tues–Sat 11am–8pm; shop and wine-tasting until 10pm; entrance charge; tel: 922 57 25 35). This former estate is now a *cabildo*-run marketing venture to promoting all of the island's wines, which are categorised into five appellations or originating areas. The low-slung, terracotta buildings house a museum, restaurant, bar and tasting room where visitors can learn something about local wine production, sample them (perhaps accompanied by traditional Canarian cooking) and of course buy them to take home. Concerts, lectures and other events are staged from time to time. Ancient wine presses and barrels stand in the courtyard entrance.

## Going west

Heading 5 km (3 miles) west of Puerto, a good road leads to an historical site, **Los Realejos** ⑳, where Guanche chiefs finally surrendered to the Spanish in 1496. The **Iglesia de Santiago**, built in 1498, is Tenerife's oldest church. Beyond the village of San Juan de la Rambla, with its Canarian houses, the road slices through banana plantations to the town of **Icod de los Vinos** ㉑, 19 km (12 miles) from Puerto. The name derives from the Guanche word *Benicod*, meaning

**Map on pages 130–31**

**TIP**

The spicy *conejo en salmorejo* (rabbit in hot sauce) served in many of Tacoronte's restaurants is highly recommended.

**BELOW:** a cool garden in Garachico.

Map
on pages
130–31

*Camel rides, which
start near Garachico,
are a popular
attraction.*

**BELOW:**
the lighthouse
at Punta de Teno.

"beautiful place", and the Spanish "de los Vinos" (of the wines) because this i
another wine-growing region. The white wine here is excellent.

According to Guanche legend, Icod was the sacred place where the gods, th
Son and the Great One, joined to create their race. Today, its principal attractio
and objective of daily coach parties is the theatrically flamboyant **Dragon Tree**
the finest example in the Canaries and estimated to be anything from 500 t
3,000 years old. If you'd like to grow one of your own, seeds are available i
shops close by – but you'll have to wait a very long time to see it in its prime

Some 5 km (3 miles) past Icod is the immaculate little town of **Garachico** ㉒
Tenerife's most important port until a volcanic eruption in 1706 laid it wast
and filled in the harbour. One building to survive this disaster was the **Castill
de San Miguel** from whose roof you can clearly see, solidified on the hill
side, two rivers of lava. The **Convento de San Francisco** was also untouche
and now fulfils the role of a cultural centre and library where visitors ca
admire the serene cloisters.

The **Isla Baja** restaurant features a model the size of a dining table, illustra
ing exactly what happened on that fateful day in 1706 and providing an excel
lent talking point among tourists as they tuck into their *gambas a la plancha*
(grilled prawns). One result of the disaster was that the residents of Garachic
became eager customers of a revolutionary new business called house insuranc
On some homes can be seen the original fire plates, dating from the 1720s
which proved they were insured with London companies.

One of Garachico's patrician houses has recently been converted into a go
geous small hotel, the **San Roque**. A world away from the egg-box concrete c
many of the resorts, this lovely building provides an imaginative setting fo

stylish art and design. Modern sculpture and grace
ful white sofas deck the inner courtyards and verar
das, while each bedroom creates a voguish, individu
setting with elegant Italianate chairs, bold colou
washes and swathes of pale calico. The bathrooms a
dashingly different. A mosaic-tiled swimming poo
and unstuffily accomplished cooking add to thi
expensive but memorable idyll. Its creation was
labour of love for its French owners, the Carayon fam
ily, but it now features in lists of the world's mo
sophisticated hotels (*see page 281*).

After Garachico the road turns its back on the se
and moves inland to the pretty village of **Los Silo**
Along the way look out for the roadside ovens, use
in the 19th century to roast the cochineal beetle into
powder which was exported to Europe as a dye.

Tenerife's most westerly town, **Buenavista** ㉓, lie
10 km (6 miles) from Garachico on a plain betwee
the deep blue sea and the dark cliffs of the **Maciz
de Teno** (Teno Massif). The road beneath crumblin
cliffs continues for another 11 km (7 miles) to th
lighthouse at the wild western tip, **Punta de Teno** ㉔
regarded by the Guanches as the end of the worl
Across the water, La Gomera can be seen in the di
tance, often with its mountains shouldering throug
billowing cloud. The rocks are a tempting spot f
watching the tremendous waves, but stand clear
the water line, it can be dangerous.

# Dragon King

Although the bizarre outburst of foliage that is the dragon tree may be found throughout the Canaries, the grandest and oldest specimen is in Icod de los Vinos where, with a height of nearly 17 metres (56 ft) and a trunk 6 metres (20 ft) round, it attracts thousands of visitors every year.

In Spanish its name is *Drago Milenario* (1,000-year-old Dragon Tree) and healthy controversy surrounds its age. Unfortunately this genus of tree, *Dracaena draco*, does not form annual rings so the method of dating relies on counting branches. But the dragon tree's system of branching occurs in an irregular, random manner rather than following a definite pattern, so it's a matter of opinion where one branch ends and another begins. This might explain why, when the German scientist Alexander von Humboldt visited Tenerife in 1799, he succeeded in dating one specimen at 6,000 years old, making it the oldest living thing in the world. The Icod giant is thought, locally, to be between 2,000 and 3,000 years old, although some botanists insist it is more like 500 years old.

But there is no disagreement that the dragon tree has played a significant role in Tenerife's history. The Guanches regarded it as a symbol of fertility and wisdom, carrying out sacred ceremonies in places such as the Valle de la Orotava. One tree they venerated there attained a height of 18 metres (60 ft) before it was blown down in 1867.

Guanches went to war bearing shields made from its bark. It had medicinal qualities too, since the resin, known as dragon's blood because it turns red on contact with air, was used both as a healing ointment, and to embalm their dead. In 1633 the herbalist John Gerarde said it was recommended for treating "overmuch flowing of the courses, in fluxes, dysenteries, spitting of blood and fastening loose teeth".

Its cosmetic properties were much appreciated by wealthy noblewomen in Venice who used it to make their hair golden. Florentine masons poured liquid dragon's blood over heated pieces of marble to stain it red; while 17th-century Italian violin-makers valued it as a rich varnish for their instruments.

The carmine resin was also believed to have supernatural powers and was burnt as an incense to thwart witches and sorcerers. The tree itself is also thought capable of foretelling events; a fine blossom supposedly means a good harvest.

The tree's curative properties have been utilised by healers who practise a special ritual for treating hernias. Patients must be taken before dawn to a tree at a crossroads. There they are lifted so they can place the bare soles of their feet flat on the trunk. Their outline is then cut in the bark with a knife. Tradition maintains that, if these cuts close up, the hernia will be cured within a year.

For all its healing gifts, the Icod Dragon Tree itself is not in the best of health, and its trunk has been shored up with concrete to protect it against storms. The road alongside has also posed problems – it has now re-routed so that the dragon can rest in peace – except for the swarms of tourists taking photographs. ❑

**RIGHT:** Stopping for a chat under Icod's famous Dragon Tree.

# CANARIAN ARCHITECTURE

*Gothic, Renaissance and Moorish elements are fused in the islands' architecture, and modern builders have added some flamboyant touches*

The Spanish conquistadors who occupied the Canary Islands in the 15th century imported their own architectural style. They arrived at a time when the new Renaissance style was coming into vogue throughout Europe, taking over from the centuries-old Gothic style. For this reason, Gothic was something of a conservative choice for San Sebastián's Iglesia de la Asunción, the church on La Palma where Columbus prayed before sailing westwards into the unknown.

More typical of the age are the civic buildings in the Plaza de España in Santa Cruz de la Palma, built in Renaissance style, based on simple classical elements, such as perfectly hemispherical arches resting on Corinthian capitals (carved with foliage patterns) and slender pillars. This being Spain, however, it was not long before purely classical concepts were being enlivened by an eclectic mix of Arabic motifs, including horseshoe-shaped arches over doors and windows, and complex arabesques, every bit as intricate as the patterns on a prayer mat.

## SCULPTING WITH WOOD

The ready availability of timber meant that wood often took the place of metal and stone. As it was a more easily carved and moulded material, local builders took full advantage of the opportunity to sculpt the elaborate wooden ceilings and beautifully carved balconies that characterise the Canaries' early churches and mansions. It is here that arabic elements are seen at their most exuberant – notably in the glorious geometry of the ceiling in the Iglesia de Nuestra Señora de la Concepción, in Santa Cruz de Tenerife.

▷ **LA OROTAVA**
Settled in the 16th century by families from Andalucia, this pretty town reflects the Arabic influence exemplified by the palace and gardens of the Alhambra in Granada.

△ **SANTA CRUZ TOWN HALL**
A colonnaded portico and richly decorated ceilings are among the features of the *Ayuntamiento* in Santa Cruz de la Palma, built in 1569.

◁ **SQUARE HOUSES**
A typical house in Garachico; modern Canarian architecture adopts the classic box shape of Moorish North African houses, clinging to the hillside like spilled sugar cubes.

△ **SAN FRANCISCO**
Garachico is a fine examp of an unspoiled 17th-cent port, with its whitewashed former convent and bell to

▷ **HOTEL BAHIA DEL DU(**
This luxury resort hotel in Playa de las Américas is b in a Disneyesque mixture styles copied from famou landmarks around the isl

## TENERIFE'S NOBLE BALCONIES

◁ TORRE DE LA CONCEPCION
The church of Nuestra Señora de la Concepción in La Laguna dates from 1502; its distinctive seven-stage tower makes an imposing landmark.

▽ SANTA IGLESIA
This 19th-century cathedral in La Laguna is neo-classical in style, contrasting whitewashed panelling with grey-black volcanic tufa.

The term "Canarian architecture" conjures up visions of old seafront mansions, with carved wooden window shutters and doors, and wonderfully varied balconies, perfect for lazing the evening hours away; or patio courtyards with noble balconies spilling scarlet and pink flowers. Their origin lies in the romantic Moorish balconies of Andalucía. Migrants from southern Spain brought this style not only to the Canaries, but also to Spanish colonies in Latin America, so it is known in Spain as a specifically colonial style of building.

That champion of rigid Counter-Reformation values, King Phillip II of Spain (1527–98), thoroughly disapproved of such un-Christian architectural practices and sent out an instruction to the Canaries demanding that the balconies be torn down. Unfortunately for those on board, the ship carrying the order never arrived, and we are the richer as a consequence, as anyone can see by visiting the Casa de Colón, in Las Palmas, or wandering around the streets of La Oratava or La Laguna on Tenerife, or La Palma's capital, Santa Cruz.

# PARQUE NACIONAL DEL TEIDE

*Visiting the strange volcanic landscape around the majestic peak of El Teide is an unforgettable experience, whether you intend to do some serious walking or just enjoy the scenery*

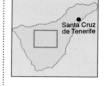

Maps:
Area 130
Park 166

There are many ways to approach El Teide, the great volcano at the heart of the **Parque Nacional del Teide ㉕**, but the most sensible way for first-time visitors is from the park's entrance, **El Portillo Ⓐ**, where the **Visitors' Centre** (open daily 9am–4pm) provides videos and information about the park and has details of the excellent signposted and guided walks available. The centre is surrounded by Moroccan cedars, and nearby is a garden of wild plants endemic to the Canaries. You can reach this point via the road from La Orotava or the long dorsal road up from **La Esperanza**, which offers tantalising glimpses of El Teide through cool forests of eucalyptus and Canary pine.

The is the route most local people prefer. At weekends many drive up from La Laguna and Santa Cruz to enjoy the walks and picnic areas. In winter snow sometimes blocks this road, built by the military in the 1940s, but for most of the year it is a beautiful drive along the mountainous spine of the island, offering clear views to both north and south, the bright light revealing the hidden colours of rock, bark and heather.

The majestic scale of El Teide becomes clear at the point where the two roads join. To the east, set atop the Montaña de Izaña, several white towers lie gleaming in the sun: the telescopes of the **Observatorio Astronómico del Teide.**

Begun in 1965, the observatory originally studied the night sky from the two smaller, silver-domed towers, but the development of Puerto de la Cruz and Reina Sofia airport has now corrupted the atmosphere to a prohibitive degree. Stellar observation transferred to La Palma where the dark night skies are now protected, and today the Izaña site is an international solar observatory. The larger white towers used for studying the sun owe their futuristic appearance to the need to isolate the instruments from the distorting turbulence caused as the surrounding land heats up.

## Montaña Blanca

Follow the marked road with the mountain known as **Las Mostazas** (The Mustards) and the domed volcano of **Rajadas** on your right. They are surrounded by a rich dark lava, often capped by the shiny black of obsidian, used by the Guanches to make *tabonas* (cutting-stones). To the left the **Mirador de San José Ⓑ**, offers splendid views, and close to the road lies the **Arenas Blancas**, a pleasant stop where everyone picnics on dunes of pumice that bear an unfortunate resemblance to cat litter.

The next viewing point, **Mirador del Tabonal Negro Ⓒ**, overlooks **Montaña Blanca**, described by

**PRECEDING PAGES:** winter on El Teide. **LEFT:** a strange rock formation. **BELOW:** uphill transport.

*A short ride on the Teléferico makes life a lot easier.*

Charles Piazzi Smyth when he found it in 1856, as "of smooth surface and light-yellow colour which every here and there has exudations of yellow and red lava which have half-stretched, half-slobbered, down the sides like so much treacle or hasty pudding." Destined to become Royal Astronomer, Piazzi Smyth scrambled up here with his Sheepshanks Equatorial to watch the Great Bear sink behind El Teide. He spent two months observing the Canary sky, discovering the astronomical advantages of "a residence above the clouds" and inspiring the establishment of observatories in the Canary Islands.

Montaña Blanca is the starting point for those wishing to climb El Teide. The construction of a **Teléferico** (cable car) **D** in 1971 makes the ascent easier for the 300,000 people who want to reach the top of El Teide every year. Cars go up from 9am–4pm, and the last one comes down at 5pm; they don't run if it's windy. The 1,200-metre (3,940-ft) ride takes only eight minutes, but expect to queue at least an hour before you get a ride.

As you wait, comfort yourself with thoughts of the arduous efforts Victorian climbers of the peak faced. A day trip then began well before dawn from La Orotava, riding on horseback by the light of the moon and pine torches. Eight hours later travellers reached the Estancia de los Ingleses on Montaña Blanca, where they cooled themselves with barrels of ice from the nearby Cueva del Hielo and took fortifying draughts of quinine prior to the steep ascent by mule to the Altavista. There the ladies and children rested in what little shade was available while the gentlemen struggled to the summit.

Modern adventurers stepping off the cable car at **La Rambleta** now find themselves part of a a busy design-conscious set. The fluorescent ski-wear and goggles favoured by the newly-chic Spanish are not essential, but neither is

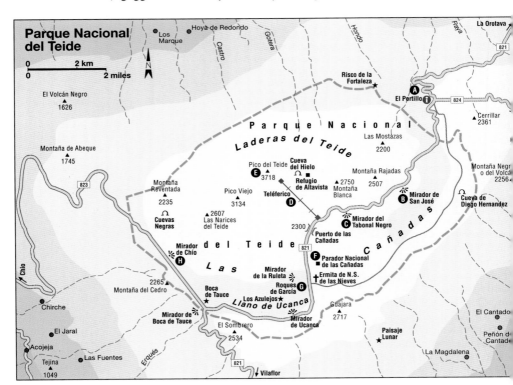

**Parque Nacional del Teide**

0          2 km
0          2 miles
N

La Orotava

Hoya de Redondo
Los Marque
Castro
Gotera
Hondo
Raya

821

Risco de la Fortaleza

**A** El Portillo ℹ          824

Cerrillar
2361

El Volcán Negro
▲ 1626

**P a r q u e   N a c i o n a l**
**L a d e r a s   d e l   T e i d e**

Las Mostazas
▲ 2200

Montaña de Abeque
▲ 1745

Pico del Teide
**E** ● 3718
Cueva del Hielo
Refugio de Altavista

Montaña Rajadas
▲ 2750     2507

Montaña Negr o del Volca 2256

Montaña Reventada
▲ 2235

Pico Viejo
▲ 3134

Teléferico
**D**

▲ 2750
Montaña Blanca

823

Cuevas Negras

▲ 2607
Las Narices del Teide

Mirador de San José
**B**

Cueva de Diego Hernandez

2300

Mirador del Tabonal Negro
**C**

Puerto de las Cañadas

**C a ñ a d a s**

Mirador de Chío
**H**

**d e l   T e i d e**

821

Parador Nacional de las Cañadas
**F**

Ermita de N.S. de las Nieves

**L a s**

Mirador de la Ruleta

Roques de García
**G**

2265 ▲
Montaña del Cedro

Boca de Tauce

Los Azulejos ★
**L l a n o   d e   U c a n c a**

Guajara
▲ 2717

El Cantado

Chio

Chirche

Mirador de Boca de Tauce

El Sombrero
▲ 2534

Mirador de Ucanca

Paisaje Lunar ★

Peñón d Cantad

El Jaral

Acojeja

Tejina
▲ 1049

Las Fuentes

Erqués

821

Vilaflor

La Magdalena

Map on page 166

vise to adopt the shorts and lager-can bravado of some British youth. Settle
or sunglasses, hat and strong-soled shoes, and make regular stops to catch your
breath: at this height the air is rare and progress slow – anyone with heart or
espiratory problems should not attempt the climb. Those in need of urgent
cclimatisation will find a bar dispenses welcome hot chocolate and brandy.

Alternatively, one can explore two short signposted paths that curl round to
ither side of El Teide. The first leads west past sulphurous fumaroles for a fine
iew of **Pico Viejo**'s crater (800 metres/2,600 ft in diameter). The second runs
ast to the **Mirador La Fortaleza**, across the *bloques* (jagged blocks) and
*ahoehoe* (ropey cords) formed by the last lava flows of El Teide.

Keen visitors should get up early to get the best from El Teide, catching the
irst car up before crowds and clouds diminish the awaiting spectacle. The best
ewards rightly go to those who slog up by foot from the base, overnighting at
ne Altavista to catch the dawn and El Teide's triangular shadow spread across
range-tinted clouds.

The summit of **Pico del Teide** Ⓔ (3,718 metres/12,197 ft) is now closed to
ne public because of erosion of the over-used paths. You have to obtain a spe-
ial permit to get to the very top. But even with this limitation, it is still a sight
nat never fails to impress.It is not simply the unsurpassed views over Tenerife;
: is also the dense line of pine winding along the dorsal ridge to Anaga, the
/hite houses of Puerto de la Cruz and the north coast, the dark circumference
f Las Cañadas, the way the lava stops short at the rugged upper cut of Teno.

There's also the sight of the other islands floating in the clouds like appari-
ons: La Palma, La Gomera, El Hierro behind, and Gran Canaria to the east.
fter all, you're not only on top of the highest mountain in Spain, but on top of

*There's plenty of information and advice for visitors to the park.*

**BELOW:**
architectural
landscape
around Vilaflor.

*Some of the rock
formations look as if
they have been
sculpted by hand.*

**BELOW:** the
Parador Nacional
de las Cañadas.

El Teide – a symbol of power that today adorns everything from cement blocks to telephones, a cloudy pillar mighty enough to uphold the classical heavens, a force that Columbus saw erupting, that brought fear to the Guanches who believed a devil lived in its bowels and would one day rise up and steal the sun.

There's also a tangible feeling the whole thing might just blow up beneath your feet, blasting you and everyone's video camera far away. El Teide is under constant observation, being monitored for unusual seismographic warnings.

Back at the foot of the Teléferico it is only a short way to the renovated **Parador Nacional de las Cañadas** ⓕ, the only accommodation available in the park. Those staying overnight can watch the glow as the sunset burnishes the yellow rocks of **Los Caprichos**, and appreciate the dark nocturnal silence of the *caldera* domed with stars. Across the road is a small hermitage, the **Ermita de Nuestra Señora de las Nieves**

## The Roques de García

A short distance away lie the **Roques de García** ⓖ, the most photographed lumps of rock in the Canaries; up to a million people come every year to enjoy the anthropomorphic shapes of their eroded strata. The route to the Roques cuts across dark lava, seemingly fresh as the day it was thrown down, that spread towards a former lake, Llano de Ucanca, and forms the first of the seven *cañadas* (small sandy plateaux) that give the park its name. Closer to the Roques some parts of the stone are tinged jade green from copper oxide, known locally as **Los Azulejos** (The Tiles).

There are two theories about how the present *caldera* (16 km/10 miles) was formed some 3 million years ago, and the **Circo**, or interior rim of the crater

Map on page 166

rovides the best clues. The first theory suggests that a greater part of the park was originally covered by a huge volcano as high as 4,880 metres (16,000 ft), he dome of which collapsed to leave a giant crater with only the southern walls emaining visible after the formation of Pico Viejo and El Teide 2 million years ater. The second theory suggests that two craters existed before El Teide's mergence, the dividing line between the two being the Roques de García.

Follow the road round and you'll come to the **Mirador de Chío ⓗ**, a gloriously dismal stop. This is a chance to catch El Teide in its darkest garb: a spent, ashen landscape, leaving its mess for all to see, with disgorged lava spilling down its cindery slopes – creation petrified. Among these black lava slides lies he gory wound of **Las Narices del Teide** (El Teide's Nostrils), the result of an ruption in 1798. You could then take the deserted road which winds down to Chío, the deathly wilderness of lava giving way to ranks of gold-green pines, hen to terraces overrun by sprawling prickly pear and euphorbia, and finally to land rich with figs and almonds.

Alternatively, descend via **Vilaflor**, from snow to sea, from lava desert above he treeline where burnt rubble lies scattered, down through pine forests. Those who know the area well like to approach the park from this side, and it is perhaps the most dramatic ascent. The thrill of this approach is that the road scales he jagged crater walls lining the whole southern side of the park before dropping into the mysterious world of the interior crater. Down a rough side-track ust east of Vilaflor lies the **Paisaje Lunar** (lunar landscape) where the erosion of pyroclastic fragments has created a coffee-and-cream wonderland of andstone cones (turn right soon after the **Mirador de los Pinos**, but be warned: t's an hour's drive on a very poor road and half an hour's tough scramble). ❑

*The Parque Nacional was formed in 1956 and the introduction of conifers began two years later.*

**BELOW:** walkers and cyclists enjoy the park trails.

## DISCOVERING TRANQUILLITY

Anyone walking or climbing in the park must take all the usual precautions, including the right clothes and quipment, getting trail maps from the Visitors' Centre, nd notifying the staff when you set out. Having done all hese sensible things, you can get a taste of the park's ranquillity by taking the track south of the Ermita Nuestra eñora de las Nieves that leads east towards Mount iuajara, a level four-hour walk that curls through Las añadas to El Portillo. At its head is the Guajara Pass, amed after a Guanche princess, which formed the ummit of the old Camino Chasna, the original link etween the Orotava Valley and Chasna (Vilaflor).

The flora of the park is one of the pleasures for walkers. winter snow decorates El Teide like icing on a bun and nly the bright faces of the Teide daisy and the carcasses f drooping *tajinaste* (viper's bugloss) punctuate the ghostly añadas. To return in May when the ever-present broom *tama del pico* blooms pink and white and the *tajinaste* ursts red is to discover a new, Technicolor world. Exemes of temperature and wind have produced a pectacular flora that blossoms briefly but brightly, giving rth to endemic species like the Teide violet and the nacious *cedro canario*.

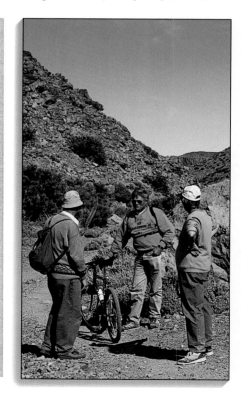

# THE EAST COAST

*Leave the dreary outskirts of the capital behind and go in search of the miraculous shrines, mysterious pyramids, fishing ports and golden beaches that lie beyond the motorway*

The fast Autopista del Sur running round the east and south of the island between Santa Cruz and the main southern resorts has little to recommend it except speed and convenience. Slicing through an arid, featureless wasteland of billboards, construction rubble and occasional candelabra cacti, most visitors experience only unremitting dreariness. If this is your first impression of Tenerife, don't give up hope – things get better. One day, this road is scheduled for a *Programa de Embellecimiento de Carreteras* intended to beautify it with trees and flowers, but it's hard to imagine this desert blooming for a while yet.

If you have more time, head for the sunny corniche road, an older inland route (C822) that jiggles its way through the flower-decked villages of Güímar, Fasnia, Arico and Granadilla de Abona with glimpses of the sea far below. These local settlements give a flavour of the real Tenerife away from the artificial holiday ghettos. Orchards and vineyards flourish beneath the shoulders of ancient slumbering volcanoes. It's much slower and more tiring to drive, but if you run out of time or energy it's very easy to rejoin the coastal motorway via any one of about ten link roads originally constructed to provide access from the hill villages to the small ports below. Several of these ports are now small-scale holiday resorts.

Heading south from the island's capital, Santa Cruz, the first few unlovely kilometres run through oil refineries and industrial estates, and it's best to stick to the *autopista*. Amazingly though, attempts have been made to attract tourists to the coast. At the twin resorts of Las Caletillas and Las Arenitas, there's a mini-forest of hotel and apartment blocks bristling beside a few patches of darkish sand in the shadow of a large power station.

## From Candelaria to Güímar

A little further south is the village of **Candelaria** ㉖ whose main attraction is a bulky modern basilica (built in 1959) housing a much-revered Virgin. In mid-August, pious islanders gather in the large square outside to celebrate the **Romería de Nuestra Señora de Candelaria** in a two-day pilgrimage (*see page 85*). Then the Virgin is removed from her glittering shrine of silver, flowers and candles to be carried on a lap of honour through the town.

She has led an interesting life, this Virgin. At the end of the 14th century her statue floated miraculously ashore at Candelaria, impressing even the pagan Guanches who placed her in a cave shrine. In 1826 a great storm washed the image out to sea again. The present carving dates from about 1830.

The smoothly paved square outside the basilica attracts skate-boarding children as well as pilgrims.

**PRECEDING PAGES:** riding the waves. **LEFT:** Guanche statue in Candelaria. **BELOW:** the church dedicated to the Virgin of Candelaria.

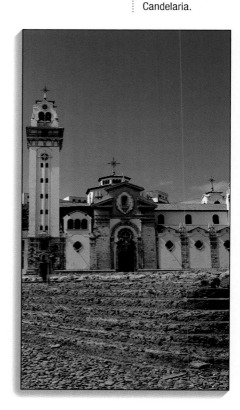

*The 18th-century church of prosperous little Güímar.*

**BELOW:** the pace of life is slow in the hillside villages.

Bronze statues of Guanche kings guard the seafront side of town, where there's a small beach popular with locals.

Heading up into the hills from Candelaria, the first village of any size is **Arafo** ㉗, a trim, whitewashed settlement on the lava slopes of the Montaña de las Arenas, which last erupted in 1706. If you catch it at the time of one of its music festivals, you'll find it vibrating to *salsa* and the sounds of Canarian folk music. Nearby **Güímar** ㉘ is a larger town, precariously built on a fault-line below another old volcano. Undeterred, settlers have lived here since Guanche times, and its mineral-rich soils produce prosperous crops of fruit, vegetables and vines. Its 18th-century prosperity is reflected in the **Iglesia de San Pedro Apóstol**, adorned inside by carved wooden apses added in 1930.

For a sense of old Güímar, walk east to the white houses and cobbled streets near the old **Dominican Convent** (now the *Ayuntamiento* or Town Hall) where a plaque commemorates Isidro Quintero Acosta, a local boy who introduced the cultivation of cochineal to the island. The town's harbour, Puerto de Güímar, is now a small resort with a sailing school and a reasonable beach.

## The Pirámides de Güímar

Just outside Güímar, a mysterious archaeological find has provoked great controversy. In 1990, the Norwegian explorer and ethnologist Thor Heyerdahl focused international attention on a cluster of six stepped pyramids, which he believed were cult-sites of the aboriginal Guanches. Test excavations fuelled hot debate, some experts declaring them of great historical significance, others dismissing them as no more than piles of rubble cleared by farmers from local fields. No convincing finds have been unearthed to confirm the origins of

Map on pages 130–31

he pyramids or their builders. But certainly as visitors see them now (much estored), they seem impressively regular structures, precisely built in neat erraces with dressed lava blocks squared at the corners rather than the random tones of the surrounding countryside. Stairways ascend to the flat summits of he pyramids, facing the rising sun, and the whole complex is oriented towards unset at the summer solstice.

Funded by Heyerdahl's compatriot Fred Olsen (a ship-owning magnate with ubstantial Canarian interests), the site has developed into a well-promoted ttraction with a modern visitor centre, which expounds pre-Hispanic theories f the pyramids, highlighting cultural parallels with civilisations in the New World. The jury is still out as far as the local tourist board is concerned, and you von't find much about the Pirámides de Güímar in any official literature. But f you're passing through the town, have a look at the pyramids and decide for ourself whether Spanish peasant settlers could have had enough time on their ands to go to so much trouble, seemingly for no other reason than to baffle uture generations.

## Cave dwellings

outh of Güímar, the **Mirador de Don Martín** gives a splendid view of the ertile valley against a backdrop of hills, with the Anaga range in the distance. 'asnia, the next sizeable place along this route, was founded in the 17th cen- ury. Bright with flowers and vineyards, it is an idyllic little spot, but has had its hare of troubles in the past: the white chapel of **Nuestra Señora de los Dolores** Our Lady of Sorrows) on the neighbouring volcanic hill was built in gratitude fter a lava flow stopped just short of the village in 1705. Around Fasnia there

**BELOW:** cactus and euphorbia cover the hillsides.

are still families living in caves, as there have been for centuries, although these dwellings now have electricity and are adorned, somewhat anachronistically, with television aerials.

The pretty village of **Arico**  is really several separate settlements, its older sector a huddle of picturesque little white houses around an exotic-looking domed church. Tomatoes and potatoes flourish on the surrounding terraces and on the coast below the port of **Porís de Abona** is turning into a bustling little resort with a lot of ongoing construction. Favoured by German visitors, it has some good fish restaurants and a neat holiday village of low-rise white self-catering units, though it is hard to fathom the attraction of these grim and shadeless beaches.

### Taking a view

South of Arico the C822 strikes further inland, trickling through **Granadilla**, where oranges and almonds grow. The roads become busier close to the large south-coast resorts; from Granadilla, a well-used route strikes up through Vilaflor towards the national park. Continuing along the C822, you pass through the cochineal village of Charco del Pino, and the terraced hill-farms of San Miguel. Between here and Valle de San Lorenzo, a wonderful view over hundreds of volcano cones can be seen from the **Mirador de la Centinela**.

The region's first *mirador*, built in 1953, it looks suspiciously as if it was made for developers to stand on as they carved up their kingdoms below, but it also demonstrates how little land the *ciudades turisticas* (tourist towns) actually occupy, clinging to the sea's skirt like timid children.

A crazy paving landscape of plastic greenhouses and water reservoirs can be seen marching south to the coast, proof that not all farmers are seduced by the sweeter fruits of tourism. Grassy fields of flowers and salad crops grow up beside the airport and, while the banana may no longer be king, it still holds a distant sway over the land. Who knows, given the changes in international trade and exports it may yet see a revival.

From the *mirador*, a long white ribbon of houses is visible winding high through El Teide's foothills, legacy of the island's aboriginal inhabitants who did not share our current obsession with the seaside. The Guanches lived inland in the natural caves formed among the *barrancos* that serrate the southern and western slopes of Tenerife.

### Back to the sea

Back on the coast, the town of **El Médano**  clearly signalled by two striking landmarks. The first is a forest of wind-powered propellers, the **Parque Eolico**, which takes advantage of the prevailing *alisios* (northeast trade winds) to provide energy to over 3,000 homes. The second is the hook-nosed **Montaña Roja** (Red Mountain), an ancient cinder-cone which all international passengers will see as they arrive at or depart at Tenerife's Reina Sofía Airport.

El Médano is a scruffy little place, but its attractions include several long golden beaches (natural blondes, with sand blown from Africa on the strong

**BELOW:**
a pretty village
house in Arico.

ds), and superb conditions for windsurfing. International competitions take
ce here, and windsurfers can often be seen zooming over the waves like
ghtly coloured butterflies.

he tiny, rocky anchorage of **Los Abrigos** ❸ is lined with excellent fish
taurants. The most popular ones fill up fast at lunchtime, especially those
h panoramic terraces. Those at the top of the waterfront road are a bit
aper and just as good. If you're catching an afternoon or evening plane
ne, you could make a meal here your last memory of Tenerife – it's just a
-minute drive to the airport.

urther west, the rocky coastline called the **Costa del Silencio** extends as
as the eye can see in a rash of sprawling low-rise self-catering holiday
velopments. The "Silent Coast" is not a very appropriate name these days,
nsidering how close it is to the airport, although at night it does, indeed, feel
et in comparison to the mega-resorts of Los Cristianos and Playa de las
éricas (*see pages 179–83*)

One of the longest-established is the Belgian-financed *urbanización* (as
se residential complexes are called) known as **Ten-Bel** and its neighbour
**Chaparral**. These are especially popular with disabled visitors, as the flat
rain is easy for wheelchairs, and families with small children. The sports
ilities are good, including several golf courses which erupt on these pallid,
sty ash-beds in unnatural splashes of emerald.

For a more genuine Spanish atmosphere, head for the fishing port of **Las**
lletas ❷, one of the few places on the south coast which retains a thriving
hing fleet and where you can still buy the daily catch to cook for yourself, or
joy being made for you in local restaurants.  ❑

Map
on pages
130–31

*Fish fresh from the
sea is on the menus
in Los Abrigos.*

**BELOW:**
the bay of Los
Abrigos at dusk.

# THE SOUTHERN RESORTS

*you like sun, sea and sand, loud music and late nights, and have
no desire to escape from the clamour of the 21st century, you
will appreciate Tenerife's southern resorts*

Map
on pages
130–31

enerife's southern corner is dominated by the Montaña de Guaza, a volcanic cone no doubt as uninterested in the developers from Los Cristianos
now snapping at its western flanks as it was when Spanish conquistadors
led here five centuries ago to accept the surrender of Pelinor, Chief of Adeje.
austere but still beautiful natural backdrop of peaks dwarfs the coastal devel-
ment, but construction work is visible on just about every section of the
thern coastline as new *urbanizaciones* gnaw into each little bay, spreading
es of mostly white modular architecture like some intractable fungal disease.
Until the mid-1960s, all that existed on this barren, treeless coastline were a
' fishing villages and the inland hill towns of Arona and Adeje. Farmers
xed a few bananas and tomatoes from the unpromising terrain, until a few
onaries glimpsed Eldorado in a brave new world of poured concrete and
ipant property speculation. A new crop went on test – tourists. And the rest,
i may think, is history. Out with the bananas, in with the pile-drivers, and real
ate fortunes blossomed overnight. But the extraordinary thing about this
elopment, unprecedented though its scale has been so far, is that it shows no
ns of stopping. A few years ago, island authorities declared that Playa de las
iéricas would soon be "finished". No more planning permission. No more
lding sites. "OK, we know we've trashed it, but
'll learn from our mistakes." As the new millen-
m dawned, however, the concrete mixers gave no
t of slowing their relentless conquest of the coast-
e, or the hills behind.

Can so many visitors, from so many countries,
lly be wrong? They come here, not just once, but
ie and time again. Obviously, this monster gives
st numbers of people exactly what they want. Not
tural interest, or history, scarcely anything recog-
ably local. Its sole purpose is *fun*, and fun it has,
m dawn until – well, the following dawn. Every-
ng visitors need – shops, beaches, restaurants, bars
d nightlife, lies within convenient reach. If older
k tire of the funshine, a younger generation
nds ready and waiting to take their place. If the
ropean time-share market is drying up, there are
nty of fresh investment wells to tap among newly
iancipated first-timers and wealthy speculators
m the former Eastern bloc. In part at least, Tener-
's booming property market is a useful place to
inder ill-gotten gains.

## ie terrible twins

ie older port of **Los Cristianos** ㉝ and the brash
w resort of **Playa de las Américas** ㉞ seem, at first
ince, to merge like Siamese twins along the coastal
ip at the foot of the arid southern hills. It's easy to

**LEFT:** Los
Cristianos, popular
with thousands.
**BELOW:** getting a
bus to the beach.

*If you need to escape the relentless pace, head to the harbour at Los Cristianos and take the ferry to La Gomera.*

**BELOW:** Playa de las Américas just grew and grew.

dismiss them as a single, stereotypical entity, but once you make sense of bewildering tangle of access roads connecting their various sprawling secto they steadily settle into clearly identifiable and discrete parts.

The two resorts tend to be marketed by foreign operators as separate holi destinations, although in practice few visitors realise exactly where one pl ends and the other begins. In fact, the official dividing line is quite distinct: the dry *barranco* which runs down to the beaches known as the **Playas Troya** (near the Hotel Troya). This is the boundary between Arona and Ade the two municipal districts which manage the resorts, named after the m older towns high in the hills, where for centuries the islanders learned to ma their homes to avoid pirate raiders. Confusingly for many visitors, the *mun pio* or regional names are sometimes used in place of the modern resorts.

## Los Cristianos

Once used to export tomatoes from Arona, the harbour at Los Cristianos bus itself with fishing and ferry services to the island of La Gomera, some 30 (18 miles) west of Tenerife. Leaflets advertising boat trips flutter from a do kiosks near the waterfront. In November it is packed with yachts awaiting favourable trade winds that will waft them to the Caribbean, just as they Columbus in the late 15th century. A close look reveals some vestiges of older fishing community immediately behind the harbour, all but submerged the densely packed holiday high-rises all around.

The seafront and the "old town" are mostly pedestrianised (the roads acc sible to traffic can become dreadfully congested at busy holiday times and it be very difficult to park). Shops, bars and restaurants line the streets aroun

Map on page 130–31

tral plaza with a modern white church. Most attention, understandably, olves around the beaches, where African traders hawk leatherware, jew-ry or sunglasses along the promenade, and amateur artists model weird igns in dampened sand.

t's quite possible to walk from one resort to another, although it can seem a g way on a hot day, and the road systems seem designed to disorient. To e your legs, there's a useful bus service (ask the tourist office how the fare icture works), and plenty of inexpensive taxis.

## aya de las Américas

the way along the seafront, artificial beaches have been created from the yish and often rocky coastline with dog-legged or semi-circular breakwaters ularly dosed with helpings of blonde imported sand. Even so, there's hardly ugh room for all the visitors to lie down in high season. Many provide tched parasols and sunbeds and offer a range of watersports from pedalos to ascending. Easily accessible are the central beaches of Troya, Bobo and stas. Those north of the harbour (Puerto Colón) such as San Eugenio, Torvis-and Fañabe are newer and rather more exclusive. **Puerto Colón** is one of the in features of the seafront, crammed with luxury gin-palaces (many of which ok as though they never sail) and excursion boats promising pirate cruises or ale-watching trips.

The sheer amount of accommodation in this huge resort is breathtaking, hough much of it is inevitably stranded far from the seafront amid chaotic ad systems. On the plus side, genuine efforts have been made to soften the ncrete with vegetation. Many of the larger and more upmarket hotel and

*As a change from the beach, try going for a whale-watching trip.*

**BELOW:** no shortage of choice when it comes to bars.

## NE LONG PARTY

ightlife is one of the main reasons for choosing Playa de las Américas as a holiday base. All night long it obs with neon and noise, especially around the raucous **ronicas** area, where more than 100 discos, nightclubs d karaoke bars compete for your eardrums within the ace of a stone's throw, and foam parties haven't yet ne out of fashion.

Naming specifically recommended ones would be a aste of time, as they tend to come and go, win and lose vour, and they are all rather similar. Many of them are cked with the *gamberos ingleses* (English hooligans) hough, as any bartender will tell you, the English don't ve a monopoly on bad behaviour.

Within many of the hotels, however, nightlife may be ore sedate, live bands giving older couples a chance to ush up on the quickstep or join in the chicken song. ne of the resort's most ambitious nightspots is the stival Latino, *Carmen Mota*, a cabaret dinner show gularly staged at the Pirámide de Arona auditorium in e **Mare Nostrum Resort**, a cluster of portentous hotels. e architecture of this place, a weighty jigsaw of classical otifs bolted together like meccano pieces, has to be en to be believed.

**Map on pages 130–31**

*Secluded grounds and private pools. Who needs the beach?*

**BELOW:**
the extravagance of the Gran Bahía del Duque.

apartment complexes have enormous and beautiful gardens with huge, invi swimming pools. Inside and out, the buildings drip with creepers and brilli flowering plants. And while some of the older blocks are truly hideous, o least show very little architectural imagination, some of the newer ones genuinely breathtaking. In a place where the only landmark buildings are ho it helps to develop an eye for them, if only to find your way around. The v ety of styles is surprising: ponderous marble neo-classicism, pastiche Canari postmodern glass-and-steel.

Two complexes are worth visiting in their own right. The **Jardín Tropi** (near the yacht marina of Puerto Colón) is a wonderful Moorish fantasy white turrets, domes and arches rambling through spectacularly gorgeous secluded grounds. A meal in one of its excellent restaurants or a visit to beach club would make a memorable treat. One of the latest additions to Pl de las Américas' hotel scene is the extravagant five-star **Gran Bahía Duque** towards the northern end of the resort: a vast compound of flamboy Italianate buildings with ritzy facilities. Direct access to a small but virtua private beach is one of its main attractions. Again, non-residents can experie something of this place at one of its six imaginative restaurants.

## Many ways to spend money

Shopping is another vital aspect of tourist entertainment in Playa de las Am cas. Few visitors to this resort will be staying far from a supermarket, newsage pharmacy, car hire office or exchange bureau to take care of the incidentals. extract more serious revenue, huge malls called *centros comerciales* stud ev sector of the development, displaying repetitive ranges of electronics, leath

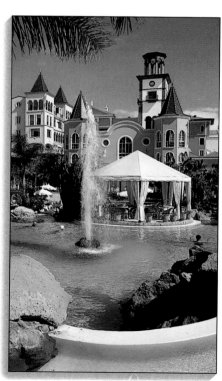

goods, souvenirs, sports kit and beachwear. Parc Santiago, San Eugenio and Fañabe are three of largest. Flea markets take place in both Los Cristia (Sunday) and at Playa de las Américas/Torvis (Thursday or Saturday), ever hopeful that visitors v invest in some of those handicrafts.

Don't expect any improving museums or highbr cultural activities. Unburdened by historical mo ments (apart from the World War II pillbox on seafront), Playa de las Américas flaunts its modern and its essential frivolity, without shame. **Pleas Island**, a multi-faceted entertainment zone for all family with mini-golf, bouncy castles, boating la and video games, says it all.

Local daytime diversions run to dolphin trips, be barbecues, donkey safaris, jeep excursions, cac parks, camel rides – brandished at visitors fr dozens of travel agencies and car hire outlets. Harle Superbowl tempts teenagers for ten-pin bowling a hamburgers near Playa Fañabe. Aquapark Octopus San Eugenio woos waterbabies with innumerab slides and chutes, helterskelters and an intrigui "magic tap" apparently floating in mid-air. L Aguilas del Teide on the Arona road offers performi birds of prey in exotically designed tropical garde And the Yellow Submarine (from Puerto Colo promises a journey to the bottom of the sea to wat passing marine life through glazed portholes.

# Building Beaches

By Mediterranean standards, Tenerife's natural beaches are poor, invariably comprising a short, pebbly shoreline with a snatch of over-populated greyish sand. So how did the island get away with a tourist miracle built on "sun and sea" holidays?

The answer lies in the ingenuity of Tenerife's developers, who over the past few decades have created artificial beaches and swimming pools out of rocks and bays all around the island. Originally the strength of the currents along the coast was considered the main problem: while these make the water clear and the waves fun they can also make swimming unsafe. One solution was to create seawater pools, using rocks and concrete to corner off part of the shore. A superlative example of this principle is at Puerto de la Cruz, where Lago de Martiánez, the lido designed by César Manrique on reclaimed land, questions the need for beaches. The lido consists of pools, landscaped gardens, bridges and paths.

A further problem was a shortage of sand: along the north coast the beaches are relatively new, and whatever black sand is formed from the basaltic lava is often washed away to leave a pebbly shingle. In the south, strong winds blow the sand inland, and while pumice lightens its colour the absence of quartz and shells prevents it from being classically "golden".

The most spectacular response to such deficiencies was made in 1970 with the construction of Las Teresitas beach to the north of Santa Cruz. Here the local pebbled beach was dramatically transformed by dumping 98,000 cubic metres (3.5 million cubic ft) of Saharan sand on top. The golden sand was extracted and shipped over using equipment from the phosphate mines of the Spanish Sahara, and a breakwater of rocks built across the bay to prevent the tide taking it straight back.

But even where such transformations haven't been made, sunbathers don't seem to mind. Privacy often appears more impor-tant than comfort or the colour of the sand. The extravagant efforts of Tenerife's developers to provide beaches are being countered by a growing desire to find undeveloped ones. Some tourists risk life and limb to get to idyllic little pebble beaches; whole families scramble out to remote coves, scaring off nudists and hippies.

But most beachmakers have returned to a more artful and well-established method: the building of *barras* or breakwaters out into the ocean. You can spot them everywhere, dog-legs of boulders branching out into the water, positioned by engineers between the currents and shore so that sand will naturally accumulate in each sheltered corner. The rocks, or *escollera*, are brought down from the hills, often in boulders big enough to fill a whole truck.

A prime example of this is the Playa de las Vistas to the west of Los Cristianos, where a man-made beach of golden sand has a rash of parasols, sunbeds, paths leading across the hot sands, and lots of contented visitors, gradually turning brown. ❑

**RIGHT:** a sandy paradise, transported all the way from the Sahara.

# THE WEST COAST

*Tranquil villages and agricultural land sit cheek by jowl with
modern tourist centres, while the Teno Massif broods
over the scene, beautiful and unchanging*

Map
on pages
130–31

Santa Cruz
de Tenerife

High in the hills, at suitably aloof distances from the boom towns they over-
see, sit the hill villages of Arona and Adeje. Both try to maintain the quiet
atmosphere of *hacienda* days, but its an uphill battle. **Arona** ㉟ has a
ew prison, where delinquent tourists are Jeeped up by the Civil Guard, drunk-
ly proclaiming their innocence. Expats now own many of its white *casas*. In
e surrounding hills successful Canarios and foreigners are building them-
lves villas, unable to live with the monster they've created on the coast.

On the other side of the 1,001-metre (3,284-ft) Roque del Conde mountain,
**deje** ㊱ sustains a more distinguished air. A fine avenue of laurels leads to the
6th-century church of **Santa Ursula**, which has some casually hung Gobe-
ns tapestries. The town was the former seat of the Guanche court from which
e island was ruled. Later the counts of La Gomera took over.

The **Casa Fuerte** at the top of the town is now only a faint echo of the forti-
ed mansion which the counts built in 1556. Sacked by English pirates 30 years
ter, it was all but destroyed by fire in the 19th century. A cannon stands out-
de the gates of the present building, in which three families still live. In one
ouse a set of wooden stocks hang on the wall, a grim souvenir of the days
hen slave-traders used the southern coast of Tenerife to corral their human
argo prior to the voyage to America.

**LEFT:** the marina at
Puerto de Santiago.
**BELOW:**
new apartments
at Los Gigantes.

## Hell's Gorge

urther up the hill is the entrance to **Barranco del
nfierno** (Hell's Gorge) ㊲, the deepest ravine in the
Canaries. Allow a good two hours for the walk, which
ecomes something of a scramble as steep gulley
alls narrow to a verdant V-shape and the path criss-
rosses a stream fringed with willow and eucalyptus
rees. The summer heat can be truly hellish, but the
lora has a paradisical abundance. At its green heart
here are cascades of babbling waterfalls that will
oothe many a soul.

Make sure you wear sensible footwear, and take
lenty of water with you. A bar-restaurant by the
ntrance to the gorge, with good views from its ter-
aces, caters for hungry and thirsty hikers with typical
Canarian dishes but you'll need plenty of liquid on
our walk.

Meanwhile, back on the coastal strip, the specula-
ors have been busy, parcelling up former banana
lantations or abandoned tomato fields for building
lots. Anything with a sea view is fair game, how-
ver dismal the scenery. From the main C822 road,
ccess tracks sprout every few hundred metres along
ormer gulleys to some new housing development or
ther on the stretch of coastline north of Playa de las
Américas now marketed as the Costa Adeje.

*Local people still lead lives largely unaffected by tourists.*

The development is solid as far as the former fishing village of **La Caleta**, an gradually the gaps of open country between more northerly points are bein narrowed. So far, it isn't a pretty sight. A glance at Playa Paraíso (Paradis Beach) will show that this resort is anything but heavenly.

## Past and present

For better impressions, stick to the good, fast high road leading to **Guía d Isora** ㊳. This attractive little agricultural centre has a typical Canarian old tow with an interesting church, the **Iglesia de la Virgen de la Luz** (Our Lady o Light), in its main square. Though recently restored, it has Renaissance origin and unusual *mudéjar* (Moorish) features; inside are several works by Tenerife' most famous woodcarver, José Lujan Perez. By the approach to the town, alon, the main road, a large craft-shop sells a huge range of Canarian products, includ ing flower perfumes, *mojo* sauces, plant seeds, music recordings and local wine – a good place to look for less run-of-the-mill souvenirs than you may find in th big resorts. Large cisterns store some of the abundant supplies of water provide by Teide's huge catchment area, which supplement Guía's naturally dry climat and irrigate the crops that flourish all around the town.

From Guía de Isora a steep winding road leads south to the deep-water po of **San Juan** ㊴. The port's streets are still quiet and sedate; locals go about thei daily life seemingly oblivious to the few camera-happy tourists who park thei cars along the promenade. On a clear day, the island of La Gomera seems jus a stone's throw away.

**BELOW:** the agricultural town of Guía de Isora.

Both San Juan and the even more local small port of Alcalá to the north ar good places to look for fish lunches served Canarian-style with *papas arrugada*

Map on page 130–31

1d *mojo* sauces. Quite a bit of construction work has taken place around San 1an's dark beaches in recent years, but the new apartment blocks are for locals 1d the place has kept its mainly Spanish feel.

Along the coast, however, it's a different story. Here, the older harbour of **uerto de Santiago** (the port of the regional centre, Santiago del Teide), has xpanded massively with large hotels and vast numbers of time-share apart-1ents which seriously threaten to overwhelm its charm. A few scrappy beaches ud the mostly rocky shore. Much more attractive is the artificial beach at **laya de la Arena ⓐ**, the southernmost section of this complex resort area, .ndscaped with palms and recently awarded a *Bandera Azul* (Blue Flag) for 1eanliness and good facilities.

Little on Tenerife equals the rapidity with which **Los Gigantes ⓐ**, the biggest :sort on the northwest coast, has been developed as a major international player .1 the Canarian tourism stakes. Los Gigantes (The Giants) takes its name from . spectacular range of huge dark cliffs that tower over the resort, plunging sheer .› the water-line and dwarfing the excursion boats that sail past on day-trips.

Land suitable for building is very limited near the cliffs themselves, and the .lack sand beach areas are small. This has kept Los Gigantes "proper" :omparatively compact and upmarket, its village-style apartments clambering .p the steep, lush slopes from the bijou marina, tucked into picturesque folds .nd terraces and accessed by a maze of serpentine roads. An artificial sea .vater lido extends the entire length of the natural beach, while the marina .›ffers sport fishing and scuba diving for its speedboat clientele. Immediately .ehind the seafront, the building facades are constructed in traditional :anarian style with wooden balconies.

**BELOW:**
you can scuba dive or snorkel at Los Gigantes.

Map on pages 130–31

*Not a man to get stuck behind on a narrow road.*

**BELOW:** Masca, a hidden village.
**RIGHT:** Masca man has seen some changes.

## The Teno Massif

A boat trip gives the best view of the precipitous cliffs (*acantilados*) marking the southern edge of the **Macizo de Teno** (Teno Massif), a peninsula of old basaltic lava-flows now sliced deep into valleys and jagged ridges by erosion. With the exception of its northern coast, Teno, like Anaga at the opposite end of the island, resisted the advances of later lava-flows and may yet halt the tide of *urbanizacion* flowing up the west coast.

Despite the increasing importance of tourism in the area, the fertile terraces that climb up to **Tamaimo** are still rich with bananas, vines and potatoes. Piles of small bright tomatoes often lie beside the road, rejected by exporters for their size but a welcome find for passers-by. Further inland is the relaxed village of **Santiago del Teide** ❷ where cacti line the roofs and Canarian balconies grace even the newest *casas*. Its small church has a gently domed roof – at Christmas the interior is decorated with poinsettias and oranges, incense wafts through the gloom and loudspeakers broadcast carols to the cows.

From here a road runs north along the edge of the massif, climbing from vines and potatoes to bramble and broom and the unfamiliar sight of grass. At its peak are small pastoral plateaux and a sign at **Erjos del Teide**, 1,117 metres (3,664 ft), marking the traditional mountain pass leading to the north coast.

Santiago del Teide can also be reached by a higher road from **Chío**, passing through the small town of **Arguayo** ❸ and almond groves that are a mass of blossom in late January. Taking this route allows inspection of the volcanic debris emitted by Montaña de Chinyero, Tenerife's most recent eruption. During 10 days in 1909 it blew ash and cinders into the sky with a noise that could be heard in La Orotava. In Arguayo there is a small ceramics and folk museum, the **Centro Alfarero** (open Tues–Sun 10am–1pm, 4–7pm; admission free; tel 922 86 34 65) where pottery is made in the simple style of the ancient Guanches, fashioned by hand without a wheel and fired in traditional wood-fuelled kilns.

## Secret village

Until recently the village of **Masca** ❹, tucked deep in Teno's folds, was one of Tenerife's best kept secrets. Its red-roofed stone houses perch on the ridges of a precipitous valley. It now has a vastly improved road whose brilliantly engineered loops and twists snake over this buckled terrain with ease, but unfortunately the route is already besieged by coach parties who clog up the passing places and crush walkers against the safety barriers. The village itself, once completely cut off from the outside world except by mule, greets its new source of prosperity with mixed and bewildered feelings. Romantics may feel the valley's isolation should have been preserved. Several restaurants invite passers-by for panoramic *al fresco* lunches. If you have time and energy to take to your feet, it's a marvellous region for walking, with magnificent rugged scenery and a great variety of interesting plants, including wild lavender, marigold and oxalis. Take water, and beware of rockfalls. A small *mirador* waits at the top of the ridge, where the land fans wide into the well-cultivated fields around **El Palmar**. ◻

# THE VIVID FLORA OF TENERIFE

*Tenerife's climate and varied topography support a wide range of indigenous plants, as well as a cornucopia of imported species*

One of the delights of Tenerife for sun-starved north Europeans is the vivid vegetation which brightens the island, even in the depths of winter. Scarlet trumpets of hibiscus bloom on terraces, sugar-pink oleander lines roadsides and multicoloured bougainvillea scrambles to the rooftops. From colonial times, new species flooded in from the New World to "acclimatise" before braving inhospitable European temperatures, and Tenerife's formal plant collections are of great interest to botanists. Away from the resorts, hot-house exotica for the cut-flower market flourish on fertile volcanic soils.

## GOVERNED BY ALTITUDE

About 2,000 species grow wild on the island, of which some 400 are endemic. Altitude stratifies them into clearly distinguishable zones. Up to about 600 metres (2,000 ft) cacti and succulents make natural rockeries of the dry ravines, hoarding scarce water in their fleshy leaves. The candelabra spurge (*Euphorbia canariensis*) and the stocky local date-palm (*Phoenix canariensis*) are typical native species. In the foothills of the Anaga, a lichen-wreathed tangle of ferns, tree heaths, juniper and laurels swirls in the mists created by the trade winds. At about 1,000 metres (3,280 ft), the Canary pine (*Pinus canariensis*) takes over, condensing airborne moisture on its long needles and providing an efficient self-irrigation system.

▷ **PRICKLY PEAR**
The prickly pear, imported in the 19th century as a host plant for the cochineal grub, has long since leapt its walled enclosures and grows wild in great profusion.

△ **HERE BE DRAGONS**
The strange, slow-growing Dragon Tree (*Dracaena draco*) is indigenous to the islands. This one, at Icod de los Vinos, is anything from 500 to 3,000 years old.

▷ **BIRD-OF-PARADISE**
Strelitzia, the bird-of-paradise, with its waxy, beak-like plumage, is the most striking of the plants produced for the cut-flower market.

## THE PRIDE OF TENERIFE

Instantly recognisable among all the strange flowers which grow under the volcano of El Teide, the giant red spires of *Echium wildprettii* make an unforgettable impact. One of its names is *Orgullo de Tenerife* (Pride of Tenerife), but it is more widely known as the *Tajinaste*. Endemic to the Canaries, it doesn't grow elsewhere, but a distant relative found in the British Isles is the viper's bugloss. In late spring, its shaggy scarlet flower-stems erupt from the arid cinder-beds to a height of 2 metres (6ft) or more, blooming spectacularly until early July before drooping earthwards like dying swans. No matter what time of year you visit the National Park, you will always see some trace of the Tajinaste, ablaze in summer or fossilised in ghostly desiccation. Like many other plants in the park, this species is endangered and strictly protected. Efforts to propagate it are continuing in a number of places, particularly at the El Portillo visitors' centre.

## CODESA

...desa (Adenocarpus ...osus) is a low-growing, ...om-like shrub which ...ws in profusion at altitudes ...m 2,000 to 2,700 metres.

## CARDON

...horbia canariensis, or ...rdón, is a variety of spurge ...ich is common in many ...ts of the Canary Islands ...ere it thrives in the arid ...ines.

### △ SABINA
The sabina is a unique kind of juniper tree which grows on El Hierro and has a peculiarly distorted shape.

### ◁ POINSETTIA
Growing to the size of sturdy trees, the vivid poinsettia hardly seems like the same flower that is widely sold in pots at Christmas time.

# LA GOMERA: INTRODUCTION

*Prepare to travel on foot if you want to discover the secrets of this wild and mountainous island*

La Gomera, the second smallest of the islands (after El Hierro) is a compact, almost circular island, about 24 km (5 miles) across. It lies just 32 km (20 miles) west of Tenerife. The long-delayed airport is open at last for domestic flights from neighbouring islands, but most visitors still come by boat from Tenerife (90 minutes by ferry, 40 minutes by hydrofoil), or from El Hierro (three hours by ferry).

The ferries bring hoards of visitors on day-trips from Tenerife, but La Gomera's special magic cannot be absorbed on a quick round-the-island coach tour. Wild and mountainous, and intricately patterned with ancient footpaths and tracks, La Gomera reveals its secrets only to those who travel on foot. Accommodation on the island encourages this, for though there are resort hotels and self-catering apartments around San Sebastián, the island's capital, Valle Gran Rey, in the west, and Playa de Santiago, in the south, the best accommodation is to be found in *casas rurales* – converted farmhouses and barns dotted round the island and often hidden in secretive valleys that feel as remote from civilisation as it is possible to be.

The highlight of a visit to the island is a trek through the mist-enshrouded laurel forest that cloaks the Parque Nacional de Garajonay. Now a UNESCO World Heritage Site, Garajonay is just one of 16 parks on the island, all protected for their rare vegetation or unique geology.

The people of La Gomera are a mix of Guanches – the original North African inhabitants of the island – and Spanish colonists, and the population has decreased significantly over the past half century due to emigration. Like the other smaller islands La Gomera has suffered extensively as a result of the fluctuating economic fortunes of the Canaries, although it is more fortunate than Fuerteventura because it is much more fertile. But staple industries, such as wine-making and the cultivation of bananas, tomatoes and potatoes only just make a profit, and many of La Gomera's interior villages are all but deserted, their few remaining inhabitants rather poor. ❏

**PRECEDING PAGES:** serene landscape on La Gomera; forest in the Parque Nacional de Garajonay.
**LEFT:** a view of San Sebastián from the ferry.

Map
on page
200

# LA GOMERA

*This little island is a walker's paradise, a place of steep cliffs
and breathtaking ravines, ancient trackways and views
that are quite simply unforgettable*

**M**any islanders from La Gomera have taken the westward passage across
the Atlantic, travelling to Venezuela or Uruguay to take up jobs in the
South America oil industry – which is why you will often hear Latino
rhythms in the island's cafés and on local radio. These adventurers are looking
for work and an income to send back to their families, but they are also following in the wake of Christopher Columbus, who embarked on his voyage of
discovery in September 1492 after stopping off at the island to collect fresh
water and food. Quite why he chose La Gomera as his last port of call before
sailing into the unknown isn't recorded. Some say that he had a whirlwind
affair with Beatriz de Bobadilla, the aristocratic daughter-in-law of the island's
governor. Others believe it was simply because La Gomera was the last known
stepping-off point for the unknown West.

## Barren doorstep

The port of **San Sebastián ❶**, the main town on the island, hasn't altered much
in size since Columbus's day. It is situated in what is probably the most barren
region of the island, and makes an untidy introduction to La Gomera; the rest
of the island only begins to become interesting once you get about 16 km
(10 miles) away from the suburbs.

The four-times-a-day ferry from Los Cristianos, in
southern Tenerife, sets the pulse of San Sebastián rac-
ing when it arrives. The MV *Benchijigua* sends waves
of traffic round the veins of the island. Day-tripping
tourists over from Tenerife, along with supplies of
beer, the post and the newspapers help warm the
hearts of the islanders as if San Sebastián had just
imbibed a slug of Venezuelan rum (which is drunk
here in large quantities at breakfast time). The island's
principle buses (to Santiago, Vallehermoso and Valle
Gran Rey) time their departures to co-ordinate with
the ferry sailings.

From the port, it is a short walk westwards, along
the promenade, past the thriving **marina** (the ghosts
of the *Niña*, the *Pinta* and *Santa María* from Columbus's fleet must surely be lurking there) to the jumble
of houses, old and new, rising sharply up the hillside,
where most of San Sebastián's 6,200 residents live.

The main square, **Plaza de Las Américas**, is wide
and uncluttered. Here there's a chance to enjoy a *café
con leche* (milky coffee), and a *bocadillo de jamón y
queso* (a ham and cheese sandwich) and watch the
pigeons fight for your crumbs. Or you can rest under
the tall palm trees while sipping a *zumo* (freshly
squeezed fruit juice).

Between the port and the plaza are a couple of grand
buildings in the colonial Canarian style containing the

**LEFT:** terraces in
the Valle Gran Rey.
**BELOW:** crenellated
building in San
Sebastián.

library and some administrative offices. The *cabildo* (local government) itself is housed in a smaller, less-distinguished, building (marked principally by the flag-poles on the exterior), a third of the way up Calle del Medio, the main road that leads northwards from the plaza. Most of the town's hotels, shops and banks are along this road, as is the tourist office (Calle del Medio 1, tel: 922 14 15 12), housed in the ancient building containing the well from which it is reputed Columbus took water for his voyages.

To the west of the plaza, standing in a small park set back from the black sand beach, is the **Torre del Conde**. This Gothic tower (now open only for occasional exhibitions) is all that survives from the fortifications built in 1447 by Diego de Herrera, the island's first Spanish governor. It served not so much for defence against external attack as for protection from the islanders, who were still far from happy at their colonisation.

It was Herrera's son, Hernán Peraza, who was married to Beatriz de Bobadilla (she who is said to have beguiled Columbus). Peraza and his wife apparently had a very passionate relationship, but despite this, Peraza fell for a young Guanche princess, Iballa, and it was while hastening to meet her in a convenient cave up

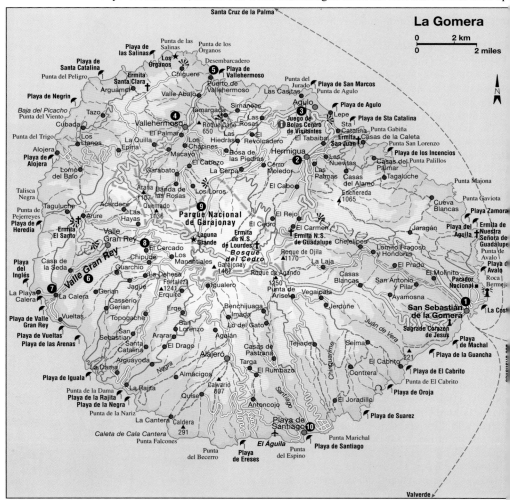

Map
on page
200

in the island's high ground (near the Roques of Agando, Zarzita and Ojila) that he was ambushed by two Guanche chiefs and thrown off the mountain; the place is still called the Degollada de Peraza (Peraza's Destruction).

The rebels then attacked the home of the Spanish colonial authorities and laid siege to Beatriz de Bobadilla, who took refuge in this tower. Eventually Spanish troops arrived from Gran Canaria, defeated the uprising and indulged in an orgy of revenge. Hundreds of male Guanches were killed, and their wives and children were sold as slaves.

Hidden from sight off the Calle del Medio are several excellent interior courtyards, known here as *patios*, one belonging to the Pensión Gomera, another to the Gomera Garden bar. In the evenings the light spills out of these doorways and the town, which seems comatose through much of the rest of the day, is remarkably alive. Out of a considerable selection of eating places the lively and atmospheric **El Pajar** restaurant at Calle Ruiz de Padron 44 (it looks like a bar from the outside) offers very good value.

Halfway up the street is the **Iglesia de la Virgen de la Asunción** (1490–1510), where Columbus supposedly prayed for the last time before setting off on his journey. The overall style is Gothic, but the construction is half-brick, half-render, giving a piebald effect to the exterior. On one inside wall is a series of elegant altarpieces and an ancient and much-faded mural (dated 1760) by Jose Mesa, a Gomeran artist, depicting the English naval attack on the island.

We haven't finished with Columbus yet: a little further up the street is the **Casa de Colón** (open Mon–Fri 10am–1pm, 4–6pm; admission free), which is supposed to be the last place that he stayed in the old world, before setting sail for the new in 1492. The unexceptional building has been bought and restored

*Watching the world go by from the steps of the Gothic church.*

**BELOW:**
San Sebastián
and its port.

by the island *cabildo*, and now houses a small collection of pre-Columbian pottery from South America, and some displays on the explorer's historic voyage. Beyond is the **Ermita de San Sebastián**, the oldest building in the town; this long, dark chapel was built to serve as the island's first church.

## Parador and playa

Directly above the harbour, on a small hill called Lomo de la Horca (literally Ridge of the Gallows) stands San Sebastián's **Parador**, one of the chain of elegant state-owned hotels, standing on the site of a former church. The Parador has the deserved reputation of being one of the best hotels on the Canaries and is consequently full most of the time. Built in island-colonial style in 1976, it has a deliberate air of antiquity created by the extensive use of dark wood. Much of the island's history is on its walls in the form of marine charts and navigational instruments. Lush sub-tropical gardens surround the swimming pool, from where there are fine views.

Beyond the Parador the road runs through modern suburbs, past the light house and becomes a track to the **Playa de Avalo**, a pebbly beach at the end of a now-deserted valley, where Tenerife's Pico del Teide can often be seen across the sea. The track winds further round the headland, past the city rubbish tip, to the **Ermita de Nuestra Señora de Guadalupe**. This lonely building, set on a low promontory surrounded by sea, houses a statue of the Virgin of Guadalupe, the focus of La Gomera's principal fiesta, which occurs in early October every five years (the next is in 2003). The statue of the Virgin is taken from here in a flotilla of fishing boats back to San Sebastián, where she is paraded through the flower-filled streets.

**BELOW:**
deep in thought.

## THE ART OF SILBO

Gomeran whistling, or *silbo*, is a language that was once widespread on the island, allowing the inhabitants to communicate complicated messages at great distances across the steep-sided ravines. In *silbo*, the pitch and duration of each whistled sound spells out a syllable, but this is not simply a coded form of Spanish: one of the many mysteries of the Canaries is that *silbo* is a language in its own right, possibly of pre-Hispanic origins (there is a theory that the original Guanches developed the language after their tongues had been cut off by the Spanish conquistadors, to stop them from hatching plots).

The language is relatively sophisticated: a French archaeologist, R. Vernau, writing in 1876, said that it allowed users to "express all their thoughts and articulate all their meanings".

Today, the art of *silbo* is fast dying out and were it not for tourist interest it probably would not have survived to the present day – you can see and hear demonstrations at the Parador, and at various restaurants in Las Rosas. However, there has recently been a move to teach *silbo* in schools, and some of the younger children are very enthusiastic about it. Perhaps this will bring about a revival in the 21st century.

## Northern route

The sun comes late and departs early from the valley of **Hermigua ❷**, a small place with 2,656 inhabitants and the rarefied atmosphere of a Himalayan village. The 450-metre (1,480-ft) tunnel that separates the two valleys also separates two worlds: where the San Sebastián valley is barren and hot its neighbour is sleepy, damp and largely overgrown.

The floor of the Hermigua Valley is cloaked in banana plantations, and trellised vines cling like cobwebs to the hillside crevices. The town itself has two distinct sections. In the upper part, where houses pile on top of each other up the hillside in an attempt to scramble into the sun, you will find the **Los Telares** apartments and the craft centre, where hand-woven rugs are particularly colourful buys. Here also is the convent of **Santo Domingo**, which contains some fine Moorish woodwork. The lower part of the town is the commercial centre, with the banana cooperative, the principal church and shops. Unfortunately, the beach is not very attractive.

*Unusual modern sculpture in Hermigua.*

Around the headland the village of **Agulo ❸** is also built in two clusters on adjacent small hills, set in a bowl of basalt. The 17th-century town centre, in the lower village, has some good examples of vernacular architecture, while the upper village has a large and unusual Moorish domed church, which dominates **Plaza Leoncio Bento**. But what really distinguishes the town is its location; one side of the basalt bowl has dropped away into the sea, giving way to impressive much-photographed views of Agulo, with Tenerife and Mount Teide in the background.

A left turn inland just before the village of Las Rosas would lead you into the Parque Nacional de Garajonay, but for the moment our route continues west-

**BELOW:**
hand-woven rugs can be bought at Los Telares.

*Some attractive
shops selling local
goods have sprung
up to cater for
visitors.*

wards on the island's main road, the TF-711, to **Vallehermoso ④** (pop. 4,516). This substantial but compact town is important as an administrative and commercial centre, but does not have much to offer tourists, except for the beach at **Playa de Vallehermoso ⑤**, where the heavy swell attracts surfers and body-boarders. Towering above it is the **Roque de Cano**, a prominent cone-shaped peak made out of solidified lava (technically this is the cone of the volcano, left behind after the volcano walls have eroded), which also features on the town's coat of arms.

Down the road is the village of **Arure**, distinguished principally by the **Mirador Ermita El Santo**, a stunning viewpoint reached down a track to the right of the road under a small bridge. From here the views extend over Taguluche and the western coast, with La Palma and El Hierro visible in the distance on a clear day. The **Mirador del Palmarejo**, further down the road, also has stunning views and an upmarket restaurant.

## Valley of plenty

Radiating out from Garajonay's central cone are numerous *barrancos* (ravines) eroded from lava by heavy rain and gushing springs and carved into terraces for growing fruit and vegetables – mangoes, avocados and the islands main export crops, tomatoes and bananas. The **Valle Gran Rey ⑥** is the most impressive example: a deep gorge that local farmers have transformed into a staircase of interlocking green plots in order to extract the maximum value from every inch of fertile soil.

From Arure you descend to this photogenic green valley, dotted with white houses and palm trees. The Valle Gran Rey has been colonised by young

**BELOW:**
local potters
in El Cercado.

Europeans, principally Germans, who have come here looking for paradise on earth. Among the valley's semi-permanent residents renting the numerous self-catering apartments are surfing fanatics, who make the most of the Atlantic waves that break on the beach; and intellectual "greens" in colourful clothes who have chosen to live out their personal ideological beliefs in this magical setting (the valley population swelled enormously after the Chernobyl disaster). This is also the closest La Gomera gets to a beach resort, with a dive centre, wind-surfing school, several restaurants and bars, and an internet café. Boats are easily hired here for trips north to **Los Organos**, the spectacular organ-pipe in the cliffs at the island's northern tip formed from sea-eroded basalt columns. Tour operators also hold out the prospect of swimming with dolphins. You may be lucky, but sightings are not guaranteed.

At the point where the long, intensely cultivated valley opens up to the sea, the little village of **La Calera ❼** sits on a hill to the right, a flower-covered jumble of houses crawling up the hill. La Calera is La Gomera's Montmartre, with small boutiques and restaurants and an abundance of spring water run-ning down roadside channels. House prices here are the highest on the island. Many of the food shops advertise locally made *miel de palma* (palm honey), made from the sap tapped almost daily from the valley's date palm trees. The sap is boiled until it forms a thick syrup. Working palms are distinguished by tin collars on their trunks, designed to keep the ants away from the sweet liquid.

Valle Gran Rey's shore towns, one at either end of the beach, have been developed with the new tourism in mind and are less attractive. **La Playa Calera** is a poor substitute for Gran Canaria's Playa del Inglés, but it has a small and clean black sand beach around the coast to the west. **Vueltas** is a fishing port of no particular distinction, apart from the fact that it accommodates numbers of tourists, has plenty of bars and restaurants, and is the departure point for the hydrofoil service to San Sebastián and on to Los Cristianos, on Tenerife.

## Approach to the park

The new road from Valle Gran Rey to San Sebastián runs cleanly down the centre of the island through a spine of forest; parallel with it is the old road, which winds through the villages of El Cercado and Chipude to the south, perched between the untouchable woods and the unfarmable barren southern slopes.

**El Cercado ❽** (The Enclosure), is built around a loop in the road, as its name suggests, and is the home of traditional pottery, made entirely by hand without the assistance of a potter's wheel. The town has a cou-ple of pleasant bars which serve satisfying, if basic, local food, and it is a good place to aim for at the end of a walk through the national park.

A good start to an exploration of the forest, how-ever, is the **Juego de Bolas Visitors' Centre** (open Tues–Sun, 9.30am–4.30pm, tel: 922 80 09 93). This means going back a few miles on the main road and taking the turning near Las Rosas (*mentioned on page 203*). Although the centre lies a little way outside the Parque Nacional de Garajonay, it is the best place to pick up information about the park. The building is a

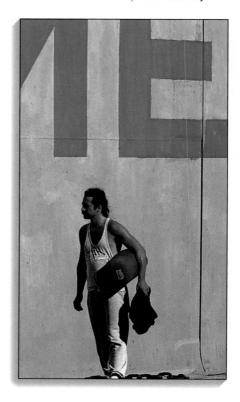

**Map on page 200**

**BELOW:** looking for Nirvana in the Valle Gran Rey.

typical Canarian structure with exhibitions explaining the geology and wildlife of the park. There is a small Ethnographic Museum, with a cut-away Gomeran house (the village houses have not changed much even today) and pottery, basketwork and weaving demonstrations (although the latter only take place when the coach parties arrive). The garden contains plants used in Canarian herbal medicine and in the cuisine of the island, and there is an enjoyable video on the island culture. Among the maps and books on sale here, the ICONA *Guide to Garajonay National Park*, with tracks and paths marked, is useful for anyone planning to go trekking.

Continue from the Visitor Centre through Acevinos to El Cedro, a route well worth the expedition. The cedar tree after which El Cedro is named has long since gone. The straggling village survives on agriculture. In a clearing in the woods above the village is the **Ermita de Nuestra Señora de Lourdes**, erected, as it says on the chapel, thanks to a donation by Florence Parry, an English-woman, in 1964. The chapel, with its tiny altar and wooden benches, is the focus for an annual pilgrimage through the forest on the last Sunday in August.

A track cuts up from the chapel to the main road near Laguna Grande, a forest clearing where there was once a lake (these days its only a big puddle even after heavy rain). The site acts as a pivotal point for walkers on the island because of its restaurant, which is reminiscent of an alpine log cabin, complete with roaring fire, and is a good place to end a long walk.

**BELOW:** traditional dress is worn for The Dance of the Drum.

## The ancient forest

At 3,984 hectares (9,844 acres), **Parque Nacional de Garajonay** ❾ is quite small compared to Spain's eight other national parks, but this ancient moss-

## THE DANCE OF THE DRUM

While many folkloric traditions are similar throughout the Canary Islands, *El Baile del Tambor* (The Dance of the Drum) is exclusive to La Gomera. The dancers, dressed in brightly coloured costumes, form a male and female line facing each other and perform a stylised dance to the rhythm of drums (*tambores*) and castanets (*chacaras*) while the drummers sing the lyrics of epic poems or romantic narratives, which tell a complete – and often very long – story, sometimes a traditional one, sometimes one created especially for the occasion. A soloist develops the story in couplets (*pareados*) which are repeated by a chorus. The dancers with the most stamina will keep going until the song ends, but they can join or leave the lines whenever they grow tired. Needless to say, staying the course is a matter of pride for some of the participants.

This type of composition used to be common throughout Spain in the 15th to 17th centuries, but the tradition has been retained only in La Gomera. If you are on the island at the time of a *romería* or village fiesta you will probably see a demonstration of the Baile del Tambor. If you are interested in tracking one down, ask at the tourist office in San Sebastián.

cloaked laurel and cedar forest is a surviving shred of similar forests that once covered the subtropical world and, as such, it is considered important enough to have been declared a UNESCO World Heritage Site in 1986. The importance of the forest is that it is the surviving vestiges of a type of vegetation that was once commonplace, clothing much of southern Europe, but it died off during the last ice age, leaving only a few remnants in the warm islands of the Canaries and the Madeiran archipelago. The term *laurisilva* (laurel wood) is used to describe the mix of fragrant evergreen plants with waxy green leaves that thrive here, adapted to the humid subtropical environment. Other plants include holly, wild olive, arbutus, juniper, and tree heath, a living fossil from the Carboniferous era, related to heather, that can grow to 15 metres (45 ft) and whose iron-hard branches are used for fencing on the island.

Walking through these woods is made more fascinating by the mossy tangle of ferns and epiphytic plants that thrive on the forest, drawing their moisture and nourishment from the semi-permanent mist that swirls across the slopes. Lime-green, yellow and orange lichens hang from the trees in hair-like hanks, creating a primeval environment from which a dinosaur might emerge at any moment – though any stirrings in the undergrowth are more likely to be the sheep or goats that are put out to graze on the undergrowth. Or maybe one of the surprisingly large and wingless Canary grasshoppers that live in the forest.

Exploring the park on foot is not difficult: most paths cross from north to south and are easy to find. The maps and guides available from the Juego de Bolas Visitors' Centre contain lots of suggestions. The main TF-713 highway cuts through the park and there are picnic points and *miradors* (viewing points) along the road where you can pull up and start a walk. The golden rule is not to

Map on page 200

*Tangled foliage and twisted trees make up the woods of Garajonay.*

**BELOW:** the Parque Nacional de Garajonay.

Map on page 200

light fires: although these woods are often dripping with mist and may look unlikely to burn, summer forest fires are a major problem. Twenty-one people, including a newly elected mayor from Tenerife, were trapped and killed here by a fire in 1984 when the wind changed direction.

Most first-time visitors head for **Alto de Garajonay**, the peak of Mount Garajonay (1,487metres/4,878 ft), supposedly named after two lovers called Gara and Jonay, La Gomera's own Romeo and Juliet, who committed suicide together on the foliage-cloaked peak rather than be separated forever by their parents, who opposed their marriage. There is a popular and well-signposted path up to the peak from **Pajarito** (which is on the bus route from San Sebastián). The peak is an hour or so on foot from here, and the reward for your efforts is a view (on a clear day) that takes in all the islands of the Canarian archipelago.

## Down to the beach

You will skirt the peak of Garajonay as you continue through Chipude, before the road dives to the sea again over barren slopes to **Playa de Santiago ⑩**, the sunniest spot on the island and the only place where tourism has taken root as firmly as on the major islands. There is a pebble beach here, but that is not the main attraction. Rather, it is the **Jardín Tecina**, an upmarket resort hotel with 330 rooms, set in white Canarian houses dotted across the hillside, with outdoor pools and jacuzzis. The Tecina is the creation of Fred Olsen, a Norwegian shipping magnate, and long-time unofficial lord of the isle (his family run the La Gomera ferry, supports the banana industry and owns all of the extensive **Barranco Benchijigua** (hence the ferry's name). The Olsens also used to run a small fish-processing business in the village and although that has since closed, fishing remains crucial to the settlement; when the boats come in, so do the lorries, and the scavenging skate, as big as barn doors, come flapping along the bottom of the fishing harbour.

**BELOW:** a rainbow arches across the *barrancos*.
**RIGHT:** the Roque de Cano and Vallehermoso.

While the Jardín Tecina looks like a new island village from a distance, there is no disguising the sad decay that the once significant village of Benchijigua itself has fallen into. It is now largely abandoned although superbly sited at the foot of the Roques Agando, Zarzita and Ojila, all three of them lava monoliths formed from eroded volcanic cones.

The Santiago road rejoins the dorsal road as it makes the long descent towards San Sebastián. For the last few miles the harbour and ferry station are clearly visible, which means that if you are visiting for the day and have miscalculated your return time, you may arrive at the top of the hill just in time to see the boat back to Tenerife disengage itself tantalisingly slowly from the quay.

The best thing you could do in these circumstances is to divert to the monument of **Sagrado Corazón de Jesús**, a 7-metre (23-ft) figure of Christ overlooking the sea, where you can watch the sun go down before finding somewhere to sleep (*see page 283 for recommendations*), having a meal, and enjoying a quiet night in La Gomera.

# LA PALMA: INTRODUCTION

*A guide to the Green Island, where trekking through the forests and the volcanic landscape is the main event*

Once the northeast trade winds brought galleons from the Spanish peninsula to the island of San Miguel de la Palma en route to South America, but now the winds bring only rain and mist to the northern slopes of the island, to the delight of La Palma's visitors and residents. The winds are the reason for the luxuriant vegetation that gives La Palma its soubriquet of "La Isla Verde" – the Green Island. By contrast with its drier neighbours, some of which see virtually no rain, this is a farmer's paradise.

The Palmeros love the beauty of their home, its green forests, its year-round flowers and its spectacular scenery. Tourist facilities are, frankly, rudimentary; there are few beaches, no tourist "attractions", and only two small resorts (at Puerto Naos, in the west, and Playa de los Cancajos, south of the capital). The experiences to be enjoyed on La Palma are simple and are never thrust upon the visitor. Trekking is the main activity, and a day spent exploring the dense Los Tilos forest, or walking around the volcanic depression of the Caldera de Taburiente is best re-lived in animated conversation in an ash-floored *bodegón* (simple restaurant), relaxing around a wooden table heaped with uncomplicated plates of grilled fish and meat, salty potatoes (*papas arrugadas*) with *mojo palmero* sauce, and strong red wine made from grapes grown a mere 200 metres (650 ft) away.

The island map is a Rorschach ink-blot test administered by a psychologist to test the mood of the viewer: it can look like a heart, or a stone axe. About 28 km (18 miles) from east to west, 46 kms (29 miles) from the rounded coast of the north to the pointed tip at the south, La Palma is the fifth largest of the Canary Islands (730 sq. km/282 sq. miles in area) and the third in population, with 80,000 inhabitants, a quarter of whom live in the capital city of Santa Cruz de la Palma. The island rises to a height of 2,426 metres (7,959 ft) at the Roque de los Muchachos, at the edge of the gigantic volcanic crater that dominates the island's northern half.

La Palma's principal road system takes the form of a rough figure of eight with a coastal road running around the island's perimeter, and a road cutting across the middle of the island, between Santa Cruz and Los Llanos de Aridane (La Palma's second city). This divides the island neatly into two, with a southern and a northern loop. It is feasible to tour each loop in a day, though there are sights enough to tempt you into lingering longer and perhaps to devote a whole week to this enchanting island. ❏

**PRECEDING PAGES:** salt pans at Fuencaliente; colonial architecture in Santa Cruz de la Palma.
**LEFT:** a harsh rocky shoreline.

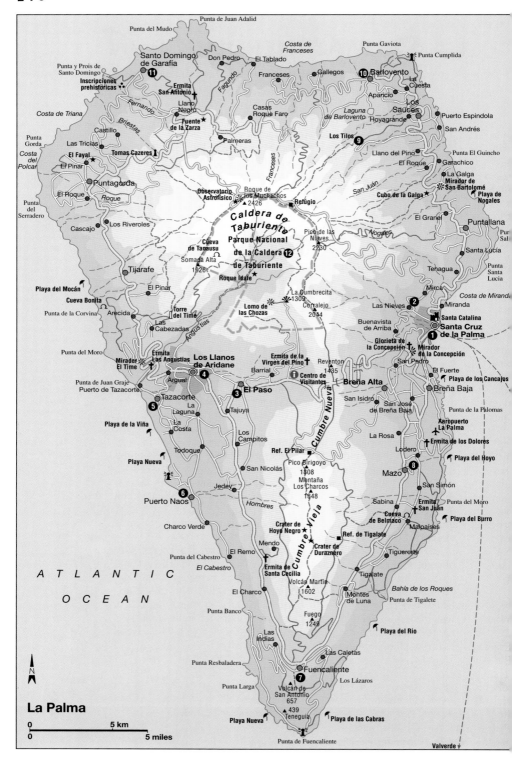

**La Palma**

0 _____ 5 km
0 _____ 5 miles

# LA PALMA: THE SOUTH

Map
on page
216

*From the pretty capital of Santa Cruz de la Palma, you can take
a trip through verdant valleys to the fishing port of Tazacorte
and down to the volcanic southern tip*

**S**anta Cruz de la Palma ❶ easily wins the prize for being the most
attractive of the Canary Island capitals. This important port has 18,000
inhabitants and sits in an amphitheatre on the slope of a volcanic crater
called La Cadereta. Modern buildings appear to dominate when you arrive, but
the harbour area and the few blocks inland from the Avenida Marítima waterfront have some fine 16th-century civic buildings and private mansions with
intricately carved and painted wooden balconies.

It is claimed that Santa Cruz de la Palma was the Spanish Empire's thirdranking port in the 16th century, after Seville and Antwerp, thriving on exports
of sugar, honey, malvasia (Malmsey wine) and timber cropped from the island's
forests. Whatever the truth of this boast, the town was rich enough to be looted
and razed to the ground in 1553 by the French pirate François le Clerc, known
by the highly piratical name of Pie de Palo ("Peg Leg"). With the aid of a royal
grant, the town was rebuilt. Since the city centre was all created at the same time,
it has an architectural unity found nowhere else in the Canaries.

The port is not only the point of entry into the city but also the centre of its
business life. At *Carnaval* (held, like Mardi Gras, on the eve of Lent) the harbour hosts the "Burial of the Sardine" (*see page 97*), a mock funeral satirising
the established authorities of church and state; a fiesta
with bacchanalian origins (the official guides never
even hint at the meaning of the tradition of throwing
talcum powder at every one in the street).

Near the port a cobbled pedestrian street, surprisingly called Calle de O'Daly (after an Irish banana
merchant), leads north to the city centre. Thanks to
their Catholic religion and American connections the
Irish did well out of New World trade from the
Canaries. This street, which at an ill-defined point
becomes Calle Real, is lined with the rich late-Renaissance houses of colonial merchants of the 17th and
18th centuries. The island's tourist office is housed in
one of them – the 17th-century Palacio de Salazar at
Calle de O'Daly 22 (open Mon–Fri 8.30am–1pm,
4–6pm, Sat 10am–2pm; tel: 922 41 31 41).

## Imperial splendour

Wander on past the shops, bars and offices housed in
Canarian mansions and you will reach the Plaza de
España, replete with echoes of past imperial splendour.
Built in the shape of a triangle, the plaza is bordered on
its long side by the Calle Real and the Casas Consistoriales (1563), now the city's **Ayuntamiento** (Town
Hall). Its arched colonnade supports an ornamented
Renaissance façade of stone carved with a bust of
Phillip II, along with the coats of arms of La Palma
and the Austrian Habsburgs. The Three Kings visit the

**BELOW:** oblivious
to the camera.

**Ayuntamiento** annually on the Feast of the Epiphany (6 January). Marking the end of the Christmas celebrations, this is also the day when children traditionally receive their presents.

Within the Town Hall's portico is a splendid wooden ceiling and, inside the building, an impressive staircase leads past murals to the office of the *alcalde* (mayor), where the flag of the conqueror, Alonso Fernández de Lugo, is preserved in a glass case. De Lugo conquered the island in 1492 on behalf of the Crown of Castille, although it took him a year to eradicate the native population. The Guanches (known here as Benahoares) exploited the island's geography to evade capture, holing up in the high peaks of the Caldera de Taburiente. De Lugo eventually won by trickery, inviting their leader to peace talks in order to ambush him, after which the remaining population were killed or exported to Spain as slaves.

## Piety, markets and museums

Facing the Town Hall is the church of **El Salvador** (the Saviour), whose Renaissance portal dates from 1503 (it survived Peg Leg's fire). The interior of the church is dominated by a *mudejar* ceiling, carved and painted by Moorish craftsmen with geometric designs originating from Portugal.

The church is regarded by the Palmeros as a cathedral, and the culmination of its year occurs on Good Friday (*Viernes Santo*). From here a procession sets out, watched by a sombre and silent crowd dressed in their best clothes. Men labour under the weight of heavy floats bearing holy statues, but the most impressive (and disturbing) of the participants are the anonymous characters shrouded in flowing black robes. They wear pointed hoods with eye slits (so that

**BELOW:** Santa Cruz de la Palma is an attractive island capital.

they may see but not be identified – being recognised would undermine the essential piety and humility of this penitential exercise). Barefoot, with anchor chains attached to their ankles and dragging on the cobbles, they carry heavy crosses or contemplate the instruments of the Passion, which they bear on black cushions. The women walk behind them dressed entirely in black and wearing beautiful lace mantillas.

Map on page 216

Calle Real is crossed by the Avenida del Puente – the *puente* (bridge) supports Calle Real as it crosses a river now tamed and running through tunnels (if it runs at all). Up the hill is the traditional **Mercado Municipal** where the produce of the island is sold – cigars, avocados, almonds, prickly pears, bananas, fish and smoked goats' cheese (*queso blanco*). On Saturday morning the flower market turns the surrounding area into a blaze of colour. At the head of the Avenida del Puente are the towers of the Bellido windmills, their sails long gone.

North of the Avenida, the street becomes the Calle de Perez Brito, winding through several small squares with fountains and crosses. These are decorated with flowers, coloured paper and satin during fiestas (particularly for the Día de la Santa Cruz on 3 May, a proud day for the residents of the city).

In the **Plaza de San Francisco**, one of the larger squares on the left, you will find the Iglesia de San Francisco (Church of St Francis), whose fine ceiling is every bit as intricately patterned as that of El Salvador. The convent alongside now contains the **Museo de Etnografía**, **Arqueología**, **Ciencias Naturales y Pintura** (Museum of Archaeology, Anthropology, Natural History and Fine Art) (open Mon–Fri 9am–2pm, 2–6.30pm; entrance charge), an amusing jumble of antiquities and stuffed animals, worth a visit for the architecture of the 16th-century Franciscan convent building alone.

*Local goats' cheese is on sale in the Mercado Municipal.*

**BELOW:**
beautiful balconies are a feature of the capital.

At the end of the Calle de Perez Brito is a building known locally as th
**Barco de la Virgen** (the Virgin's Boat), housing the **Museo Naval** (Maritim
Museum) (open Mon–Fri 9.30am–2pm, 4–6.30pm; entrance charge). Built in th
shape of a boat, the museum is in fact a full-sized concrete replica of the *Sant*
*María* in which Christopher Columbus sailed to America. Palmeros like t
believe that Columbus visited La Palma en route to the New World, but in fac
he didn't (although he did visit neighbouring La Gomera, where his ships wer
stocked with provisions and he was entertained by the Countess Beatriz d
Bobadilla, notorious for her numerous lovers). The Barco plays an importan
role in the Virgen de las Nieves fiesta (*see pages 238–39*).

Across the valley on a promontory overlooking the mouth of the river ar
the ruins of the **Castillo de la Virgen**, and as you walk back towards the centr
of the town along the sea front (Avenida Marítima) you will pass the star-shape
**Castillo Real** (also known as the Castillo de Santa Catalina). Both castles wer
used to fight off the attacks of pirates, raiders and corsairs between the 16th an
18th centuries. Sir Francis Drake, whose piratical attack from the sea wa
repelled by the guns of these castles in 1585, did not manage to set foot on th
island. South of the Castillo Real, on the waterfront, are some of the Canar
Islands' finest façades, with traditional wooden balconies.

## Looping the loop

The southern part of La Palma is still volcanically active, and numerous erup
tions over the last few thousand years have filled the valleys with lava and
jumble of basalt rocks, while deep drifts of ash have smoothed the steep volcani
contours. You can see this if you head out of Santa Cruz on the main C-832 roa

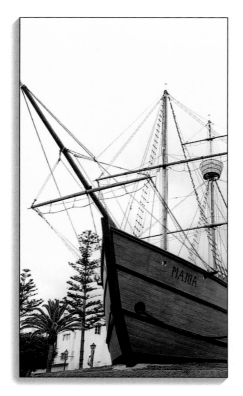

**BELOW:** a replica of
the *Santa María*,
Columbus' ship.

## LA PALMA'S PARADOR

**P**aradors, Spain's chain of high-class state-run hotels
are usually housed in historic buildings, but some hav
new, purpose-built premises. La Palma's parador is one c
the latter: it used to occupy one of the splendid seafror
mansions of Santa Cruz but in 1999 it was relocated to
brand-new building on the coast at El Zumacal, midwa
between the airport and Santa Cruz.

Though modern, the parador is built in the tradition.
Canarian style, and is set in a spot from where there ar
sweeping coastal views from the shaded balcony (parado
are renowned for their wonderful vistas). The comfortabl
65-room hotel offers a swimming pool and attractiv
landscaped gardens stocked with indigenous Canaria
plants (for more details and bookings, tel: 922 43 58 28 c
dial the paradors' central reservation number in Madri
tel: (3491) 516 6666).

If you cannot afford the four-star luxury of the parador, c
if you simply prefer something more informal, you will fir
numerous *casas rurales* (literally, rural houses) dotte
around the island, providing comfortable accommodation
converted farm buildings (further information is availab
from the tourist office in Santa Cruz, or from the Asociacić
de Turismo Rural, tel: 922 43 06 25).

Map on page 216

heading south. The road loops back northwards as it climbs and enters a tunnel that cuts through the wall of La Caldereta. This is an old volcanic crater that has been compacted through being overlaid by recent eruptions and then re-exposed by wind erosion and by the sea; as a result the crater has been sectioned as if by a knife. It is well worth stopping on the edge of La Caldereta, at the **Mirador de la Concepción**, to take this in and to enjoy the view of Santa Cruz.

Just beyond this point, a side road leads north to **Las Nieves ❷**, the village that contains the **Real Santuario de la Virgen de las Nieves**, the spiritual centre of La Palma (you can also walk here from the centre of Santa Cruz: it's an uphill hike of around 3.5 km/2 miles). Above the altar in the whitewashed church is the statue that is the focal point of religious devotion. Not far from the modest chapel, the **Chipi Chipi** restaurant (closed Wed, tel: 922 41 10 24), with its terrace and flower-covered wooden cabins, offers a chance to take in the views over a coffee or a snack.

Back on the main road (TF-812), there is a choice of routes. The simplest is to head west, following signs to El Paso. After 5 km (3 miles), the road dives into a tunnel through Las Cumbres, the mountainous ridge that forms the backbone of the island. As well as forming a watershed, the mountains mark a climatic divide: it is a strange sensation to enter the high tunnel on the east in mist and cloud, and burst out of the other side in the bright sunlight. From the western side, you can often look back to the central ridge and see the cloud flowing over the peaks like a waterfall (a *cascada* in Spanish, which is the name of a nearby bar from which this sight may be enjoyed).

Alternatively, if you are confident enough of your car to take it on twisting roads, you can head south and drive to El Paso via San Pedro (visit the

**BELOW:** the Santuario de las Nieves, surrounded by trees.

embroidery workshop and sales centre for fine traditional designs), Breña Alta, San Isidro and then over Las Cumbres to **El Pilar**. This is a clearing in the mountain forest which is quiet enough on weekdays but which bustles on Sunday and fiestas, when Palmeros come here to enjoy a picnic – not fruit and sandwiches, but often an entire meal: *sopa de garbanzos* (chick pea soup), perhaps, followed by roast suckling pig.

## The route of the volcanoes

El Pilar marks the boundary between the Cumbre Nueva (New Summit) peaks to the north, and the older volcanic peaks of the Cumbre Vieja (Old Summit) to the south. If you want to explore the latter, you can follow the **Ruta de los Volcánes**, a demanding 7-hour ridge trial that heads south from this point, skirting the crater of Hoya Negro, and descending eventually to Fuencaliente at the island's southern tip. Alternatively, you can walk the first mile or so to get a feel for the character of the volcanic landscape and to take in the panoramic westward views.

Above El Pilar the road passes through a lunar landscape of ash ejected from the eruption of **Tacande**, when an enormous lava stream flowed westwards to dominate the landscape towards El Paso. The date of this eruption is usually given as 1585, but recently established carbon-14 dates obtained from trees embedded in the ash and lava give a pre-conquest date. It is now known that the Tacande eruption took place at some time between 1470 and 1492. The historical records of the 1585 eruption have been misidentified and refer, in fact, to part of a twin lava stream at Jedey, near Puerto Naos, most of which was from the eruption of 1712.

**BELOW:** a *romería* in El Paso.

At the summit of this road there is a magnificent view westwards and north-wards into the **Caldera de Taburiente**, La Palma's central caldera, which is covered in the next chapter. White blobs atop the vertical far wall of the caldera mark the observatory domes at Roque de los Muchachos (*see pages 233, 237*).

Continuing west, a wide road, lined with golden California poppies, bypasses **El Paso ❸**, but the narrow side roads of the village take you past little houses built in traditional style with pointed roofs and ornamental chimneys, reminiscent of Thai spirit houses. The prickly pear cacti which infest the uncultivated gardens are left over from earlier times when the cactus was cultivated to host the cochineal insect, harvested to make reddish-pink food colouring and dyes. The insects cling to the succulent leaves in grey, mould-like clusters. Just beyond El Paso, keen gardeners and lovers of tropical birds will enjoy the **Parque Paraiso de las Aves** (open daily 10am–6pm; entrance charge), signposted off the TF-812 El Paso–Santa Cruz road on the way to Los Llanos.

## Fertile valley

Some 6 km (4 miles) further on lies **Los Llanos de Aridane ❹**, La Palma's somewhat anonymous-looking wine-rich second city (pop. 16,000), which has a pleasant church and some traditional Canarian buildings set around the central square. It is situated in the middle of a fertile valley filled with almonds, figs, avocados and banana plantations. The well-built houses are fronted by a colourful blaze of exotic flowers and shrubs, including scarlet poinsettias, hibiscus and bougainvillea. On the El Paso side of the town, the **Pueblo Parque de Palma** (open Mon–Sat 10.30am–5pm; entrance charge) is a botanical garden with some 6,000 subtropical plants, and a few handicraft shops.

Map on page 216

*Prickly pears flourish beside cultivated maize around El Paso.*

**BELOW:** rug-weaving is one of the local crafts.

## Down to the coast

From Los Llanos you can explore the rift valley that was formed some 400,000 years ago when the volcanic cone at the centre of the island collapsed to form the Caldera de Taburiente (*see page 234–36*), but our route continues south towards the coast. If you have time to spare, however, it is worth going a short distance northwest, through banana plantations and almond orchards, pink with blossom in January, to **El Time**, on the edge of the rift valley that forms the outlet of the *caldera*. A restaurant balcony perches precariously over the sheer drop, with a view into the crater, over Los Llanos and Tazacorte, and south over the banana plantations of the western plains. The peninsula, formed as the 1949 lava flow cooled in the sea, is now covered with bananas, irrigated by water from the mountains. This is carried through pipes which drop almost vertically down the valley wall and feed the tanks which dot the landscape below – a reminder that La Palma is the most water-rich island in the archipelago.

On the coast below is the port of **Tazacorte** ❺. This is where Alonso Fernández de Lugo, the conqueror of Gran Canaria, landed in 1492 and wrenched control of the island from the native Guanche king. Now, fishing boats and yachts tie up in the well-protected harbour and, at the seashore itself, restaurants offer whatever fish have been caught that day – *samas* and *viejas* may be untranslatable but they are very palatable species available on local menus. Tazacorte village across the valley is lovely, with steep streets of traditional houses decked with balconies. In the central square men both old and young play chess and cards beneath a flowery arbour.

The coast around here is peppered with white houses, surrounded by gardens of green banana plants, scarlet poinsettia, pink and cream oleander, blue morn-

*The Roman philosopher Pliny called La Palma Pluvalia, because it received so much more rain than the other islands.*

**BELOW:**
fishing at Tazacorte.

ıg-glory and geraniums of every hue. Above the coast, the foothills of the ıountains are cut with terraces, some abundant with crops of vegetables and uit, some sad and neglected (many Palmeros have fled to better-paid jobs in ıe cities of peninsular Spain and of Venezuela).

A detour south from here leads to **Puerto Naos** ❻, which has the biggest each on La Palma, with fine black sand. Because of this, Puerto Naos also ıas a rash of unsightly hotels and comes as close as you get on La Palma to ɛing a tourist resort. The road south of town is still blocked by the lava flow f 1949. To continue south you have to return to Los Llanos de Aridane and take ıe C-832 for Fuencaliente. Just above San Nicolás, look out for the **Bodegon 'amanca** (tel: 922 46 21 55), a typical Canarian restaurant that has been built ıto a series of wine caves cut into the hill-side. The large barrels are still used ɔ store the wine that you may drink with a *parilla mixta* (mixed grill) of sev-ral kinds of spicy sausages and meats.

Map on page 216

*The vineyards around Volcán San Antonio produce a rich, sweet wine.*

## ıouthern volcanoes

ıt the southern point of the island two packed-ash (*picòn*) roads lead to the eaks of two volcanoes. They are safe to drive on as long as you stick to the ıgnposted routes – if you stray, you risk bogging the car up to the axles in ust. Passing through vineyards you reach the perfectly formed cone of the **ʻolcán de San Antonio.** You can easily walk around the circumference, which ommands wonderful, if cold and windswept views of the coast and the Atlantic ɔouthwards there is nothing between here and the Antarctic). If you're not **ʟ**austrophobic, you can slide into the quiet centre of the cone and listen to the entle brushing of the pine needles, the only sound there is.

**BELOW:** the Volcán de San Antonio.

Map on page 216

About 3 km (2 miles) further south are the jagged rocks, lava flows and coloured basalt of **Teneguia**. This is the volcano that erupted on 26 October 1971 – the most recent eruption in the Canary Islands. The throat of the Teneguia eruption is easily accessible, and you can experience geothermal energy in the flesh by sitting on a rock for a few minutes.

**Fuencaliente** ❼ is the main town on the island's southern point. The name means Hot Spring, although this has long gone. From here a road (paved most of the way) zig-zags down beneath Teneguia, through steep slopes rich in succulent flowers, to **El Faro de Fuencaliente**, a deserted lighthouse overlooking turbulent seas and a stony, steeply-shelving seashore. The lighthouse still bears the scars of the 1971 eruption, which created new beaches of sterile *picòn*.

Nearby, a beach house that survived destruction by a matter of a few metres when the lava flow stopped is now an informal restaurant, serving delicious fresh fish and local wine. El Faro also has sea-water evaporation tanks, used to produce salt. There are very few sea birds here because the cliffs plunge almost directly into deep ocean waters – the island lacks the warm shallow waters that produce the food the birds need.

## Signs of the Guanches

Northwards from Fuencaliente, a pretty drive leads through pine forests with sea views and dramatic wayside flowers. Beyond Malpaises, right beside the road, the **Cueva de Belmaco** is a cave once inhabited by Guanches. The oven now built into the cave is recent, but the carvings on the stone faces are ancient. Nobody knows what these carvings of meandering mazes and spirals represent, if anything at all. Other carvings elsewhere have the superficial appearance of a written language.

In the scree falling from the cave are small fragments of dark brown Guanche pottery. At **Mazo** ❽, a couple of miles further north, the **Cerámico Molino** produces highly sought-after replicas of the few score Guanche pots and scoops that have survived intact enough to copy. The black oil-rubbed surfaces of the ceramics are decorated with complex and rhythmic patterns of simple, impressed lines. Mazo is also the production centre for the local cigars, called *puros* that are widely smoked all around the island.

Mazo celebrates the fiesta of **Corpus Christi** (60 days after Easter Day) by decorating the village with arches and carpets of flowers, seeds, leaves, lichens, fruits and sand. The priest leads a procession on the fragrant carpet, starting at the church, which is also filled with the scent of flowers.

Returning to Santa Cruz, the main road passes the beach of **Los Cancajos** (near the army barracks where crowds of people from Santa Cruz gather on Sunday between Mass and lunch, enjoying the fine view of the city across the harbour and protected from the surging sea by the rock pools. The black-sand beach here is the reason why this coastal strip between airport and capital, has developed into a resort, with apartment blocks, restaurants, bars and two discos, making Los Cancajos, the least-typical but most lively spot on the island.

**BELOW:** replicas of Guanche pottery are made at Mazo.
**RIGHT:** Mazo has flower carpets to rival those on Tenerife.

# LA PALMA: THE NORTH

*You can explore the dramatic national park of the Caldera de Taburiente where wild flowers cover the bare volcanic slopes in spring and the night skies are exceptionally clear and dark*

Map on page 216

The highlight of this northern route is a drive over the mountain road to the Caldera de Taburiente. At any time of the year the mountains can turn cold and in winter (January to April), it will certainly be icy and covered with snow on the mountain top: take warm clothes on this trip, no matter how fine it appears to be when you set out. You may also want to take swimming gear as there are some inviting bathing spots along the northeastern coast.

From Santa Cruz, the C-380 road curves in a series of hair-pin loops around the deep-cut, water-eroded valleys that lie to the north of the capital. Magnificent scenery is guaranteed as you negotiate Puntallana and San Bartolomé, passing through a landscape that is the oldest on La Palma, in geological terms. Hidden off the road near Puntallana is the island's best beach, Playa de Nogales. Difficult access, plus the fact that the beach is shaded by high cliffs from the middle of the day, means that it might escape development: follow signs from Puntallana to Bajamar and then to Playa de Nogales before parking at the end of the road and scrambling down the cliff track to the beach.

**PRECEDING PAGES:** harvesting bananas is dirty work. **LEFT:** the Caldera de Taburiente. **BELOW:** a river runs through it.

## Interesting options

Two interesting options are open to you when the road forks beyond the Mirador de San Bartolomé. You could take the left fork to stay on the main road, and turn off to **Los Tilos** ➒, just before you reach Los Sauces. The woodland park at Los Tilos has preserved a small amount of the original laurel forest of the Canaries. Entirely natural, the woods contain plant species not found anywhere else in the world, flourishing in the wet mist among the mossy tree trunks.

The park's **Centro de Visitantes** (open Mon–Fri 9am–5pm) can provide maps showing the several walking trails that start from this point. The most challenging, but also the most rewarding of these is the 12-km (7-mile) there-and-back trek southwest to the **Caldera de Marcos y Cordero.** If you plan to walk here, remember to bring waterproofs and torches. Follow the water channels upstream as they run around the steep sides of the *caldera.* The flowery, metre-wide path is scratched into the vertical cliff face and tunnels darkly through rocky outcrops, dripping with water. At the source, water cascades into the channel from the heart of La Palma.

The alternative to Los Tilos is to take the right fork after San Bartolomé, which leads to **San Andrés,** a delightful little town of cobbled streets and whitewashed houses. East of San Andrés there are a number of exposed headlands, but shelter is available at Puerto Espindola, where **El Charco Azul,** a natural swimming pool, is breathtakingly

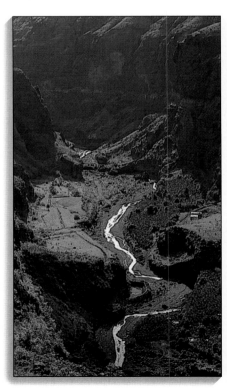

blue and calm in the encircling protection of the cliffs and constantly replenished by the waves from the seaward side.

## Guanche carvings

Back on the main road, **Barlovento ❿** is a straggling village with a reservoir that holds 5 million cubic metres (35 million cubic feet) of water. From here the winding road passes through a quiet area of livestock and agriculture. Some 5 km (3 miles) after Roque Faro, you will come to the new visitors centre at **Fuente de la Zarza** (open Mon–Fri 9am–5pm), where you can learn all about the mysterious Guanche rock carvings which can be found nearby, before following the trail to the site of some of the best-preserved examples.

The next stop is **Santo Domingo de Garafía ⓫**, which is now connected to the island capital, Santa Cruz, by a dorsal road that climbs to the highest point on La Palma, the Roque de los Muchachos. Until the completion of this road a generation ago, Garafía was one of the most isolated communities on earth. The inhabitants communicated weekly with the rest of the island by means of a messenger who rode a mule – or walked with it – across the mountains. To maintain contact with the rest of the world, boats sailed in and out of the tiny port below the village.

Downhill from the cemetery, the road gradually deteriorates; take your car as far as you dare and walk on to the edge of the cliffs, to view the offshore islands and the sea surging through natural archways. Ospreys nest on this coast. On top of the cliffs, a litter of steel cabling represents the remains of a bosun's chair that was once used to haul cargo from boats bobbing in the white water below. Crumbling steps lead down the cliffs to the dock.

**BELOW:**
waves lash the
coast at Garafía.

Map on page 216

## The highest peak

The island of La Palma languished in rural isolation for much of the 20th century, and it has continued to resist the tourist development that characterises some of the other islands in the Canaries. There are few concrete apartment blocks, and no billboards outside the confines of the airport complex. The island is governed with concern for ecology, and there is even a law preserving the light from pollution by artificial light. La Palma has stewardship of the darkest, clearest skies in Europe, and from the Roque de los Muchachos observatory above Garafía (*see page 237*), astronomers from several European nations peer into the depths of the universe.

It was Garafía's own mayor who welcomed the Spanish monarch (Juan Carlos) at the observatory's inauguration in 1985, handing him the walking stick that signified the temporary transfer of authority over the town while the king was in Garafía. A small man, the mayor swelled to the king's great height when embraced by him. As the two men stood shoulder to shoulder, the moment was captured on film by an aide, using the mayor's own Kodak Instamatic camera. No doubt it is a picture that the mayor has cherished ever since.

The **Observatorio Astrofísico** itself is strictly off limits to visitors (although if you want to know what it is up to you can visit the Isaac Newton Group's website at www.ing.iac.es), but the road up to the dome-shaped building also takes you to the peak of **Roque de los Muchachos**, the island's highest point (at 2,426 metres/7,959 ft). The Muchachos (the Boys) themselves are the columns of solidified mud on the peak. From here the horizon is wide as you look down on the sea and onto the tops of the white cloud, perhaps pierced to the south west by the island of El Hierro, and to the southeast by La Gomera; almost certainly

*From the Roque de Muchachos on a clear moonless night, you may see the cone of the zodiacal light stretching upwards from the point on the horizon where the sun disappeared. This is sunlight scattered off a dusty nebula which surrounds the sun; it is seldom seen in Europe.*

**BELOW:** there are attractive rural houses to rent.

to the east by the peak of El Teide on Tenerife. The silence of the Roque in summer is emphasised by the sound of swifts in flight overhead, and by the distant bells of herds of goats. It is not unusual to see a *mouflon* (a wild sheep)

## La Caldera de Taburiente

Somebody has calculated that La Palma is the world's most mountainous place because it has so many high peaks in relation to its size. Like the Roque de los Muchachos, most of the highest peaks lie within the **Parque Nacional de la Caldera de Taburiente** ⓬, renowned for its spectacular scenery and as a classic example of volcanic erosion.

To get to the park's **Centro de Visitantes** (Visitors' Centre, open Mon–Fri 10am–2pm, 4–6pm, Sat 10am–3pm) you should circle round to the south side turning off the TF-812 near El Paso. At the centre you can pick up literature and maps detailing walking trails, before heading north on the road that leads up to the magnificent viewpoint at the **Mirador de la Cumbrecita**. There is also an information booth at the Mirador selling the Ministry of the Environment's map of the park, showing hiking routes, such as the one that goes to the **Mirador Lomo de las Chozas** lookout, about 1 km (⅔ mile) west.

You can also approach the caldera from Los Llanos (*see page 223–24*) where the Río de las Angustias flows through a rift valley. It is fed by two tributaries the Río de Taburiente and the Río de Almendro Amargo, which meet at the junction called Dos Aguas (Two Waters). The first part of the route is easy to follow: a paved road goes north from near the church, passing through plantations of avocado trees. The road becomes more adventurous and unpaved as it enters the rift valley, and is only passable on foot or in a 4-wheel-drive vehicle. The

**BELOW:**
bearing the load
on stony tracks.

Map on page 216

rack descends sharply to the river, where the rocky bed of grey stones is usually fordable, except after storms or when the spring melt-water pours from the mountains. Then the river runs deep and fast with brown water, which carries the very substance of La Palma out into the sea.

On the other side of the river, the road ascends through tobacco farms and their drying sheds to a look-out virtually in the centre of the crater, below the Roque de los Muchachos. As the setting sun casts long dark shadows and the orange of the evening light intensifies the colours in the rocks, a chill strikes from the evening air and the sky darkens. In the distance, the spire of the **Roque Idafe** monolith stands up from the crater floor. It was regarded as a sacred place by the original Guanche inhabitants of La Palma who made offerings there to their god, Abora.

## Exploring the crater

The caldera (which means kettle or cauldron in Spanish) consists of the central hollow of an extinct volcano, revealed when the peak of the volcano collapsed – the "roof material" now lies fractured and jumbled as a series of hills and rocks on the crater floor. The collapse, which was far larger than the similar 19th-century explosion of Krakatoa, occurred 400,000 years ago and stopped further volcanic activity in the northern half of La Palma: more recent activity has been confined to the southern portion of the island. The crater is 9 km (5½ miles) across. It is not, as is sometimes claimed, the largest in the world, but it is perhaps the most impressive. The inner wall of the *caldera* is an almost sheer drop of 900 metres (2,300 ft). The strata of the innumerable volcanic eruptions before the collapse have been revealed in these inner walls.

*Making cigars (puros) from the tobacco grown on local farms.*

**BELOW:**
a tile picture depicts the arrival of the treacherous conquistadors.

## TREACHERY IN THE CALDERA

It was below the look-out in the centre of the caldera that the Spanish conqueror of La Palma, Alonso Fernández de Lugo, tricked the Guanche chief Tanausu and consolidated his victory in 1492. On landing at Tazacorte, de Lugo had received the immediate surrender of the tribes of Aridane, Tihuya, Tamanca and Ahenguardeme; he then fought and conquered the Tigalate tribe, thus subduing the southern half of the island. But in the wooded hills of Acero (the Guanche province within the caldera) de Lugo met stiff resistance from Tanuasu and, realising that he could not win by fair means, he ignobly descended to foul.

He sent a messenger inviting Tanuasu to negotiate with him. Ignoring the wise words of his advisor, Ugranfir, Tanuasu agreed to meet for talks. At the designated meeting place in the Barranco del Riachuelo he was ambushed and captured by de Lugo and his troops. After a battle in which there was considerable bloodshed, Tanuasu was sent into exile. Repeatedly crying out "Vacaguare, vacaguare" (I want to die), he refused to eat during the voyage to Spain after he had lost sight of his island, and eventually died of hunger. De Lugo's victory over La Palma was complete.

Map on page 216

A road circles the caldera rim to the east of the island. Occasionally the rim of the crater narrows down alarmingly to little more than the width of the road. At one point you enter the cutting known as **Los Andenes** (the Railway Platforms) from where there are views into the caldera to the south and, on the other side, down to the northern coast. Wherever there are cuttings, you can see how walls of basalt have been formed by molten lava welling up through cracks in the ash deposits. These walls have been exposed as the ash has eroded away and now form dykes that can be seen standing in the surrounding country, including **Pared de Roberto** (Robert's Wall), erroneously described as archaeological remains in some guide books. The cuttings also reveal "bombs" of volcanic lava which, spinning through the air, solidified into spheres and were then buried in the wind-drifted ash.

The road passes red and yellow drifts of ash, formed into fantastic shapes, some given fanciful names (look out for the formation known as the Yellow Submarine). Look out, too, for yellow or orange ash that has been covered with hot flowing lava and baked red from the top. At this height, and above 2,000 metres (6,500 ft), the soil is bare except for a few isolated juniper trees. The rocks are covered with flat, plate-sized, thick-leaved aeonium plants, some flowering with golden blooms.

## Mountain blooms

As the road descends, the vegetation becomes less sparse. Stunted pines give way to heavier woodland, with views across to Tenerife. In the spring pink and white cistus blooms for several weeks and the almost ubiquitous small shrub, the *cordeso*, is covered with a mass of fragrant bright yellow blossoms. You can

enjoy the view and the flowers from Fuente de Olen (Olen's Spring), a picnic area, within which are the ruins of a cylindrical stone-lined pit, which was used in the days before refrigerators to store winter ice for later use. The pines here are beautiful, hung with what the English call Spanish moss, but the Spanish know as Englishman's Beard.

Canary pines give way to laurel forest as you descend by a series of zig-zags down a deep cut valley with views to Santa Cruz. At one point the road crosses a narrow-gauge railway line, used to extract mineral water from the mountain (the owner tunnelled horizontally until he found a descending stream of water, which he now bottles and sells at Mirca). You might pass a gang of labourers cutting the coppiced *faya* trees – these stakes are a mainstay of banana growing, holding the easily bruised bananas away from the main trunk of the plant; and a prop for the building industry where they are used as scaffolding.

If you are lucky you may see one of La Palma's unique *pininana* flower, with its 4-metre (13-ft) high spike of blue florets. The *pininana* is a biennial plant that flowers in the spring. It is related to Tenerife's scarlet *Tajinaste*, known as the Pride of Tenerife. At some stage you are almost certain to enter the mist of the cloud layer as you make your descent into **Mirca**, past a pretty little church surrounded by eucalyptus, before finally returning to Santa Cruz.

# The Observatory

Inaugurated in 1985 by the king of Spain and the crowned heads and presidents of several European states, the Observatory on La Palma contains astronomical telescopes for studying the sun and the universe. It is the home of the William Herschel Telescope, the largest in Europe and the third largest in the world.

The observatory was founded by the Instituto de Astrofísica de Canarias (in La Laguna, Tenerife). It is here because the heights of the western Canary Islands are among the half-dozen best places in the world for astronomical viewing, with the darkest sky against which to pick out the faintest, most distant quasars and the clearest, steadiest atmosphere through which to see sharp detail.

The reason for these excellent astronomical conditions is the special geographical location of La Palma. It is under the influence of the oceanic climate of the northwest Canary Islands, with cloud tops below the mountain peaks 80 percent of the time. The clouds trap dust and mist at the surface of the sea below. In the sea itself, the cold Canary Current flows southwards from the latitudes of the British Isles, past Portugal, and stabilises the air across the Roque de los Muchachos.

You can confirm for yourself the clarity of the air by looking through binoculars. El Teide is 130 km (80 miles) away, but it is possible to see the headlights of individual cars driving in Las Cañadas, as well as the brighter lights of Playa de las Américas on the shore. At night you can also see the lights of aircraft as they approach and land at Madeira, 400 km (250 miles) north.

There is no access to the observatory for members of the public, but from the Roque de los Muchachos you can see the large dome of the William Herschel Telescope. The dome opens as the sky darkens and the telescope's giant 4.2-metre (13.8-ft) mirror is able to record light from exploding galaxies at the edge of the universe. In the foreground is the small building containing the

**RIGHT:** dawn light illuminates the observatory near the Roque de los Muchachos.

Carlsberg Automatic Meridian Circle, moved here from Denmark. If the computer inside senses that the weather is suitable, the shed will roll to one side, and the telescope will automatically seek out and measure the positions of the stars.

On a spur to the north of the Roque de los Muchachos is the Nordic Optical Telescope, with a 2.5-metre (8.2-ft) mirror. A tower to the right of the William Herschel Telescope holds the Swedish Solar Telescope, which points upwards to examine the sun via a mirror called a coelostat – you can see it atop the tower. Beyond the solar telescope are the Swedish Stellar Telescope, the Isaac Newton Telescope (UK-Holland) and the Jacobus Kapteyn Telescope (UK-Holland-Eire).

Astronomers from all over the world visit the observatory and study here. Those who work through the night sleep in the *residencia* near the observatory gate during the day. Stern notices ask you to keep away at night so as not to disturb the delicate observations with car lights, and in the daytime so as not to disturb the astronomers' sleep. ❑

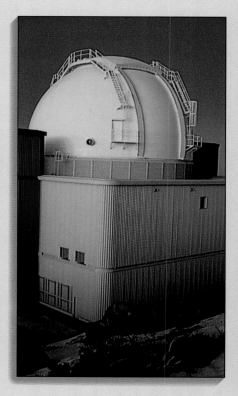

# THE FIESTA OF NUESTRA SEÑORA DE LAS NIEVES

*The Virgin descends only once every five years and the people of La Palma don't pass up the opportunity to celebrate in grand style*

Nuestra Señora de las Nieves, the Virgin of the Snows, the patroness of La Palma, takes her name from a 4th-century miracle in Rome when the Virgin appeared during an August snowstorm. On 5 August each year her statue is carried from her sanctuary to the square where a huge crowd greets her with a cacophony of church bells, fanfares and fire crackers.

## THE MAIN EVENT

It is only once every five years that the major event takes place – the Bajada de la Virgen (the Descent of the Virgin). The sacred image is carried in a lavish bier down the hillside to the Iglesia del Salvador in Santa Cruz, accompanied by *romeros*, or pilgrims, dressed in traditional costumes. Musicians serenade the Virgin with stringed instruments, among them the *timple*, a kind of small guitar, played like a mandolin, which is indigenous to the islands.

The Bajada, which has been taking place since 1680, is accompanied by a lengthy fiesta. There are processions and dances of giants and dwarves, all wearing enormous false heads, and displays of lucha canaria, folk dancing and arts and crafts, as well as a great deal of eating and drinking.

▽ **SHARING SECRETS**
"Dwarves" mingle with the crowds, some of whom are emigrants who return from Latin America especially to celebrate the fiesta.

△ **ROMEROS EN ROUTE**
A group of *romeros* in the traditional dress of La Palma, with cummerbunds, scarves and intricate embroidery.

▷ **COURTLY WAYS**
Richly dressed participants stage a courtly 18th-century tableau as part of the celebrations, which go on for several weeks.

◁ **DANCING FOR THE VIRGIN**
The most spectacular part of the fiesta is the stately Dance of the Dwarves, who manoeuvre with three-cornered hats balanced on their over-sized heads.

△ **DRESSED IN STYLE**
A member of a folk group, dressed in the characteristic La Palma costume with flower-bedecked straw hat, waits her turn to entertain the crowds.

## THE SEÑORA'S SANCTUARY

The sanctuary of Nuestra Señora de las Nieves on the outskirts of Santa Cruz de La Palma was founded at the time of the 15th-century Spanish conquest, although the present church was built some two centuries later. It's an interesting little building, but the pièce de resistance, indeed, the reason why the church is here at all, is the 14th-century terracotta image of the Virgin, dressed in bejewelled robes, which is kept above a baroque altar, and venerated throughout the island. You may sometimes see altar boys outside on the church steps, polishing the silver altar pieces with loving care until they can see their faces reflected in them. Naive paintings inside the church depict the numerous incidents in which the Virgin saved ships and sailors from storms at sea. There is no doubt about the place Our Lady has in the hearts of the islanders -- and it's not just because they enjoy a good fiesta.

**FAITHFUL FOLLOWERS**
e statue of the Virgin, eceded by a priest, is companied by enthusiastic owds as it is carried in lendour down the hillside.

▷ **STANDING TALL**
Gigantes (giants) weave their way carefully through the crowds with all the dignity that that this great occasion demands.

# EL HIERRO:
## INTRODUCTION

*El Hierro isn't hard to reach, yet it still feels as if it sits at
the edge of the earth – and that's its attraction*

Once upon a time, before the world was round and when the
Americas weren't even a twinkle in Christopher Columbus's
eye, the little-visited island of El Hierro was the furthest
westerly point known to man. Its lighthouse, Faro de Orchilla,
was officially the end of the world and the anchor of the zero
meridian, which has since moved back to Greenwich.

Approached by ferry, this could be the world's beginning. Austere,
unforgiving tan flanks rise steeply from a dark froth of lava in a steel
blue sea, past wind-contorted juniper trees bleached bone-white by
the sun and into scrubland inhabited only by lizards and dust-devils.
The capital Valverde is drawn across the hillside at cloud level like
white beads of perspiration. There is an almost mythical beauty here,
but El Hierro's picturesque poverty has receded thanks to European
Union funding, poured into the island in an attempt to halt the haem-
orrhaging of its population. The roads are smooth and new, in a land
where smoothness doesn't come naturally.

It's the smallest island in the archipelago (only 278 sq. km/107
sq. miles) and a large proportion of the population lives over the top
and down the other side of the island from Valverde, in the remains
of a huge volcanic crater called El Golfo, to be linked eventually to
Valverde thanks to a massive tunnelling project. Most of El Golfo has
long since crumbled away into the sea, but the crater rim is breathtakingly wild and windy, while on what remains of the crater floor,
way down below, the days are calm and the land fertile.

El Hierro can be an intense experience for the traveller, and in
many ways, despite the modern roads, it feels unchanged since it
perched on the edge of the known world. Yet it's not that remote: the
Trasmediterránea ferry from Tenerife calls four times a week at
Puerto de la Estaca, and there's an airport, built on reclaimed land in
1972, just to the north of the port, to which three Binter Canarias
flights wing in daily from Tenerife – although they are somewhat
susceptible to wind. Most of the car hire offices are in the airport,
although hire representatives also meet the ferries. There is practically no public transport but most villages have a taxi.

There is a small but helpful Tourist Office at Calle Licenciado
Bueno 1, 38900 Valverde, tel: (22) 55 03 02, fax: 55 10 52; and there
are several hotels, ranging from the beautifully situated Parador
Nacional El Hierro to the idionsyncratic Hotel Puntagrande at Las
Puntas, said to be the smallest hotel in the world. ❑

**PRECEDING PAGES:** Valverde, the island capital.
**LEFT:** a man at peace with himself.

# EL HIERRO

*On your way round El Hierro you'll find pine woods and junipers, avocados and bananas, the world's smallest hotel and a place that breeds the largest lizards*

Map on page 246

he seaward point of entry to El Hierro is the small harbour at **Puerto de la Estaca ❶**, where Trasmediterránea's ferry brings passengers across from Tenerife four times a week, so this little port is many people's introduction to the island. Very little seems to have changed here since the 1930s when steamers regularly called at its cobbled quay to collect figs, wine, almonds and goat-skins, and it remains vulnerable to south-easterly winds.

First impressions as you drive out of the port or from the airport (which lies just to the north of it) will be of smooth new roads laid across a rocky sea-blown wilderness crocheted with lava walls. This is a fairly inhospitable flank of the island, and there are only a couple of destinations of note.

The only route south along the coast passes a few scattered houses, a couple of bars, and a small black sandy beach at Timijiraque before burrowing through the womb of a mountain to emerge by the photogenic **Roque Bonanza**, a lava arch which appears regularly in guidebooks and postcards.

The Roque de la Bonanza is at one end of a bay called **Las Playas** (The Beaches), effectively the remains of a semi-submerged crater; at the far end is the **Parador Nacional ❷**, built in 1976 just above the shoreline where the surf rolls rocks of lava around with its tongue. This must be one of the finest locations of any in the state-run Parador chain, but it is also exposed to the worst of the weather. A freak storm in 1999 routed the full complement of guests, and pounded the swimming pool to pieces. The pool has since been rebuilt and the parador re-opened – this time with a new breakwater out to sea.

North of the airport is **Tamaduste ❸**, with a rare and sheltered beach which attracts locals down from Valverde on Sundays. La Caleta on the other side of the airport offers a similar lava-scaped pool, some breeze-block houses and a bar which usually seems to be playing Leonard Cohen songs. If these places seem deserted mid-week, it's because many Herreñan families have summer houses on the coast and use them only at weekends.

## The sleepy capital

The island capital, **Valverde ❹**, is strung across the side of the hill 800 metres (2,625 ft) above the port and airport. The only Canary Island capital which is not on the coast, it was originally sited here for safety's sake, and the tower of the church of Nuestra Señora de la Concepción (open daily) was reputedly built in 1767 to keep watch for pirates.

Valverde is not a busy place, and when the Victorian adventurer and travel writer Olivia Stone arrived in 1884 (*see page 55*) there wasn't even an inn. "All is poverty," she noted, deducing from her reception that

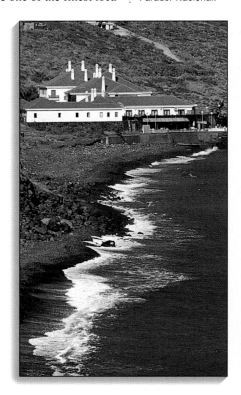

**LEFT:** the bell-tower at Frontera.
**BELOW:** the seaside Parador Nacional.

*Valverde was built on the site of the ancient Bimbache settlement of Amoco .*

she was probably the first Englishwoman to set foot on the island. Mrs Ston would have seen the newly-built windmills (their site is now a football pitch used to grind maize into the flour that is toasted to make *gofio*, but she wa two years too early to see the new clock, brought all the way from Paris i 1886, and installed in the church tower.

Today Valverde has a youthful atmosphere (there are two discos an numerous, bars as well as a small cinema) which is generated by the island' high school students, who come in from the surrounding villages and board i the capital during the week. Be warned, though, that it also has a confusin one-way system and a severe shortage of parking.

The town's heroes did not all win fame on their native soil. The **Plaza d Quintero Nuñez**, built in 1913 above the church, was named after an Herreñ who rose to become the mayor of Manila. He was just one of many Canar islanders who emigrated in search of a better life, although more went to Lati America than to the Philippines. The inconspicuous Tourist Information offic (open Mon–Fri 8.30am–2.30pm, Sat 8.30am–1pm) is on the main street at Call Licenciado Bueno 1. The English-speaking staff can provide you with map and bus timetables.

El Hierro's cuisine is simple but good. Try the **Noche y Dia** restaurant for quintessentially Herreñan meal: the pungent straw-coloured *vino herreñc solomillo* (sirloin steak) and *piña* (pineapple). Look out too for local *quesadillc* a cheesecake flavoured with vanilla, aniseed and lemon, and for musty Her reño cheese, made from a mixture of cow's, goat's and sheep's milk, whic comes in three kinds, *ahumada* (smoked), *curada* (mature) and *blanco* (white The *curada* is the most popular of the three.

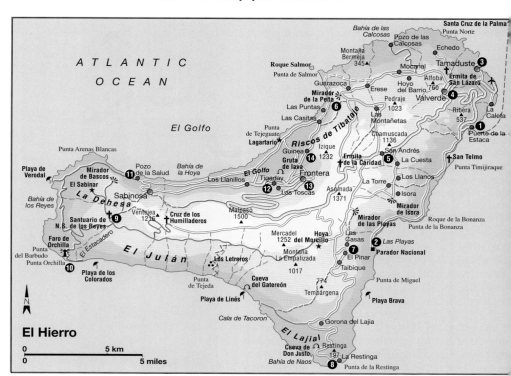

### entral spine

rom Valverde the road climbs further onto the high spine of the island, the isdafe, which at its highest point reaches 1,500 metres (4,920 ft) above sea vel. This is essentially livestock-rearing territory, and a bleak tracery of dry one walls and lava-slab tracks decorate the pastureland. In days gone by, many rmers migrated up here each summer to grow cereals and graze livestock, turning later to the coast to harvest figs and vines. The cowboy town of **San ndrés ❺** bears the raw stamp of farm life high up on a windy meseta, where ncient prickly pear bushes and fig trees are hallowed by stone circles, and ick capes and hats shroud their owners.

Agriculture still dominates the island, from the old men forever cropping *gasaste* (albuminosa) for fodder, to the new lorries now taking *queso her-ño* to the ferry. The new Cooperativa Ganadera (by the road junction to Isora) nnot produce enough local cheese to meet demand.

Water has never been abundant and conserving it has proved crucial to the land's survival. This is epitomised perhaps by its emblem, the Garoë tree, rowing in a valley to the north of San Andrés. Surrounded by small pools of ater, the present tree (a lime) planted in 1957 marks the site of an earlier aroë destroyed by a hurricane in 1610. Cartographers of the time frequently epicted El Hierro as the mysterious island of Pluvialia, with its rainy Arbol anto, the sacred tree whose leaves could distil water and bring life to a water-ss land. In fact the phenomenon is not so rare; water condenses on many trees nd plants here as the trade winds swirl clouds across El Hierro – enough to pro-ide an annual 2,000 litres a sq metre (40 gallons a sq. ft), more than eight mes the island's rainfall.

Map on page 246

*Farmers sometimes find road transport is quicker than herding.*

**BELOW:** sheltered harbour at Tamaduste.

The only coastal destination of note north of here is **Pozo de las Calcosas** with a steep walk down to a peculiar, semi-deserted shanty town of thatche houses and a man-made seawater pool.

West of the Garoë tree the road to the Mirador de la Peña curves past th deserted village of Las Montañetas, with tightly bunched houses and lava wall well-preserved by the climate, and fruit trees still blossoming although there no-one left to harvest the fruits. This is one of several abandoned villages on th Nisdafe; their inhabitants have long since emigrated, or descended to an easie life in El Golfo.

## Easy living in El Golfo

Just how different **El Golfo** is becomes clear if you stop off at the **Mirador d la Peña ❻**, which is graced by a restaurant designed by Lanzarote artist Césa Manrique, who died in 1992 (*see page 268*) in a characteristic harmony of loca wood and stone. Only when you stand at its edge, with precipitous cliffs drop ping sheer below, do you sense the full drama of El Hierro. For the sky falls nc to shadow-bright sea but to a fertile lowland crescent pawed out of the moun tains, a green secret lying low in the up-thrust crater of an extinct volcano. I contrast to the rest of the island, life in El Golfo is carefree and easy. Access wi be far easier, too, when the massive tunnel project already under way at Mocana is completed, as it is due to be in 2005.

But stay up on the high ground, for there is more Nisdafe to see south of Sa Andrés. The **Mirador de las Playas** has the opposite aspect to La Peña, wit long-range views to La Gomera and El Teide. Its giant pine trees are impressiv examples of the ancient pine woods that cover much of the central Nisdaf

**BELOW:** a shepherd guards his flock.

Map on page 246

their floors soft underfoot and inches deep in long needles. Many walks lead through these sweet-smelling woods – a good starting point is the picnic site at **Hoya del Morcillo**.

Pine woods also give their name to the southern town of **El Pinar** ❼, its steep streets now closely entwined with its neighbours Taibique and Las Casas. The village is well-known locally for its folk-dancing residents. At the top of the town (turn hard right uphill by the Calle El Lagar) the **Museo Panchillo** (No. 53) has a display of local curios and sells honey and figs (no set opening hours; knock on the house door for entry). Behind it the **Artesania Cerámica** (follow the sign of the snail) sells pottery and hand-made jewellery.

South of El Pinar the land gradually falls toward the sea and pines give way to a scorched no man's land of volcanic clinker. Unbelievably there's life at the end of the road – just. **La Restinga** ❽ is a small fishing port with a black sand beach and two diving centres, which benefits from the Teutonic desire to get to the end of things. It was a German who set up the first bar (now the **Kai Marino Pension**) in the 1960s, even though running water didn't arrive until 1974. La Restinga's restaurants have excellent fish – try the *peto* (similar to tuna) or the small white *cabrillas*, a member of the grouper family, which is usually grilled whole. And don't be put off *lapas a la plancha* (limpets) by the fact that the dish is sometimes evocatively translated as grilled slime – they can be very tasty.

It was at the nearby **Bahía de Naos** (the coast has been designated a Marine Nature Reserve) that the Norman adventurer Jean de Béthencourt first landed in 1403. His main problem in conquering the island's aboriginal inhabitants, the Bimbaches, was not fighting them off, but finding them. This was partly because

*Laying out nets to dry in La Restinga.*

**BELOW:** La Restinga, an idyllic fishing village.

they were able to hide in the mountainous Nisdafe which they knew so well, but also because they were so few, many of them having been carried off by Moorish slave-traders.

In the end de Béthencourt used a captured Bimbache as an intermediary to invite their leader Armiche to peace talks. Armiche agreed to what seemed reasonable terms, and he and more than 100 of his men surrendered their arms, whereupon de Béthencourt promptly imprisoned them – teaching them a hard lesson in the duplicitous ways of conquerors.

Centuries later, El Hierro learned some more unpalatable ways of the world when English sailors landed here in April 1762, four months after England declared war on Spain in what was to become the Seven Years' War. An early alarm, signalled across the mountain-tops to Valverde, resulted in the capture of the island, along with nine rifles that became the focus of a preposterous dispute. Requisitioned by the Tenerife government, the arms were only returned to the islanders after the intervention of Carlos III, a king who became almost as popular in the Canaries as the brandy named after him, a powerful brew served in liberal quantities and sometimes used to give a bit of extra strength to a small cup of black coffee.

About 1.5 km (1 mile) north of La Restinga lies the **Cueva de Don Justo**, a labyrinthine system of volcanic tunnels which is believed to total over 6,100 metres (20,000 ft), making it the sixth largest complex in the world. A concealed entrance to the tunnels lies below the red cone of the **Montaña de Prim**. Although the entrance is accessible to the public, it is inadvisable to go inside without an experienced guide; the tourist office in Valverde (*see page 243*) will arrange for a guide to accompany you.

**BELOW:** a twisted *sabina* tree.
**RIGHT:** succulents grow even where the soil is poor.

## Rough shores

The southern coast of Hierro is known as **El Julán**, a line of barren, windswept slopes falling sharply to steep cliffs. Curiously, the remotest part of the island is also home to **Los Letreros** (open daily 9am–3pm), a bizarre set of primitive inscriptions made in the flat surfaces of lava-streams. As yet undeciphered, their alphabet-like doodles have also been found at La Caleta and at other sites on the island. Some think their authors belonged to an early Berber civilisation, others link them to similar inscriptions in La Palma and the Cape Verde Islands. Vandals have had their say too and Los Letreros are now guarded – you'll need your passport if you want to view the site, and you must be prepared for an 8-km (5-mile) walk each way.

Map on page 246

Towards the end of El Julán lies a remote *ermita* (hermitage), the **Santuario de Nuestra Señora de los Reyes ❾** (open daily), home of the island's spiritual patroness. The diminutive figure of Our Lady of the Kings sits in the silver sedan chair used to carry her down to Valverde for a fiesta held in her honour. The procession takes a full day to wind across the Nisdafe.

The legend of Our Lady tells how a French ship was becalmed off El Julán for weeks on end, its crew only kept alive by the generosity of the Herreñans who took food to the stranded sailors. Having no money, the captain gave the islanders the statue of the Virgin Mary from his ship. That same day, 6 January 1577 (which is Epiphany, the Day of the Kings), a breeze suddenly blew up, and the ship sailed on to safety.

*A wayside marker on the Virgin's path.*

A track north from the ermita leads to another of El Hierro's surprises, **El Sabinar**, a grove of *sabinas* (juniper trees) bent double by persistent winds. Bowed but not defeated, every tree is stunted, its twisted trunk worn silver-

**BELOW:**
the sanctuary of
Nuestra Señora
de los Reyes.

smooth. Further ahead lies the lookout point of **Mirador de Bascos**, also known as El Rincón (The Corner), bright with wild flowers and giving fine views over El Golfo.

But there is no easy way down here, and the end of the world still to see, so turn back to the El Julán road and go west to **Punta Orchilla** ❿, its name derived from the orchil (a moss-like lichen found on rocks and used for dyes) which was once El Hierro's second export product (slaves were the first). Here the waves attack a coast of lava badlands covered with numerous species of euphorbia, almost the only plant which will grow here.

This coastline looks sufficiently sinister to suit its former status as the outer edge of the known world. In AD 150 Ptolemy placed his zero meridian through El Hierro, a line universally accepted right up to the late 19th century, when it was finally transferred to Greenwich in 1884. A sign commemorating this lonely corner of the world stands by the lighthouse, and you can get a dated certificate of your visit from the tourist office in Valverde.

Head up around the western end of the island and you are on your way to easier living, although it may not seem like it. The island's best beach, **Playa del Verodal**, is out here, the fortunate result of a recent landfall, when red gravel was pushed down to the sea during a project to build a coastal road.

### Water and wine

Up on the north coast, the **Pozo de la Salud** (Well of Health) ⓫ is a briny well with a picture of the Virgin set alongside a new spa hotel, among the fall-out from the island's most recent volcanic eruption (1793). Towering cliffs are striped with rockfalls and mountains are streaked with dark cinders. In the

**BELOW:** the Faro de Orchilla, site of the zero meridian.

Map on page 246

1890s this health-giving well developed a reputation as a therapeutic spa thanks to the radium content of its waters. An analysis of 1915 suggested it could treat everything from indigestion to venereal disease, and recommended hot baths and daily draughts washed down with chicken soup. The new hotel offers some of those treatments and has a large solarium and swimming pool.

By now the land is opening up into El Golfo, and the road cuts through fields growing bananas and pineapples on ground once dead with lava. Here a Finca de Experimentación researches into new crops that could help the island's vulnerable economy; strawberries, papaya and avocados are current favourites.

The village of **Sabinosa**, steep and covered in flowers, is the prettiest on the island. Beyond it, Los Llanillos and Tigaday seem like luxurious, busy towns after the austerity of the western end. Vines and wine presses reveal **Tigaday** ⑫ as the centre for Herreñan wine. One of the few things known about the Bimbaches was that they were the only early Canarians to distil alcoholic liquor (using laurel berries) – a tradition continued in the local *mistela*, a wine fortified with sugar and spices. Another surviving sign of Bimbache intelligence is a skull which was found in the Cueva de los Jables (now in the Museo Arqueológico in Santa Cruz de Tenerife), showing that they practised a rudimentary kind of brain surgery.

Tigaday is where the main route from Valverde – until the opening of the Mocanal tunnel – finally relaxes into fertile ground, having climbed the Nisdafe and made the long switchback descent of the crater cliff. Near the bottom it passes through one of El Hierro's most interesting villages, **Frontera** ⑬. Locals sometimes confusingly use the name Frontera to refer to the whole of the El Golfo area. The village is best-known for the 19th-century church of **Nuestra**

**BELOW:** rural houses in Guinea.

Map on page 246

**Señora de la Candelaria** (open daily), remarkable for the bell-tower placed on the volcanic cone behind. The grey amphitheatre beside the church is the *lucha canaria* stadium with the best view in the world; *lucha canaria* (Canarian wrestling) is followed with passion on this island (*see pages 85–87*).

## Largest lizards, smallest hotel

To the north of Frontera, the cliffs called **Riscos de Tibataje** are the last refuge of a "giant" lizard which was until recently considered extinct (*see opposite*). Various rescued specimens are being cared for in the new **Lagartario** (open Mon–Thurs 10am–2pm, 4–6pm; entrance charge), situated at the foot of the cliff on the road to Las Puntas. They may not seem very big, but apparently they are still growing!

Also near the base of the cliffs is the restored village of **Guinea** , one of the original settlements of the Norman colonists brought over by de Béthencourt in the 15th century. An ambitious modern project along the coast here – a complex of sea-water swimming pools – stands unused.

This circuit of the island ends at the **Hotel Puntagrande** at **Las Puntas**, under the eye of the Mirador de la Peña. Once recognised by the *Guinness Book of Records* as the smallest hotel in the world, it stands on the old *embarcadero* where, up until the 1930s, many of the island's supplies where shipped in. Once the home of El Hierro's customs officer, the four-room property qualifies as a hotel thanks to its bar, restaurant and lounge, a glass-walled conservatory right on top of the building. It is not easy securing a room, but even if you don't get to stay, try to stop off here for an evening meal of salad, soup and the fish of the day, and watch the sun disappear. ❏

*Lucha canaria bouts are avidly followed on El Hierro.*

**BELOW:** the smallest hotel in the world.

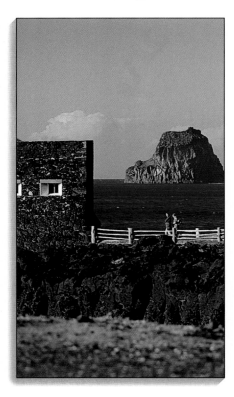

## HERREÑAN HANDICRAFTS

Apart from fishing, the cultivation of fruit and vineyards, and the care of sheep, goats and cattle whose milk is turned into excellent cheese, El Hierro has no productive industries. What it does have, in abundance, is a lively tradition of handicrafts.

Thread is still spun, then woven on fairly primitive wooden looms to produce colourful rugs, bedspreads, tablecloths and shoulder bags, which are very popular with tourists these days. Pottery is another island craft, and some creative pieces are being produced by potters in Valverde, Guarazoca and El Pinar, alongside the traditional earthenware vessels.

There is also a certain amount of woodcarving: mulberry, pine and beech are most commonly used to make domestic utensils, as well as a local form of castanets called *chácaras*. Basket-making also flourishes, although this is tough on the hands and the wicker has to be softened first in sea water for a considerable period before being worked.

During the summer months you will often find a handicraft fair going on in one of the island villages, when sales of goods are accompanied by folk music and dancing. Check with the tourist office if you'd like to visit one.

# El Hierro's Lizards

**B**efore the Spanish conquest of El Hierro the island was populated by cave-dwelling islanders, the Bimbaches, and a species of lizard that grew up to 1.5 metres (about 5 ft) long. The Bimbaches didn't survive for long, but the giant lizards fared rather better, until a combination of introduced wildcats and woodland clearance reduced their number to a brave few living in safety on the offshore Roques de Salmor. When the last Salmor specimen died in the 1930s, his skull was sent to the British Museum.

That should have been the end of that. The fact that it wasn't is due to a German biologist who arrived here in the early 1970s, his curiosity aroused by papers detailing the passing of the species *gallotia simonyi simonyi*. But several goatherds maintained that a population did still exist, in one very inaccessible part of Riscos de Tibataje, the crater cliff of El Golfo.

In due course the lizards were tracked down, but proved to be so much smaller than their ancestors – maximum 60 cm (23 in) – that their finders concluded they must be a subspecies. DNA tests, however, have shown that they are indeed from the original stock, but that years of persecution and clinging on to a cliff-face had simply stunted their growth.

A decade later, European money was made available to try to save the lizard from extinction. Twelve adults were captured and brought down to a new recovery centre – the Lagartario – at the foot of Fuga de Gorreta, on the road from Frontera to Las Puntas. The Lagartario is open to visitors, who get a brief explanation and guided tour.

Juan Pedro Péres, with a grin like a crevasse and fists like meat safes, is the man-mountain who mans the mountain. Known as *Periquin* (Little Parrot), he is the brother of *Pollito* (Little Chicken). Both are celebrated *lucha canaria* fighters, and the objects of local reverence. The Lagartario's biologist is one of Periquin's biggest fans, after the latter saved his life, pinning him to the rock face with his stick after he had lost his grip.

The centre has made its first release of captive-bred lizards, back onto the protected offshore Roque Salmor. The first mainland release is scheduled for the remote area of La Dehesa, at El Hierro's wild western end, but only when the factors which caused the lizards to die out in the first place have been resolved.

Despite their final size, the lizards grow slowly and are far less streetwise than their relatives, the more aggressive common lizards. For the first three years of their lives they are soft targets for the island's predators. If the project wants to re-establish them on La Dehesa then they will have to deal with the kestrels and the wildcats first.

Meanwhile, though, the inmates of the Lagartario are enjoying their new, five-star accommodation. Juan Pedro's original 12 have had 400 offspring, and show no signs of stopping there. Moreover, most of these children are already bigger than their parents, and still growing. Perhaps one day they'll get back to the size of grandad whose skull is ensconced in the British Museum.  ❏

**RIGHT:** the lizards are smaller than they used to be, but they are getting bigger all the time.

Map on page 264

# THE EASTERN ISLANDS

*If you have the time and the inclination to tear yourself away from the hills and beaches of the western Canaries, their eastern neighbours are only a short ferry ride away*

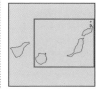

An imaginary line in the sea between Tenerife and Gran Canaria divides the Canaries into Eastern and Western provinces. To the east lie Gran Canaria, Lanzarote and Fuerteventura, islands whose hot dry African climates make them very different in character from the lush and green islands of the Western province. It is not just the arid environment and sparse vegetation that makes them like Africa: sandy Fuerteventura, closest to the African mainland (96 km/60 miles) is quite literally a chip off the block of the Sahara, while Gran Canaria has massive dune systems at Maspalomas (and yet the highest points in the mid-north of Gran Canaria occasionally receive snow in the winter, to the exhilaration of the locals).

Having sand and sea in abundance, these islands are perfect for beach-lovers and for watersports – the south-facing beaches tend to have gently shelving shorelines for novice windsurfers, while the north has swells and buried reefs that create waves mighty enough to attract keen surfers. Gran Canaria also has a number of attractive spots well away from the crowded sands: the mountainous interior hides some spectacular volcanic landscapes, and there are wild undeveloped beaches with excellent fish restaurants in the north. Lanzarote's volcanic landscape is enhanced by the wonderful creations of local artists César Manrique, whose murals, mosaics and sculptures turn many a dull roundabout into a work of art. All this lies within 35 to 50 minutes of Tenerife, with an average of three flights a day to each of the islands from Tenerife Norte airport.

## Gran Canaria

The third largest of the Canary Islands (1,532 sq. km/592 sq. miles) **Gran Canaria ❶** is often described as a miniature continent because it has every type of landscape. It also has a population of 714,000, almost 50 percent of the Canaries' total. A large African population adds colour to a vibrant Hispanic culture, and the year-round warmth brings holidaymakers from all over Europe bent on partying all night and making the most of a one-week break.

**Las Palmas ❷** (pop. 500,000) is the seat of Canarian government (the cause of a certain amount of inter-island rivalry) and is a major city in anyone's terms. It has major traffic problems, extensive slums, and all the problems you would associate with a major port, including a reputation for being one of the worst cities in Spain for drug addiction and drug-pushing; it also has an active red-light district. On the positive side, it has a compact and atmospheric downtown area of narrow streets overhung with Canarian balconies, and a modern quarter packed with elegant cosmopolitan shops and department stores.

**PRECEDING PAGES:** central mountains of Gran Canaria; Playa Canteras; the dunes of Maspalomas. **LEFT:** local farmer. **BELOW:** a view of Las Palmas.

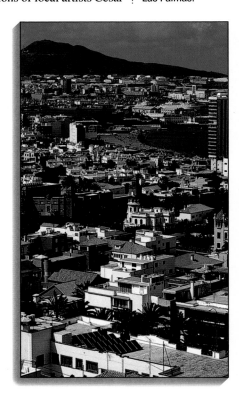

*Ferries link the islands and bring visitors from the mainland to Las Palmas.*

The city sits on a narrow peninsula with sea to east and west, and a sea frontage over 9 km (6 miles) in length. The sea-front promenade links the older Vegueta and Triana quarters (in the south) with the modern city that lie further north along the eastern side of the peninsula. **Parque San Telmo**, in the Vegueta quarter, marks the site of the old port where Columbus is said to have landed en route to the Americas. Some local historians (from Tenerife province) maintain that Columbus never set foot in Las Palmas at all, but that has no discouraged the city authorities from designating the 15th-century governor's house (in the beautiful street called Calle de los Balcones) as the **Casa de Colón** (Columbus Museum, open Mon–Fri 9am–6pm, Sat and Sun 9am–3pm; entrance charge). The museum has exhibits on pre-Columbian America, models of Columbus's ships and details of his voyages, plus material on the role of the Canaries as a stepping stone to the New World and the development of Las Palmas as a city).

In the same street, or just off, are the colourful municipal market (open morning only), the cathedral and Museo de Arte Sacra, the Atlantic Centre for Modern Art (with a lovely interior patio) and the **Museo Canario** (open Mon–Fri, 10am–5pm, Sat 10am–1pm, Sun 10am–2pm; entrance charge), with interesting models and displays on the cave-dwelling life of the Aborigens, the island's pre-Spanish inhabitants.

Pedestrianised Calle de Mayor de Triana, five blocks north of the cathedral is where you will find the city's most elegant shops, plus pavement cafés and street entertainers, but the big department stores (including Marks & Spencer and El Corte Inglés) and the duty-free outlets are concentrated around Avenid Mesa y Lopez, further north.

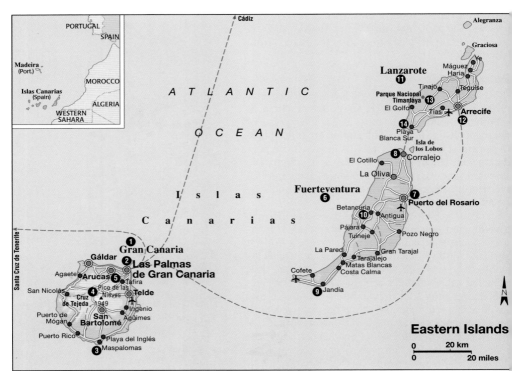

Eastern Islands

Map on page 264

To the west lies **Playa de las Canteras**, the capital city's own resort, one of the oldest on the island and the most popular with the Spanish themselves.

Surrounding the capital are various semi-industrial areas for warehousing, assembly and manufacturing, and you will have to travel some miles down the southeast coast before getting clear of the sprawl. Half-way down this coast, and slightly inland, the **Barranco de Guayadeque** is a long ravine honeycombed with caves (some of which are still inhabited), which have proved a treasure trove of Aborigens' remains. Towards the northwestern end of the ravine, the **Fortaleza de Ansite** is a volcanic rock that looks like a fortress, and marks the site where the Aborigens were defeated in 1483 in the final battle in the Spanish campaign to conqueror the island. **Santa Lucia**, the next village north, has a museum displaying Aborigen artefacts and weapons, and reconstructions of old Canarian houses.

Continuing north to San Bartolomé then heading due south will take you along the dramatic **Fataga Valley**, a miniature version of the Grand Canyon. Halfway down, the Camel Safari Park alerts you to the fact that you are approaching package-tour territory. Playa del Inglés and **Maspalomas** ❸ together form a continuous belt of urbanisation around the island's southern tip. Tourism has taken root in the south because of the sun and sand – notably the famous dunes at Maspalomas. Local tour agents offer camel excursions into this Sahara-like expanse of blown sand, but if you want to escape the commercial buzz the best way to do so is to walk across the dunes to the lighthouse at the western end of the resort.

Further round the coast are the smaller resorts of Puerto Rico and Puerto de Mogán, beyond which the west coast becomes wilder, with most inhabitants

**BELOW:**
the exterior of
the Casa de Colón.

pursuing their original livelihoods of fishing or agriculture. In the northwest the two attractive towns of **Agaete** and **Galdar** are important centres for the island's cultural life, with festivals and Arborigen remains.

Inland Gran Canaria has a landscape to rival the best of Tenerife, with patches of ancient forest and a cluster of peaks rising to 1,949 metres (6,394 ft) at **Pico de las Nieves**. Good paved roads allow you to reach the summit without physical exertion, but there are well-defined footpaths linking **Cruz de Tejeda** ❹, where the island's **Parador Nacional de Tejeda** is located (with a good, if expensive, restaurant), and to the distinctively shaped peaks of the Roque Bentaiga (to the west) and the Roque Nublo (to the south).

In these inland areas, some islanders still live in caves, like their Aborigens forefathers. Cave dwellings and a cave church can be visited at **Artenara**. At **Tejeda**, cave houses cluster along the ridge, though the whitewashed exteriors can make cave houses difficult to distinguish from more conventional ones. For a complete contrast, return to Las Palmas via **Santa Brigida** and **Tafira** ❺ where some of the island's best restaurants and most atmospheric hotels are to be found, many of them a legacy from an era when the British dominated Gran Canaria's trade and industry.

## Fuerteventura

Although it is the second largest island in the Canaries (1,731 sq km/668 sq miles), **Fuerteventura** ❻ has a permanent population of just 25,000. Sand – masses of it – is the reason why the island has little agriculture, but also why it has enjoyed a renaissance as the perfect destination for a laid-back beach holiday. The island used to be more prosperous, and its higher land was at one

**BELOW:** windswept landscape of Fuerteventura.

:ime wooded with palms, but over the last few centuries the climate has ɔecome increasingly unkind to plants, though more accommodating to anyone ḻesperate for sun, especially in winter.

The capital city of **Puerto del Rosario** ❼ (where most visitors arrive via ƒerry from Gran Canaria), is a straggling and rather unattractive place, although ıt has a shady square and narrow cobbled streets in the old quarter. It is home ṯo the 1,000-strong Spanish Foreign Legion, which has been stationed here since 1975, and whose huge barracks looks like a desert fortress.

The road north passes first through lava fields, beside a coast where craggy cliffs overhang brilliant blue waters – popular among diving enthusiasts – then ṯhrough sand dunes, to the former fishing village of **Corralejo** ❽, at the north-ern tip of the island. Thanks to the strips of white sandy beaches, this is where ɱany of the resort areas are located, and also where ferries from nearby Lan-zarote deposit visitors.

To the south of Puerto del Rosario lies the elegant Parador Nacional, over-ḻooking Playa Blanca, an appealing sweep of white sand. Shortly afterwards ḵsome 6 km/4 miles from the city) you come to the international airport.

The remainder of the island's resorts are along the sheltered southern coast, whose long golden beach stretches 25 km (15 miles), in a great uninterrupted ɪsweep, from Costa Calma in the north to Jandia in the south. **Jandia** ❾ is a great place for watersports because of the strong offshore breezes.

Inland the main attraction is **Betancuria** ❿, the island's first capital, home to the cathedral, two small museums, and craft workshops where local wine, cheese, fruit liqueur and cactus jam can be sampled. Nearby Antigua has another crafts complex set around a windmill once used for grinding toasted maize

**Map on page 264**

*Puerto del Rosario used to be known as Puerto de Cabras – Goat Port – until 1957, when the name was changed to its present more attractive one.*

**BELOW:** Hotel Tres Islas at Corralejo.

(*gofio*) for bread-making. South of Antigua, the Valles de Ortega has been turned into a green oasis of palm trees and fruit plantations.

## Lanzarote

**Lanzarote** ⓫ has a population of 50,000. Despite its modest proportions, the island has no less than 300 volcanic cones and an arid landscape, of which the islanders have made ingenious use, piling up lava boulders and painting them white to construct houses, flattening the rock for road surfacing material, making sturdy walls of it for fields and powdering it into sand for beaches. They also use the volcanic ash instead of earth (and manage to grow a surprising quantity of vegetables in this unpromising material).

One plant that thrives here naturally is the prickly pear cactus, which is widespread on the island, either growing wild or cultivated and hosting colonies of cochineal beetle, which live in a kind of white dust on the side of the plant. The beetle is a source of food dye; once a major industry, cochineal export died almost completely with the introduction of synthetic colouring, and now staggers on only for the benefit of those few who prefer natural food colouring.

Lanzarote's aridity has been brilliantly enhanced by the colourful and energetic creations of the artist César Manrique, whose name and work crops up wherever you go on the island. Born in Arrecife in 1919, he built an artistic reputation in Madrid and New York before returning home in 1968. Here he devoted his creative vision and energy to the construction of many of the island's most memorable sites and attractions. Manrique died in a car crash in 1992, but his legacy lives on: it is no exaggeration to say that the appeal of the island owes much to his imagination.

**BELOW:** ploughing the lava fields is heavy going.

Map on page 264

Others would argue that **Arrecife** ⓬ is the main attraction, a place that Manrique condemned as an urban disaster, but which attracts holidaymakers by the thousands for its sandy beach, its shopping and its nightlife. The golden sands here are in stark contrast to the black and red of the island's volcanic rock and soil. If you are coming from Fuerteventura you will probably arrive in Arrecife (unless you took the crossing to Playa Blanca).

Going north, you can visit Manrique's home, now the **Fondación César Manrique** (open Nov–June, daily 10–3pm, July–end Oct, 10–7pm; entrance charge) near **Costa Teguise**. Formed from solidified lava bubbles and collapsed lava tubes, the distinctive house makes the most of views out over the surrounding lava fields, and is full of Manrique's own colourful works.

His **Jardín del Cactus** (Cactus Garden) (open daily 10am–6pm, Jul–Sept, till 7pm; entrance charge) at **Guatiza** was formed by terracing a worked-out quarry and planting it with cacti which were chosen for their sculptural qualities.

About 15 km (10 miles) further north, Manrique transformed the **Cueva de los Verdos**) (the Greens' Cave) (open daily 10am–5pm, July to Sept till 6pm for 50-minute guided tours; entrance charge) into a visitor attraction, consisting of a 2-km (1-mile) walk though a network of caves and lava tubes. The cave is named after the Green family who once lived here, not because of any ecological associations.

Lanzarote's peaks do not reach to the heights of neighbouring islands but they compensate for their lack of height by their fiery hues and lunar appearance. **Parque Nacional Timanfaya** ⓭ results from volcanic eruptions that took place as recently as 1730. Here the *malpais* or "badlands" are so bad that barely a patch of moss or film of lichen manages to grow, and the park area is littered

*César Manrique's work and influence is ubiquitous.*

**BELOW:** Manrique's sign at the Parque Nacional Timanfaya.

Map on page 264

*A boat bobs in the water at Playa Blanca.*

**BELOW:**
covered up in a Moroccan street.
**RIGHT:**
Carnival disguises in Lanzarote.

with the cinder-like rocks that spewed out of the Montañas del Fuego, the Fire Mountains. Visitors can drive to **Isolate de Hilario**, where park rangers demonstrate that the volcano is far from extinct by pouring water into a tube in the ground: seconds later the water is forcibly ejected in the form of a column of steam. The park's restaurant, El Diablo, cooks with volcanic heat.

You can take a 45-minute guided tour on a park bus, visiting the area's main landmarks, and walkers can join free guided walks, but it is essential to book in advance. Call the visitor centre at **Mancha Blanca** (open Mon–Fri 9am–3pm; tel: 84 08 39). The 3-km (2-mile) walks (held on Mon, Wed and Fri) explore the volcanic formations around **Yaiza**, which is also the departure point for 15-minute camel rides. Yaiza is probably the prettiest village on the island, fresh with flowers and cleanly painted houses.

From Yaiza the road goes west to the jagged coast where you'll find the fishing village and the stunning green lagoon of **El Golfo**. A turning to the south takes you through **Las Salinas**, great salt pans where coarse salt is extracted by evaporation. Once this was a thriving industry but is considerably less important now. The road ends at **Playa Blanca** ⓮ from where ferries sail to Fuerteventura. Alternatively, head east from Yaiza, back to Arrecife.

## Going to Africa

Although politically part of Spain since the late 15th century, the Canary Islands are geographically a part of northwest Africa. Fuerteventura, the closest island to the West African coast (just 100 km/60 miles away) and, to a lesser extent, all the other islands, are geologically of a similar quality to the desert regions of the north and west of Africa.

The islands' first inhabitants, variously known as Guanches, Arborigens and Benahoares, are closely related to the indigenous inhabitants of modern-day Morocco and Mauritania. Theories abound concerning the original settlers, but it is believed that a Berber tribe, known as the Canarii, came to the islands from North Africa 6,000 years ago, following the decay of their forests and vegetation. This belief is supported by similarities in the appearance of the Guanches and the Canarii (tall and with a fair complexion), the similarity of their language and symbols, their worship and burial habits, their tools and weapons and their methods of animal and crop husbandry.

Despite the close proximity, the many African influences and the large number of African nationals now living and working in the Canaries, excursions to the African continent are not commonly made by locals or tourists, and flights are surprisingly expensive.

Royal Air Maroc (tel: 928 26 84 64) offers a regular service from Las Palmas on Gran Canaria to both Agadir and Marrakech, but if you have time to spare and are determined to see Morocco while you are in this part of the world, Royal Air Maroc package holidays, sold by travel agents in the Canaries, are the best value: for less than the price of a normal return flight to Marrakech, you can buy a whole week's holiday in that city, including flights and half-board hotel accommodation. ❑

# INSIGHT GUIDES
# TRAVEL TIPS

# New Insight Maps

Maps in Insight Guides are tailored to complement the text. But when you're on the road you sometimes need the big picture that only a large-scale map can provide. This new range of durable Insight Fleximaps has been designed to meet just that need.

### Detailed, clear cartography
*makes the comprehensive route and city maps easy to follow, highlights all the major tourist sites and provides valuable motoring information plus a full index.*

### Informative and easy to use
*with additional text and photographs covering a destination's top 10 essential sites, plus useful addresses, facts about the destination and handy tips on getting around.*

### Laminated finish
*allows you to mark your route on the map using a non-permanent marker pen, and wipe it off. It makes the maps more durable and easier to fold than traditional maps.*

### The first titles
*cover many popular destinations. They include Algarve, Amsterdam, Bangkok, California, Cyprus, Dominican Republic, Florence, Hong Kong, Ireland, London, Mallorca, Paris, Prague, Rome, San Francisco, Sydney, Thailand, Tuscany, USA Southwest, Venice, and Vienna.*

## 🦉 INSIGHT GUIDES
*The world's largest collection of visual travel guides*

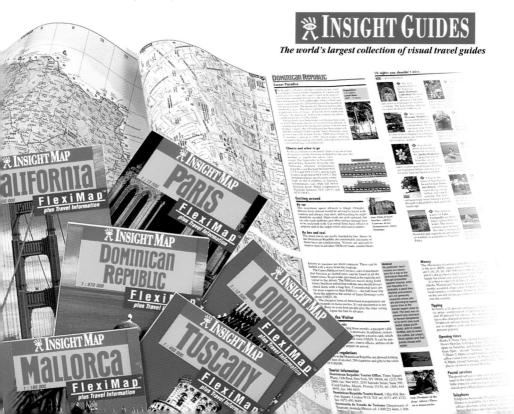

# CONTENTS

# Getting Acquainted

## The Place

**Area:** Tenerife has an area of 2,354 sq km (790 sq miles), and is the largest island in the Canarian archipelago, which consists of seven main islands and six smaller ones, with Africa some 96 km (60 miles) to the east.
**Capital:** status is shared between the cities of Santa Cruz (Tenerife) and Las Palmas (Gran Canaria).
**Highest mountain:** Pico del Teide at 3,718 metres (12,197 ft).
**Population:** 700,000.
**Language:** Spanish.
**Time zone:** Tenerife, in common with all the other islands in the archipelago, follows Greenwich Mean Time throughout the year.
**Currency:** Spanish pesetas.
**Weights and measures:** metric.
**Electricity:** 220 volts.
**International dialling code:** 34 922.

## Climate

The Canaries are known for their equable climate, which varies little throughout the year. Temperature averages range from 18°C (64°F) in winter and 24°C (75°F) in summer, though they can reach 30°C (86°F) in the sunniest months of July and August. There can be heavy rainfall from mid-October to February, though this mainly falls in the north of the islands.

Northern Tenerife has a wetter climate than the south and is consequently much greener. The south coast gets little rain and its desert-like landscape is only broken by greenery where holiday developments have introduced tropical palms, shrubs, flowers and golf courses. During the winter months snow often covers the peak of the Pico del Teide.

## The Economy

The Canarian economy is based on tourism, commerce and agriculture, with bananas, tomatoes, avocado pears, flowers and – more recently – fresh herbs being the main exports to mainland Spain and the rest of Europe. The port of Santa Cruz handles over 50 million tonnes of shipping cargo annually. Tourism is the main growth industry and, over the last three decades, this has greatly increased the islanders' standard of living, assisted by grants from the European Union.

## The Government

The Canary Islands are an Autonomous Region of Spain (one of 17 such regions). They are integrated into the European Union, although certain differences apply because of their position and traditions. For example, import duties and VAT are low to compensate for the high cost of transporting goods to the islands.

Santa Cruz de Tenerife is the administrative capital of the islands of Tenerife, La Palma, La Gomera and El Hierro, while Las Palmas de Gran Canaria is the administrative capital of Gran Canaria, Lanzarote and Fuerteventura. The Presidency of the Canary Islands alternates between the two cities, every four years (coinciding with regional elections). The 60-member parliament meets in Santa Cruz, while Las Palmas has the Supreme Court, and the various departments of the regional government are split equally between the two island capitals (though some maintain office on both). Each island has its own *cabildo insular* (island council).

## Etiquette

The Canarian people are outgoing and friendly – to pass a Canarian you know even by sight and not greet them is an insult. A "*buenos*

## Fascinating Facts

- The Pico del Teide is the highest mountain in Spain. It can be explored by cable car.
- The exotic *Strelitzia* (bird-of-paradise) is the symbolic flower of the Canary Islands.
- The dragon tree known as Drago Milenario (literally "1,000-year-old dragon") at Icod de los Vinos is reputed to be between 500 and 3,000 years old and was revered by the original Guanche people as a symbol of fertility.
- The Barco de la Virgen naval museum in Santa Cruza de la Palma is a concrete reproduction of Columbus' flagship, the *Santa María*.
- In La Gomera, the sap of the *Phoenix canariensis* (palm tree), which has a daily production of 6–12 litres (10–21 pints), is made into a dark "honey" – delicious with local bananas.
- In AD 150 Ptolemy placed his zero meridian line through El Hierro at the Faro de Orchilla.
- It is the custom on New Year's Eve at the stroke of midnight to sip champagne and eat grapes – one for each strike of the clock for a "happy month" in the new year.

*días*" or "*hola*" (good morning/hello) and a handshake will get an immediate response. If you know someone well, a kiss on both cheeks is expected. The islanders are very family-oriented, so a remark about their children is always appreciated.

Football is the main topic of conversation in bars, with fanatical support for Tenerife, Real Madrid and Barcelona teams – derogatory remarks are not welcome.

Do not expect anyone to hurry in the Canaries: the *mañana* (tomorrow) attitude remains strong. The locals think of themselves very much as Canarios, not Spaniards, whom they refer to as Penínsulares.

# Planning the Trip

## What to Wear

There is no need to pack heavy clothing. Even on the odd wet, windy day, a windproof jacket will suffice for going up to the Pico del Teide or on a boat trip. Footwear should include comfortable walking shoes as the inland terrain can be rough. For the beach, loose sandals are necessary as the sands can become burning hot. A sun hat, sunglasses and sun protection creams are essential. Lightweight cottons are the most comfortable clothes. Smart casual wear is best for evenings. Beach clothes must not be worn when visiting a church.

On Tenerife the major tourist shops have a wide range of clothing for all age groups. It is also easy to buy camera film, reading and writing materials, toys, and beach and sports equipment. Many international brands of food are available, including PG Tips tea, Nescafé coffee, Cadbury's biscuits and Heinz tomato soup.

## Entry Regulations

For a stay of up to 90 days, citizens of EU countries, the USA and Canada need only valid passports or a national identity card. For longer stays you must obtain a visa from the Spanish consulate in your home country. Citizens of Australia, New Zealand and South Africa need a visa.

## Health

Adequate medical insurance is recommended. European Union citizens are entitled to reciprocal medical benefits and should obtain the relevant documentation before leaving home. In the UK, form E111 is available from main post offices. Your hotel or free local newspaper will supply the name of a nearby doctor or dentist. Some practitioners in the Canaries speak good English and advertise in the local papers. Remember to get a receipt if you wish to make an insurance claim. If you require special medication, take sufficient supplies with you or bring a detailed prescription. Bottled water is widely available. There are no dangerous animals or snakes in the Canaries and insect bites are rare. Hangovers, upset stomachs and sunstroke are the most common problems.

## Money

The currency is the Spanish peseta. Bank notes are issued in 1,000, 2,000, 5,000 and 10,000 peseta denominations. Coins are issued in 1, 5, 10, 25, 50, 100, 200 and 500 peseta denominations.

It is best to bring with you some pesetas for immediate use on arrival. Most hotels, shops and some restaurants in the tourist resorts accept credit cards and traveller's cheques. Banks and exchange bureaux do not normally charge a commission – but remember to take your passport. Automatic cash dispensing machines can be found in the majority of towns, even on the smaller islands.

## Getting There

### BY AIR

All seven main Canary Islands have airports, the newest one being that on La Gomera, which started operating in autumn 1998. Most of the international flights go to Tenerife, Lanzarote and Gran Canaria, with the other airports being used principally for inter-island flights.

The Spanish national carrier, **Iberia Airlines**, offers scheduled flights to Tenerife, though this usually means changing in Madrid or Barcelona.
**UK office**
Venture House
27–29 Glasshouse Street
London W1R 6JU
Tel: 020 7830 0011
Fax: 020 7413 1261.
**Central enquiry line** on Tenerife:
902 40 05 00.

## Public Holidays

All banks and government offices including post and tourist offices are closed on public holidays. In the popular tourist spots some of the food stores and souvenir shops open for part of the day. Buses and taxis run as usual, but be warned that the roads will be very busy.

The main public holidays are as follows:

| | |
|---|---|
| ● New Years Day | **1 January** |
| ● Epiphany (Twelfth Night–Tres Reyes) | **6 January** |
| ● San José | **12 March** |
| ● Good Friday | **variable** |
| ● Easter Monday | **variable** |
| ● Labour Day | **1 May** |
| ● Corpus Christi | **variable** |
| ● San Pedro y San Pablo | **29 June** |
| ● National Day | **18 July** |
| ● Santiago Apostal (St James's Day) | **25 July** |
| ● The Assumption (Feast of Our Lady Of Candelaria) | **15 August** |
| ● Día de la Hispanidad (Columbus Day) | **12 October** |
| ● All Saints' Day | **1 November** |
| ● Constitution Day | **6 December** |
| ● Immaculate Conception | **8 December** |
| ● Christmas Day | **25 December** |

In some towns and villages, everything may close for the local saint's day, which can be any time of the year.

**Iberia Airlines' sales offices:**
Avda Anaga 23
Santa Cruz de Tenerife
Tel: 922 28 11 12
Fax: 922 27 13 74
Reina Sofía Airport
Tel: 922 75 92 85
Fax: 922 75 92 86
Los Rodeos Airport office
Tel/fax: 922 63 58 79.
The latter airport is used for some inter-island and mainland flights to Spain.
**Airport information**
Reina Sofía Airport
Tel: 922 75 90 00
Los Rodeos Airport
Tel: 922 63 58 00.
   The islands are a 4-hour flight from the UK. The majority of visitors use charter companies, which operate from nearly all of the UK's regional airports, offering flight-only tickets and package holidays that include flight, accommodation and (sometimes) car hire.
**Independent travellers** If you would prefer the services of a small independent specialist, try:

## Bringing Your Car

Any size of vehicle, including motor-homes and caravans (also boats) can sail on the Trasmediterránea ferry from Cadiz. A vehicle can be imported for six months provided the vehicle registration documents, green card, insurance certificate and Spanish Bail Bond are in order. To board ship you may have to reverse your vehicle up the ramp.

Travellers' Way
The Barns, Hewell Lane,
Bromsgrove
Worcs
B60 1LP
Tel: 01527 559000
Fax: 01527 836159.
This company specialises in rural tourism, and has a good selection of hotel and self-catering holidays on the islands, with converted farm buildings (*casas rurales*) at reasonable prices.

## BY SHIP

### *Long Distance Services*
The only passenger and vehicle shipping line to operate a regular service between mainland Spain and the Canary Islands is the ferry company **Trasmediterránea**, which runs several services a week from Cádiz to Gran Canaria, Lanzarote and Tenerife.
   Trasmediterránea's UK agent is:
**Southern Ferries**,
First Floor
179 Piccadilly,
London W1V 9DB
Tel: 020 7491 4968
Fax: 020 7491 3502.
Early booking is essential for school holidays and carnival time (February). Tickets include all meals during the voyage (48–72 hours). Pensioners get a 20 percent discount.
   Trasmediterránea's head office in Spain is at Calle Alcala, Madrid, CP 28014. There is one central phone number for all passenger

## Useful telephone numbers

### *General*
**Medical emergency:** 061
**Directory enquiries:** 1003
**International directory enquiries:** 1025
**Narcotic hot line:** 902 10 10 91 (office hours)
**Police emergency:**
   National police: 091
   Local police: 061

### *Medical/Hospitals*
**24-hour emergency medical services:**
64 12 00
**Social Security Hospital,**
Santa Cruz:
60 20 00
**General Hospital,**
Santa Cruz:
64 10 11
**Children's Hospital,**
Santa Cruz:
28 65 50
**Centro Médicos del Sur,**
Playa de las Américas:
79 10 00

**Centro Médico Salud,**
Puerto de la Cruz:
38 76 65
**Duty Chemist:**
28 24 24 (24 hours)

### *Ambulances*
(*Cruz Roja*/Red Cross)
Santa Cruz: 28 18 00
Puerto de la Cruz: 38 38 12
Las Américas: 78075
Los Cristianos: 79 05 05

### *Consulates*
**British Consulate**, Tenerife:
Plaza Weyler 8 (1st Floor),
Santa Cruz,
tel: 922 28 68 63
(Monday to Friday, 9am–noon, also 24-hour emergency telephone)
**American Consulate**, Gran Canaria:
Calle de Martinez de Escobar 3 (office 3), Las Palmas,
tel: 928 22 25 52
**Irish Consulate**, Tenerife:
Calle del Castillo 8, Santa Cruz,
tel: 922 24 56 71

### *Town Halls*
(*Ayuntamientos*)
Santa Cruz: 60 60 00
Playa de las Américas: 71 01 20
Puerto de la Cruz: 38 04 28
Los Cristianos: 72 55 00

### *Fire Brigade*
North: 33 00 80
South: 71 62 06

### *Post and Telegraph Offices*
Santa Cruz: 24 51 16
Puerto de la Cruz: 38 25 68
Playa de las Américas: 75 05 84
Los Cristianos: 79 10 56

### *Stolen Credit Cards*
(Madrid numbers)
Eurocard: 915 19 60 00
American Express: 915 72 03 03
Visa/MasterCard: 915 19 21 00

### *Bus Stations*
Santa Cruz: 21 56 99
Puerto de la Cruz: 38 18 07
Playa de las Américas: 79 54 27

information and bookings; ring this in preference to contacting local offices in Spain and the Canaries: tel: (34) 90 245 4645.

On Tenerife, Trasmediterránea's office is at:
Est Marítima Muelle de Ribera,
Santa Cruz de Tenerife,
CP 38001
Tel: (34) 90 245 4645
Fax: 922 84 22 44.

### Inter-Island Services

A complex network of inter-island ferries and hydrofoils links the main islands of the Canaries. Schedules change frequently, so it is not possible to publish a definitive schedule. Most of these services are operated by:
**Trasmediterránea**, all passenger enquiries, tel: (34) 90 245 4645; see Long Distance Services opposite for office details.
Website: www.transmediterranea.es
**Fred Olsen Line**
Edificio Fred Olsen,
Poligono Industrial Añaza s/n,
Santa Cruz de Tenerife
Tel: 922 62 82 00
Fax: 922 62 82 53
Website: www.fredolsen.es.

The local airline **Binter Canarias** provides regular inter-island flights. They can be contacted at:
Aeroporto de Los Rodeos
Tel: 922 26 43 46
Fax: 922 25 35 42
Website: www.bintercanrais.es

# Practical Tips

## Business Hours

Banking hours vary but core hours are Mon–Fri, 9am–1.30pm and Sat, 9am–12.30pm in winter (many banks do not open on Saturdays between June and the end of October). The same times apply to public offices. Post offices are open Mon–Fri, 9am–2pm; Sat, 9am–1pm. Most food stores and supermarkets are open 8.30am–1.30pm and 4–7.30/8pm. Some food and souvenir shops, mainly in tourist resorts, are also open Sundays 10am–1.30pm.

## Tipping

Tipping is expected: 10 percent is normal for taxi drivers and waiters. A service charge is added automatically at some restaurants. In bars, if you sit down at a table the waiter will bring you la cuenta (the bill) and expect a tip. In English-style pubs you pay as you drink and tipping is optional.

## Media

### NEWSPAPERS AND MAGAZINES

English daily and Sunday newspapers are available in the main tourist resorts on the afternoon of publication. There are several local newspapers published in English, including the daily Island Sun, which covers events from abroad as well as on the islands, and La Gaceta de Canarias, which has a weekend edition in English and German. The Canarian is published weekly and Island Connections and Tenerife News are both fortnightly newspapers, often

circulated to hotels and given away free at tourist offices. The glossy Canary Island Gazette has a useful "What's On" section. A broad range of magazines and books printed in English is available.

## RADIO

Oasis 101 FM is the local English radio station. Broadcasting to the north and south of Tenerife, it includes world headlines, local news and announcements interspersed with pop music. Reception for the BBC World Service is usually good.

## Internet

Public access is now available to the Internet by using a computer from a local technical service: **Atlantis Net**, Calle del General Franco 36, Los Cristianos. Net cafés can be found in several towns on Tenerife.

## TELEVISION

Programmes from America, England, Germany, Italy and Spain, plus local Canarian stations, are on offer with good reception aided by satellite dishes.

## Telecommunications

### POST OFFICES

Most open Mon–Fri, 9am–2pm; Sat, 9am–1pm. Stamps (sellos) can also be purchased at tobacconists and most hotel receptions. Post boxes are painted yellow.

### Mail Boxes

MBE, Calle Antigua General Franco 16, Los Cristianos, offers mail boxes and redirecting services, tel: 922 75 24 96; fax: 922 75 04 39.

### TELEPHONE

There are plenty of public telephone boxes (painted blue) but sometimes they get jammed with too many coins. More reliable are the larger *cabinas* (booths) marked **Telefonica Internacional**, where calls are monitered by an assistant who you pay when you finish your call. Open 9am–1pm and 4–9pm. All public phone boxes have instructions in English.

For the UK, dial **00**, wait for a high-pitch tone, then **44** followed by the area code (omitting the initial 0) and the telephone number.

**Country Codes**

| | |
|---|---|
| Australia | 61 |
| France | 33 |
| Germany | 49 |
| Ireland | 353 |
| Italy | 39 |
| New Zealand | 64 |
| USA and Canada | 1 |

To make a reverse charge telephone call to Britain via an English-speaking operator, dial **900 99 00 44** for a freecall to British Telecom International, who will place your call for you.

## Tourist Offices

### United Kingdom

Spanish National Tourist Office, 22–23 Manchester Square, London W1M 5AP, tel: 020 7486 8077; fax 020 7486 8034.

### USA

665 5th Avenue, New York 10103, tel: (212) 265 8822; fax: (212) 265 8864.
8383 Wilshire Boulevard, Suite 960, Beverly Hills, Los Angeles, California 90211, tel: (213) 658 7188; fax: (213) 658 1061.
Water Tower Place, Suite 915 East, 845 North Michigan Avenue, Chicago, ILL 60611, tel: (312) 642 1992; fax: (312) 642 9817.
1221 Brickell Avenue, Miami, FL 33131, tel: (305) 358 1992; fax: (305) 358 8223.

### Canary Islands

**Tenerife**
Adeje: Avda Rafael Puig 1, tel/fax: 922 75 06 33.
Aeroporto Reina Sofia, tel: 922 39 20 37.

Candelaria: Avda del Generalísimo s/n, tel/fax: 922 50 04 15.
El Médano: Plaza de los Príncipes de España, tel/fax: 922 17 60 02.
La Laguna: Plaza del Adelantado 194, tel: 922 63 11 94.
La Orotava: C/Carrera del Escultor Estevez 2, tel: 922 32 30 41; fax: 922 32 11 42.
Los Galletas: Avda Marítima, tel/fax: 922 73 01 33.
Los Cristianos: Centro Cultural, C/General Franco s/n, tel: 922 75 71 37; fax: 922 75 24 92. Also at Playa de Las Vistas, tel: 922 75 06 69.
Puerto de la Cruz: Plaza de Europa s/n, tel: 922 38 60 00; fax: 922 38 47 69.
Playa de las Américas: Centro Commercial "City Centre", tel: 922 79 76 68; fax: 922 75 71 98. Also at Playa de las Vistas, tel: 922 75 06 69.
Santa Cruz: Cabildo Insular, Plaza de España, tel: 922 23 95 00; fax: 922 23 98 12.
Santiago del Teide: Centro Comercial "Seguro del Sol", Calle Manuel Ravelo 20, tel/fax: 922 86 03 48.

**La Gomera**
San Sebastián: Calle Real 1, tel: 922 14 01 47; fax: 922 14 01 51.

**La Palma**
Santa Cruz de la Palma: Calle O'Daly 23, tel: 922 41 31 41; fax: 922 41 21 06.

**El Hierro**
Valverde: Calle Licenciado Bueno 1, tel: 922 55 03 02; fax: 922 55 10 52.

**Gran Canaria**
Las Palmas: Parque de Santa Catalina, tel/fax: 928 26 46 23.

**Lanzarote**
Arrecife: Parque Municipal, tel/fax: 928 80 15 17.

**Fueteventura**
Puerto del Rosario: Avenida de la Constitución 5, tel/fax: 928 85 10 24.

## Embassies & Consuls

### What a Consul Can Do

- Issue emergency passports.
- Contact relatives and friends to help with money and tickets.
- Advise how to transfer funds.
- In an emergency, advance money against a sterling cheque supported by a bankers card.
- Provide a list of lawyers, interpreters and doctors.
- Arrange for next-of-kin to be informed of an accident or death and advise on procedures.
- Contact British nationals who have been arrested.

### What a Consul Cannot Do

- Pay your hotel, medical or any other bills.
- Pay for travel tickets, except in very special circumstances.
- Give legal advice.
- Investigate crime.
- Obtain accommodation or work permits.

For embassy details, *see Useful Telephone Numbers.*

## Police

There are three different kinds of police. The Policía Nacional wear brown uniforms and rule the streets. The Policía Municipal, the traffic police, wear blue uniforms and white caps. The Guardia Civil, in green, are very important and rule everywhere else. They talk in Spanish but understand English and will speak it, if necessary.

## Security and Crime

The Canarian authorities are well aware that their crime rate figures have an effect on the tourist industry as well as the local population. With the increase in the number of visitors to the island, the crime rate has gone up. Drug-related crime, car theft, burglaries and handbag snatching are constantly being reported – mainly in the tourist resorts.

The majority of hotels and apartments have security boxes and it is advisable to use them at all times. Remember to lock your apartment doors and windows. Never leave valuable articles in your car, even in a locked boot. Take care with unattended articles on the beach. Having photocopies of your important documents, such as your passport and driving licence, and making a note of credit card numbers is a wise precaution. Never carry large sums of money or handbags on the road side as you walk – body belts are useful. Keep to well-lit streets at night.

Should you be unfortunate and become a victim of criminal activity, report it immediately to your tour representative who will know what is the correct procedure. If you are an independent traveller, make your way to the nearest Policía Nacional or Guardia Civil police station: these days they understand English. If you have any witnesses to the crime, be sure to get their written statement. Insurance companies require police proof of the incident.

If involved in a road accident do not remove injured people until an ambulance or police van arrives. Even if there are no personal injuries, make sure that insurance details are exchanged. Do not have the car repaired until you have an assessment of the damage and the insurance claim settled.

Be heartened by newspaper reports that the police in the Canaries are almost at the top of the Spanish league for solving crime. Efforts are being made to keep people, property and the streets safe. The police now keep a high profile and patrol tourist areas by day and night.

For **Emergencies** see Useful Telephone Numbers.

## Lost Property

You should report any loss to your holiday representative or hotel reception, then the local police. Lost property can be claimed from bus stations or the Policía Municipal.

## Medical Services

Considerable improvements have been made to medical services for visitors to Tenerife, but it is still necessary to have a good holiday medical insurance policy. All five hospitals on the island will give you the same emergency treatment on your E111 form as you would obtain in England. They have English-speaking staff. Ask at your hotel reception or look in the local English papers for your nearest médico (doctor).

### CHEMISTS

For minor problems farmacías (chemists) will give advice as well as medication. They are also allowed to dispense a wide variety of drugs on prescription. A consultation with a chemist may be quicker and cheaper than consulting a doctor. Chemists are open shop hours. Look for a green cross; they have a rota for after-hours service (see Useful Telephone Numbers).

### RED CROSS

The Cruz Roja operates the ambulance services (see Useful Telephone Numbers). Centro médico or clinica are private clinics. Most have English-speaking doctors and nursing staff and British insurance is accepted. Local newspapers and hotels advertise the nearest clinics.

## Dental Treatment

The Spanish National Health Service does not cover dental treatment so it must be paid for immediately, then claimed on your insurance. Emergency treatment will be dealt with almost immediately.

The Spanish word dentista doesn't correspond exactly to dentist: ask for an odontólogo. Hotels and local newspapers have lists of practitioners.

# Getting Around

## Arriving by Air

Reina Sofía Airport, the arrival point for the majority of visitors, can be chaotic – despite recent improvements to its facilities. The airport is at its busiest on Tuesdays and Fridays when the bulk of British tourists arrive. However, there are plenty of free luggage trolleys and little or no inspection of incoming luggage by Customs. There is an information desk, car hire outlets, souvenir shops, cafeterias, toilets with facilities for babies and the disabled, and an escalator to a viewing terrace.

Taxis outside the building are mostly large white Mercedes and operate in a strict queue. Travel from the airport to Playa de las Américas takes about 25 minutes, and to Puerto de la Cruz around 1 hour 40 minutes. A regular bus service runs between the airport and Santa Cruz, where you must change buses to reach Puerto de la Cruz. Buses also run to Los Cristianos, Playa de las Américas and further west. The last bus leaves from the airport at 10pm. During the night, a taxi or a hire car are the only options. Offices at the airport close at 11pm.

Reina Sofía Airport Information, tel: 922 75 90 00.

## Arriving by Ship

When arriving by sea, there are plenty of taxis in port waiting to meet incoming ships. During office hours car hire firms are open in the port terminal buildings, which also have telephones, toilets, bookstalls and refreshments.

## Public Transport

Tenerife's main bus service, TITSA, is efficient and covers the island well. Most of the vehicles are new, air conditioned, clean and painted white and green.

A bus is called a *guagua* (pronounced '*wah-wah*') and a bus stop is a *parada*. The express routes along the *autopistas* from Puerto de la Cruz or Playa de las Américas are worth using for day trips to Santa Cruz.

A book of *bono* (voucher) tickets valid for up to a year can be bought at main TITSA offices. This gives 30 percent discount on any journey along regular routes. The bus driver also collects the fares. Passengers enter at the front and depart by the rear door.

Central bus station: Avenida Tres de Mayo, Santa Cruz, tel: 922 79 54 27.

### TAXIS

Look out for a green light on the car roof and an "SP" (Servicio Público) plate. All taxis have meters and fares are published in the local free newspapers. For long journeys and day trips ask to see the *tarifa* (rates) or negotiate the cost. There are surcharges for putting luggage into the cab boot and for late-night travel.

Any complaints about taxi drivers should be lodged with the Policía Municipal, who keep a register of all taxi owners and drivers. Remember to take the registration number. However, processing of complaints can be slow.

### CAR HIRE

Compared to Britain and the rest of Europe, car rental is cheap. Vehicles range from the small Seat Pandas to jeeps and mini-buses: the cost rises with the size of the vehicle. Hire can be for one, three or seven days, or more. Usually there is a discount for longer periods and it is worth looking

around for special offers.

Child seats and roof racks are available. Drivers need to be over 21 years, although some companies make it 25 years old. Have your current driving licence and passport handy. Get fully comprehensive insurance, otherwise you will have to pay up even if someone hits you.

Mopeds, motorbikes and bicycles can be rented in the larger resorts. Avis SA, Hertz SA and Bettacar SA have offices at Reina Sofía Airport and on the smaller islands. It can be easier and cheaper to rent your vehicle from their UK offices.

Despite the large number of rental firms on Tenerife, it can be quite difficult to hire a car at peak times such as Christmas, so book before you travel if possible.

## Local Car Hire Firms

**Sanasty SA**, Cristian Sur 4, Los Cristianos, tel: 922 76 55 79.
**Sunnyland Travel**, Tenerife Royal Garden, Local 2-A, 38660 Playa de las Américas, tel: 922 751190
Parque Santiago III, Local 14, 38660 Playa de las Américas Tenerife, tel: 922 751190
**Avis SA**, Paraiso del Sol-Playa, Playa de las Américas, tel: 922 79 10 01.
**Hertz SA**, Plaza Constitución, Puerto de la Cruz, tel: 922 38 45 60.
**Occa SA**, Calle Fernandez Navarro 15–17, Santa Cruz, tel: 922 23 04 99.
**Tenerife Rent-a-Car SL**, Poligono Industrial, Las Chafiras, San Miguel de Abona, tel: 922 73 52 99

## Driving

Driving is on the right-hand side of the road. The use of seat-belts is compulsory. It is prohibited to drive when using a hand-held telephone or to throw cigarette ends or any object out of the window – expect an on-the-spot fine. Driving in towns is busy but fairly straightforward

## Speed Limits

| | |
|---|---|
| Motorways | **120** km |
| Highways | **100** km |
| Other roadways | **90** km |
| Urban streets | **50** km |
| Residential areas | **20** km |

and signs are international. Motorway junctions are sometimes complicated by endless "Give Way" signs and bends.

Some petrol stations close on Sundays, others stay open for 24 hours. Not all take credit cards. Pay-and-display parking areas known as *Zonas Azules* (Blue Zones) have been created in the busy streets in Santa Cruz, Puerto de la Cruz, Los Cristianos and Playa de las Américas.

Driving in the countryside is less busy during the week and there are plenty of places to take picnics and go for walks. Driving on the smaller islands can be a pleasure, but take it slowly in the mountains as the roads can be dangerous – there have been a large number of fatal traffic accidents on the island in recent years.

# Where to Stay

## Accommodation

The choice of accommodation on the islands is extensive, ranging from elegant five-star luxury hotels in green and peaceful surroundings alongside beautiful sand dunes, to simple one-star pensions in small villages.

More modest apartments and pensions can be located either in the towns or inland villages. Recently a number of old *fincas* (farmhouses) and *casas rurales* (rural houses) have been converted into places suitable for tourists to rent and brought into a goverment-run certification scheme. In most instances they are in quiet locations with delightful settings, perhaps overlooking a deeply terraced valley or green banana plantation or with a sea view.

Information centres and reservations for rural tourism: **Aricotour**, Carretera General 11, 38580 Arico, tel/fax: 922 16 11 33; and **Atrea**, Turismo Rural, Carretera General de Tacoronte-Tejina, La Estación Tacoronte, tel: 922 57 00 15; fax: 922 57 27 03.

Because there has been a movement among the Canarian authorities – together with local hotel groups – to take the tourist industry up-market and get away from the image of just being for bucket-and-spade families and football lager louts, the trend in the last few years has been to build only four- and five-star hotels and high-grade apartments. Cheap accommodation, therefore, is getting harder to find.

The following is a list of hotels giving an idea of what is on offer. Facilities and charges are, of course, always liable to change.

## Price Categories

Double room per night:
**Expensive** more than £100
**Moderate** £50–100
**Inexpensive** under £50

## TENERIFE

### Expensive
#### Costa Adeje
**Hotel Gran Bahía del Duque,**
Playa del Duque.
Tel: 922 71 30 00
Fax: 922 712616.
Luxury hotel in a secluded position by the sea, offering privacy on a grand scale. Elegant suites and 362 air-conditioned terraced rooms set around colourful gardens and pools. Many facilities including exercise, health and beauty salons plus nightly entertainments.

#### El Médano
**Hotel Médano**
Playa del Médano.
Tel: 922 17 70 00
Fax: 922 17 60 48.
It is fascinating to stay at this old-fashioned hotel which is partially built on stilts over the sea – it's rather like being on a cruise. A large sandy seashore is good for swimming and wind-sailing. A long flat promenade and some excellent fresh fish restaurants are nearby.

#### Garachico
**San Roque**
Esteban de Ponte 32.
Tel: 922 13 34 35
Fax: 922 13 34 06.
This gorgeous little hotel is family-run and entirely unstuffy, yet finds its way into lists of some of the best hotels in the world. In a lovely historic house in Garachico's old quarter, it has been beautifully restored. Stylish but relaxing, each bedroom is a delight.

#### Los Cristianos
**Estefania**
Crta de Arona (2km), Chayofa.
Tel: 922 75 13 22
Fax: 922 75 15 93.

A peaceful bolt-hole in colourful gardens, high in the hills above Los Cristianos, with cool, stylish décor and Mediterranean architecture. Italianate furniture, ceramics and exquisite white sofas deck public areas and bedrooms. The palm-shaded pool terrace offers superb views.
**Hotel Princess Dacil**
Calle Penetración s/n.
Tel: 922 79 08 00
Fax: 922 79 06 58.
One of the first of the high hotels to be built in the south, a number of regulars enjoy long stays during the winter. Always busy, yet it is at the quieter end of the development with a pleasant 10-minute seafront walk to the harbour.
**Apartments Tenerife-Sur**
Ctra Las Galletas s/n.
Tel: 922 79 14 74
Fax: 922 79 27 74.
These apartments comprise a twin-bedroom, lounge/dining room area with a kitchenette, bathroom and balcony or terrace – some have a sofa-bed to sleep two extra people. Large central pool and supermarket.

#### Los Gigantes
**Royal Sun Apartments**
Geranio 16.
Tel: 922 86 72 72
Fax: 922 86 72 48.
Lavishly equipped apartments high over the marina with superb views of the resort and the adjacent cliffs. Facilities include a nightclub, hairdresser, launderette and sports club; courtesy taxi service into the resort. Apartments have sound systems, circular baths and modern kitchens.

#### Playa de las Américas
**Jardín Tropical**
Gran Bretaña.
Tel: 922 74 60 00
Fax: 922 74 60 66.
One of the most beautiful and enjoyable hotels anywhere in the Canaries. Though right in the heart of Playa de las Américas, it feels amazingly secluded in its delightfully landscaped gardens. Moorish arches, domes and turrets create an eyecatching fantasy

skyline, while inside, elegant furnishings ramble through an endless series of wings and spaces. Several excellent restaurants and a waterfront beach-club.

### Puerto de la Cruz
**Hotel Melia Botánico**
Calle Richard J Yeoward.
Tel: 922 38 15 00
Fax: 922 38 15 04.
Recently refurbished, this long established plush hotel with glistening chandeliers is in a quiet position on a hill above the town. Close to the famous Botanical Gardens. Conference rooms, Olympic-size swimming pool and evening entertainments.

### Santa Cruz
**Hotel Mencey**
Avda Dr. José Naveiras 38.
Tel: 922 27 67 00
Fax: 922 28 00 17.
Legendary elegant old building frequented by kings and queens, the rich and famous. In a tranquil part of the city. Beautifully appointed, 286 bedrooms and suites. First-class cuisine. Conference and banqueting rooms. Tennis, sauna and swimming pool, plus tropical gardens.

### Moderate
### Güímar
**Finca Salamanca**
Crta Güímar, El Puertito Km 1.5.
Tel: 922 51 45 30
Fax: 922 51 40 61.
Skilfully converted from an old avocado farm, this rural haven offers smart, imaginative accommodation and an excellent Canarian restaurant within easy reach of the Pyramids of Güímar. Mexican hardwood furniture, rustic pottery and contemporary fabrics fit surprisingly well into the traditional surroundings.

### Playa de las Américas
**Hotel La Siesta**
Avenida Marítima.
Tel: 922 79 22 52
Fax: 922 79 22 20.
This is a well-run hotel with friendly staff. All rooms have air conditioning, spacious terraces and satellite TV. Three swimming pools, sports, music and shows. Easy level walk to the beach and shops.
**Apartments Parque Santiago IV**
Avenida Litoral s/n.
Tel: 922 75 28 26
Fax: 922 79 30 60.
Large complex of well-furnished apartments within an easy flat walk of the promenade and beach. Huge choice of shops, bars and restaurants at hand.

### Los Gigantes/Puerto de Santiago
**Aparthotel Tamaimo Tropical**
Hondura, Puerto de Santiago.
Tel: 922 86 06 38
Fax: 922 86 07 61.
An attractive apartment complex with good facilities in local style. Public areas are colourful and comfortable, and apartments are light and fresh with well-equipped kitchens and decent bathrooms. Large pool terraces; shops and restaurants within walking distance.

### Puerto de la Cruz
**Apartments Pez Azul**
Ctra Botanico.
Tel: 922 38 59 49
Fax: 922 38 59 80.
These 135 apartments on four floors (two lifts) are above the town. Maid service. Large pool with adjoining solarium, snack bar and restaurant. Easy walk to local shops, bars and restaurants.
**Hotel Marquesa**
Calle Quintana 11.
Tel: 922 38 31 51
Fax: 922 38 69 50.
Built in 1712 and carefully refurbished in 1984, this 91-room hotel is full of old-world charm, potted plants and courteous service. The busy restaurant has an outside terrace where you can dine by candlelight and watch the world stroll past.
**Hotel Monopol**
Quintana 15.
Tel: 922 38 46 11
Fax: 922 37 03 10.
Situated in the centre of Puerto, this is a small family-run hotel in a typically Canarian building, with attractive carved wooden balconies and a beautiful indoor lounge. Sun terrace and bar by small swimming pool. Two-minute walk to seafront and shops.
**Hotel Tigaiga**
Parque Taoro, 28.
Tel: 922 38 35 00
Fax: 922 38 40 55.
Long established as one of the finest hotels in Puerto, the Tigaiga occupies a prime position with views of Teide and overlooking the town. It is noted for courteous service and the exotic palm tree garden where folk dancing and *lucha canaria* (Canarian wrestling) exhibitions are held.
**San Telmo**
Paseo San Telmo 18.
Tel: 922 38 58 53
Fax: 922 38 58 99.
Located on the pedestrianised seafront in the centre of the resort, this little place enjoys excellent views of the rocky coast and lido, especially from its open-plan bar-lounge upstairs. Decor is cosy and welcoming, with wood panelling and floral chintzes. Bedrooms are simple but clean and light with good bathrooms.

### Pico del Teide
**Parador Nacional Cañadas del Teide**
Las Cañadas del Teide.
Tel: 922 38 64 15
Fax: 922 38 23 52.
Central reservations: tel: (34) 915 16 66 66; fax: (34) 915 16 66 57.
This state-run hotel, now enlarged and refurbished, has a superb location close to the summit of Teide. A place to enjoy the peak, which is seen at its best at dawn or in the pink evening glow, after the tourist coaches have departed. Enjoy the Canarian menu and a blazing log fire.

### Santa Cruz
**Contemporaneo**
Rambla General Franco 116.
Tel: 922 27 15 71
Fax: 922 27 12 23.
This attractively designed modern business hotel stands near a quiet park, with easy access to central

shops and sights. Less expensive than the luxury Mencey immediately opposite, it is stylish and comfortable inside with a bright bar-café and restaurant downstairs.

### Inexpensive
#### Los Cristianos
**Hotel Andreas**
Calle General Franco 26.
Tel: 922 79 00 12
Fax: 922 79 42 70.
Close to the town hall and shopping area, this 42-room commercial hotel makes a good base for short-stay holidays. Meals are taken in the public restaurant or pizzeria. Nearby are taxis, buses and the tourist office.
**Pension Corisa**
Edificio Andreas.
Tel: 922 79 07 92 (no fax).
Small simple pension in same block as the Hotel Andreas. Five-minute walk to the beach and harbour going past shops, bars and restaurants.

#### Puerto de la Cruz
**Hotel Tejuma**
Perez Zamora 5.
Tel: 922 38 36 13 (no fax).
Small and clean. Situated towards the west of Puerto, on a road leading downhill to the seafront. A ten-minute walk to the town centre.

#### Santa Cruz
**Hotel Horizonte**
Santa Rosa de Lima 11.
Tel: 922 27 19 36 (no fax).
A small friendly Canarian commercial hotel with 55 rooms. Close to shops and restaurants. Useful for business or short stays to see the capital, which has a large old-fashioned park and interesting museums.

## LA GOMERA

### Expensive
#### Playa de Santiago
**Hotel Jardín Tecina**
Lomada de Tecina.
Tel: 922 14 58 50
Fax: 922 14 58 65.
Set among banana plantations and

overlooking a little fishing port where tuna fish are landed, this luxury hotel was built by the Fred Olsen shipping company. Three attractive swimming pools, bar, lounge, music, dancing and live entertainments. Children are welcome.

### Price Categories

Double room per night:
| | |
|---|---|
| **Expensive** | more than £100 |
| **Moderate** | £50–100 |
| **Inexpensive** | under £50 |

#### San Sebastián
**Parador de Gomera**
San Sebastián.
Tel: 922 87 11 00
Fax: 922 87 11 16.
Central reservations: tel: (34) 915 16 66 66; fax: (34) 915 16 66 57.
On a headland looking out to sea and the Pico del Teide, this state-run hotel has a quietly nautical decor due to the island's association with Christopher Columbus. The outdoor swimming pool is sunken and surrounded by gardens with tall palms. A place to relax and rest.

### Moderate
#### Playa de Santiago
**Apartments Tapahuga**
Avda Marítima.
Tel/fax: 922 89 51 59.
Canary-style decor with attractive wooden balconies and potted palms gives a welcome feeling to these nice modern apartments by the harbour. Small pool and sun terrace on the roof. Supermarket next door.

#### Valle Gran Rey
**Hotel Gran Rey**
Calle La Punta.
Tel: 922 00 34 22
Fax: 922 80 56 51.
The first hotel to be built beside the sea at this, until recently, undeveloped tropical valley. Now tourism is catching up with it and turning it into a beach resort. Come here to enjoy fresh fish and Canarian cuisine in the rather expensive La Pareda restaurant.

### Inexpensive
#### Hermigua
**Ibo Alfaro**
38820 Hermigua.
Tel: 922 88 01 68
Fax: 922 88 10 19.
A small, friendly, rural haven, which is an excellent walking base. A former manor house, this little building has been cheerfully and elegantly renovated in local materials. All the bedrooms are simple, but pretty and personal, named after local flowers. Popular with German walking parties, but takes a mix of independent travellers.

#### San Sebastián
**Hotel Garajonay**
Calle Ruiz de Padron 17.
Tel/fax: 922 87 05 50.
In the centre of town, quiet, clean and plain with comfortable beds. Restaurants, bars and shops nearby. Easy walk to the port.
**Hotel Villa Gomera**
Calle Ruiz de Padrón 68.
Tel: 922 87 00 20
Fax: 922 87 02 35.
In a central position, this hotel offers 16 unsophisticated clean rooms in one of the town's main streets. No dining room.

#### Vallehermoso
**Hotel de Triana**
Triana s/n.
Tel: 922 80 05 28
Fax: 922 80 01 28.
A surprisingly chic new venture in an old house at the back of a small inland village. With stripy wicker and exposed stonework, it is cool, bright and airy. The stylish modern bedrooms have kitchen facilities. A little restaurant offers evening meals.

## LA PALMA

### Expensive
#### Brena Baja
**Parador de le Palma**
El Zumacal.
Tel: 922 43 58 28
Fax: 922 43 59 99.
Central reservations tel: (34) 915

16 66 66; fax: (34) 915 16 66 57.
In a fine coastal position this new
65-bed *parador* is built in Canarian
style with well-stocked gardens
surrounding a swimming pool.

## Price Categories

Double room per night:
**Expensive**    more than £100
**Moderate**    £50–100
**Inexpensive**    under £50

### Los Llanos de Aridane
**Hotel Sol Elite La Palma**
Puerto Naos.
Tel: 922 40 80 00
Fax: 922 40 80 14.
Large modern hotel with comfortable
rooms suitable for a family holiday, it
lies beside a black sand beach.
Plenty of hotel entertainments.
Coach excursions are arranged.

### Moderate
*Barlovento*
**Hotel La Palma Romántica**
Topo de las Llanadas.
Tel: 922 18 62 21
Fax: 922 18 54 00.
A hideaway honeymoon hotel, also
suitable for anyone interested in
using the small astronomical
observatory and a modern
gymnasium. Built as a traditional
Canarian *casa*, it has wood floors
and pine balconies. Take a light
sweater as the mists come down
quickly.

### Brena Baja
**Apartments Costa Salinas**
Playa de los Cancajos.
Tel: 922 43 43 48
Fax: 922 43 45 10.
Close to a black sand beach and 15
minutes' drive to the capital.
Modern comfortable flats with maid
service, rental TV. Restaurant has
buffet service.

### Los Concajos
**Hacienda San Jorge**
Playa de los Cancajos 22.
Tel: 922 18 10 66
Fax: 922 43 45 28.
An attractive apartment complex in
local style amid large, colourful

gardens. Facilities are very good,
with a health and fitness centre and
a useful on-site supermarket. The
boldly refurbished apartments feel
quiet and peaceful. The main
restaurant overlooks the beach just
beyond the gardens.
**Tabiente Playa**
Playa de los Cancajos.
Tel: 922 18 12 77
Fax: 922 18 12 85.
Under the same management as the
Costa Salinas apartments, this
large seaside hotel is unexpectedly
comfortable and imaginative inside,
with plants festooning the foyer, and
murals and goldfish ponds.
Bedrooms are tastefully furnished in
green-stained wood with matching
fabrics. Spacious pool terraces.

### Inexpensive
*Santa Cruz de la Palma*
**Apartamentos La Fuente**
A Perez de Brito 49.
Tel: 922 41 56 36
Fax: 922 41 23 03.
A series of simple apartments
scattered throughout the old town
in a number of older houses. They
vary in style and size, but have
been thoughtfully renovated to a
good standard by a resident
German owner, and feel spacious,
clean and full of charm. In the heart
of a charming Canarian town near
shops and restaurants.
**Pension Canarias**
Calle Cabrera Pinto 27.
Tel: 922 38 70 00 (no fax).
In a quiet narrow, winding back
street of the capital, with 16 rooms.
Approved by the tourist office.

### Los Llanos de Aridane
**Hotel Valle de Aridane**
Glorieta Castillo Olivares 3.
Tel/fax: 922 46 26 00.
Typical Canarian hotel with cheerful
staff and good service. Near the
market and town centre.
Spectacular views of the mountains.
An ideal base for exploring.

---

## EL HIERRO

There are no expensive hotels on
the island.

### Moderate
*Valverde*
**Parador del Hierro**
Las Playas.
Tel: 922 55 80 36
Fax: 922 55 80 86.
Central reservations: tel: (34) 915
16 66 66; fax: (34) 915 16 66 57.
Set in almost total isolation
beneath a high volcanic backdrop,
this 50-bedroom hotel is the ideal
place for budding authors who want
solitude in comfortable
surroundings. Seafront swimming
pool with sun terraces and
gardens.

### Inexpensive
*Frontera*
**Hotel Ida Ines**
Del Hoya Belgara Alta.
Tel: 922 55 94 45
Fax: 922 55 60 88.
Attractive little hotel with modern
facilities and small rooftop
swimming pool. Magnificent views,
interesting walks, very peaceful.
**Hotel Punta Grande**
Las Puntas.
Tel: 922 55 90 81
Fax: 922 55 92 03.
Claims to be the smallest hotel in
the world, just four rooms (also
apartments nearby). With wild seas
around, it was originally a fort, then
a warehouse; now it has nautical
decor with old diving equipment in
the excellent restaurant – the fish is
really fresh.

---

*Valverde*
**Boomerang**
Dr Gost 1.
Tel: 922 55 02 00 (no fax).
This simple but sprucely kept place
on a quiet side-street in the town
centre makes a convenient touring
base. Bedrooms are clean and
spacious with rustic wooden
furnishings.
**Pension Cananas**
San Francisco 9.
Tel: 922 55 02 54 (no fax).
A friendly welcome awaits you but
little English is spoken. Pleasant
light rooms are sparkling clean. On
the capital's main street, with
simple bars, cafés and
supermarkets.

## Restinga

**Pension Kai Marino**
Puerto de la Restinga.
Tel: 922 55 94 45
Fax: 922 28 50 01.
By the small port, close to a tiny
black beach. Small bright rooms
with friendly staff and good food in
a simple bar/restaurant. Isolated
position on the island.

### Campgrounds

Tenerife and the Western Canary
Islands have only one official
campground, but the Tenerife
*Cabildo* (local government) is
planning 20 new sites.

Every year a trickle of stalwart
campers – either backpackers or
motor-caravanners (the terrain is
not suitable for towing caravans) –
make the journey from Europe and
elsewhere. Around the islands are a
number of unofficial places where
parking is tolerated, provided that
not too many congregate.

In the forests of Tenerife, La
Palma and El Hierro, basic camping
areas are provided by the
authorities. With drinking water,
cold showers, toilets and wood for
barbecues, they are often used by
school groups. Permission is
needed to stay in the forests (for
limited periods) and the tourist
offices can provide the latest
details about camping on the
islands.

**Camping Nauta**, Class 1
Cañada Blanca, Ctra 6225 (Km
1.5), Las Galletas, Tenerife.
Tel: 922 78 51 18
Fax: 922 79 50 16.
Geographically in the centre of
southern Tenerife amid banana
plantations; 15 minutes' drive to
the coast. On clear winter days
there is a glorious view of the
snowy peak of El Teide. Pitches are
level and terraced with electric
hook-ups. Modern shower blocks,
laundry, supermarket, swimming
pool, games and TV room plus
wooden chalets for hire.

# Where to Eat

### What to Eat

The Canary Islands, like other
popular tourist destinations, have
bowed to demand and now
international dishes can be found in
almost every café and restaurant,
but you can find local food if you
look. Tenerife in particular can
provide the widest of choices for
eating out, both in the kind of venue
and cuisine.

### Canarian Cuisine

For genuine Canarian cooking it is
best to hire a car and drive up to
one of the mountain villages. Even
if your Spanish is non-existent, a
smile and a gesture is usually
enough to get you into the kitchen,
where the cook will be delighted to
lift the lid off a huge cooking pot to
let you enjoy the aroma of a
delicous *conejo en salmorejo* (rabbit
in a spicy sauce).

Be sure to try the *papas
arrugadas*, little Canary potatoes
gently boiled in their skin in very
salty water (sea water can be used).
When cooked they have wrinkled
skins and should be eaten with
*mojo rojo* sauce, which is made
with crushed hot red peppers,
garlic, cumin and saffron – very
piquant. Another Canarian sauce,
traditionally served with fish, is
*mojo verde*, a mild creamy green
sauce with parsley and fresh
coriander.

The eating habits of the locals
differ from those of most visitors.
Canarians, like the Spanish, do not
eat large breakfasts but prefer to
have just a hot drink before going to
work. At around 9.30am they go to
the nearest bar or café to enjoy
*desayuno* (breakfast). This will

consist of tea or more likely coffee
and a *bocadillo* (sandwich) of
salami or cheese plus a *pastel*
(cake).

At about one o'clock it is time for
*tapas*, those tasty little snacks that
line the counter of many bars. This
is an excellent way to have a light
meal and try some unfamiliar
dishes.

The midday meal, *almuerzo*
(lunch), will be taken about 3
o'clock. Usually it will be a hearty
meal, possibly *sopa de pescado*
(fish soup) with *pan* (bread),
followed by *ensalada* (salad) and
maybe a *chuleta a la brasa* (char-
grilled chop), and finally a *tarta de
almendras* (almond tart). It is
always a leisurely meal.

In the evenings, German tourists
are often the first to arrive in the
restaurants, followed by the Brits
and then other tourists. At about 9
o'clock, the Canarians appear full of
chatter after having *aperitivos* –
because like all Spaniards they eat
late. *Pescado* (fish) is the most
popular food among the locals.
Once *cabra* (goat) roamed the
hillsides, but now it is hard to find
succulent *cabrito asado* (roast kid).

A great deal of fish is still caught
off the coast of the Canaries and in
the nearby waters off West Africa.
All the town markets include stalls
of fresh and frozen fish – go early to
get the best.

*Mero*, *cherne* and *abade* are all
Spanish names for sea bass, *sama*
and *sargo* are fleshy sea bream,
and *atun* and *bonito* are types of
tuna. Probably the most popular
fish is *lenguado* (sole) which is
found on most menus. Seafood
enthusiasts should look for
*calamares* (squid), *mejillones*
(mussels), *gambas* (shrimps) and
*langostinos* (huge and expensive
deep-sea prawns).

### Tips for Visitors

Most restaurants have printed
menus outside in several
languages, plus a national flag,
while at the resorts eating places
also have pictures showing various
dishes with the prices.

The *menu del día* (menu of the day) is often an easy way of ordering a meal. It will consist of a starter, main dish and probably the national favourite pudding: a flan (caramel pudding). These days you may have to pay for the bread rolls and butter.

It is helpful when ordering to ask for the dish by pointing at the number on the menu – if you try to use your halting Spanish the waiter will probably insist on answering you in near perfect English, even if it is with a Liverpudlian accent!

## Where to Eat

### IN THE RESORTS

The local papers have advertisements and lists of restaurants, while in the streets, hand-outs touting for custom will give an idea of what to expect. Another source of information is the holiday company representative at your hotel, who will have first-hand reports from other clients. Whatever your tastes, Tenerife can provide for them – be it full English breakfast, roast Sunday dinners with Yorkshire pudding, bangers and mash or fish and chips – even Kentucky Fried Chicken, Pizza Hut and McDonald's, if you must.

European and Asian restaurants abound, top of the list (after Spanish) being Chinese, followed by Indian, Italian, German, French, Scandinavian, Thai, Korean, and Mexican. Popular with the Canarians are Venezuelan restaurants – try their freshly prepared *arepas*, savoury South American pancakes.

Every Canarian town and village has a bar or two and practically all will be able to produce food, so one never needs to go hungry. In the capital Santa Cruz, the bars and restaurants cater mainly for the islanders and the atmosphere is more restrained than on the seafronts of Puerto de la Cruz, Los Cristianos and Playa de las Américas. Santocruceros like to be neat and tidy and tend to be rather formal when visiting restaurants.

## EATING AROUND TENERIFE

At the weekends Canarians like to relax and enjoy large family picnics in the forests or go to the *playas* (beaches) for late fish lunches.

Other popular places are in the north of Tenerife, around La Esperanza and Agua Garcia, and along the C-820 old road, which runs parallel with the Autopista del Norte. Between La Laguna, Tacaronte and El Sauzal are some more good restaurants with high-class menus, serving good-quality meats and fresh fish. They are always very busy at weekends, so it is wise to book a table.

In the south, with so many five-star hotels, there is no lack of sophisticated venues where the ambience is smart and the wine list requires a decent bank balance.

Los Abrigos, close to the airport, is famous for its fish restaurants. Go on a warm starlit night to sit at a table overlooking the lapping waves – very romantic. If you wish to dance after your meal then make for Playa de las Américas and the **Banana Garden** restaurant (tel: 922 790365), next to the Troya Hotel – you can stay there until late. At Los Cristianos you will see Chinese lanterns on many streets, lighting up the entrances to Chinese restaurants. Vegetarians will find they are not neglected and the ubiquitous pizza can be enjoyed at places such as **Pasta a Go-Go** at Puerto Colón and **Little Italy** in Los Cristianos.

The list of eating houses below, while by no means exhaustive, offers a sampling of the various types of food available.

## TENERIFE

### Expensive
### *Cabo Blanco*
**San Martin**
Calle la Iglesia.
Tel: 922 72 01 70.
Friendly, informal restaurant, specialising in roast suckling pig,

leg of lamb, grilled chicken. Folk dancing on Wednesday. Reservations.

### *El Medano*
**Avencio**
Chasna 6
Tel: 922 17 60 79.
Splendid typical fresh fish restaurant near the seafront. Always busy but no table reservations taken. Closed Monday.

### *Playa de las Américas*
**Mamma Rosa**
Aptos, Colón II.
Tel: 922 79 48 19.
Smart decor, well-dressed clientele. International menu includes fresh pasta, vegetarian meals, steaks. Large wine list. Reservations.
**Restaurant Las Rocas**
Hotel Jardin Tropical, Gran Bretana.
Tel: 922 74 60 64
Glorious wave-side location. A pricy but elegant place for seafood at sunset. Best to book ahead for a terrace table.

### *Puerto de la Cruz*
**La Parilla**
Hotel Botánico, Avda. Richard Yeoward.
Tel: 922 38 15 00.
An international restaurant with an extensive menu and wine list. There are also Thai and Italian restaurants in the same five-star hotel. Smart clothes requested.

### *Rural Restaurants*
**Clarets**
Chayofa (5 minutes north of Los Cristianos).
Tel: 922 79 49 80.
Attractive rural restaurant, open for light lunches and afternoon teas. Dinner from 6pm (closed Wednesday). Extensive *à la carte* selection. Dinner dances on Sunday.
**Los Limoneros**
Los Naranjeros (near Los Rodeos airport).
Tel: 922 63 66 37.
Well-established, high-class, beautifully appointed restaurant with attentive service. Canarian and international cuisine. Busy at weekends. Reservations.

## Culinary Traditions

When the Guanches lived in caves they used clay pots to cook the meat of wild animals. Some of these pots can be seen in the Archaeological Museum in Santa Cruz. At the School of Craftmanship, Cerámico Molino, at Mazo in La Palma and in the village of Chipude in La Gomera, artisans are making replicas of the same clay pots – still without a potter's wheel or oven.

Another relic of the culinary past is *gofio*, a finely ground toasted wheat or maize which is still served in rural restaurants and sold in some supermarkets. Canarians sprinkle it on their food, put it in stews and use it to thicken soups. Deep in the forest of Garajonay, La Gomera, at La Laguna Grande, there is a little bar that serves delicious watercress soup, with a dish of *gofio* always on the table.

### Meson de Isora
Carretera 822 de Guía de Isora Km 95.
Tel: 922 85 04 50.
A large roadside restaurant and grill in Spanish style; specialities include fresh meats and Iberian cold cuts. International menu with a good wine list.

### Moderate
### *Los Cristianos*
**Rincón del Marinero**
Muelle.
Tel: 922 79 35 53.
Look for the boat outside. Well-established fresh fish menu in plain surroundings, always busy and service can be slow. Closed Monday.
**Overseas**
Apartment San Marino 11.
Tel: 922 79 20 13.
One of many pleasant Chinese restaurants in the area. Cheerful service. Takeaways available. Open daily 1pm–midnight.

### *Los Gigantes*
**Tamara**
Avda Maritima

Tel: 922 86 00 11
A relaxed, quiet place with a grandstand location above the resort. A mix of snacks, drinks and full meals, accompanied by piano music.

### *Playa de las Américas*
**Ambassadeur**
Calle Starco.
Tel: 922 75 16 65.
International menu including vegetarian dishes. Cocktail bar, live entertainment and dance floor. Open 6pm–3am. Kitchen closes at midnight. Closed Sunday.
**Molino Blanco**
Avda Austria 5, San Eugenio Alto.
Tel: 922 79 62 82
A popular tourist venue set back from the seafront near the *autopista* but still not far to walk from the centre. Recognisable by the white windmill feature outside. Romantic ambience – sit under orange trees with strumming violinists. Wide menu with some unusual dishes.

### *Puerto de la Cruz*
**Hotel Marquesa Terrace**
Quintana 1.
Tel: 922 38 31 51
The terrace of this charming old hotel is often the best place to enjoy the lively atmosphere and street entertainment near Puerto's church square. You can have just a beer, or a full meal here.

**Casa de Miranda**
Plaza de Europa.
Tel: 922 37 38 71
One of Puerto's finest old mansions, containing an informal tapas bar in rustic style and a more elegant and beautifully furnished upper dining room with balconies overlooking the street. Faultless service and excellent food.

### *Parque Nacional del Teide*
**Parador de Cañadas del Teide**
moderate bracket Tel: 922 38 64 15
Exceptional regional cooking in an attractive restaurant, or daytime snacks and drinks at a useful self-service café overlooking the Roques de Garcia. Views to die for.

### *Rural restaurants*
**Bodegón**
Hirache-Gara, Vera de Herques.
Tel: 922 85 10 25.
On a mountainside near Guía de Isora, a large friendly restaurant used by locals for wedding receptions. Specialises in roast rabbit in garlic, Argentine pork sauages and spit-roasted chicken. Closed Monday.
**La Baranda**
Casa del Vino, El Sauzal, (off Autopista del Norte Km 21).
Tel: 922 56 33 88 (Note: the restaurant has a different phone number from the Casa del Vino wine museum.)
Canarian cuisine. Nice views from the terrace. Open Tuesday–Saturday.

## Price Categories

Meal for two with house wine:
**Expensive**     over £40
**Moderate**     £25–40
**Inexpensive**  under £25

### Inexpensive
### *Los Cristianos*
**Don Armando**
San Telmo.
Tel: 922 79 61 45
An authentic, traditional *tapas* bar. The menu caters for tourists in several languages, but at least avoids picture food. An attractive terrace gives a fine vantage point over Playa de las Vistas.
**Papa Luigi's**
Avda Suecia 40.
Tel: 922 75 09 11
An easy-going Italian place in the heart of the old town, with cosy terracotta and gingham. Friendly service and popular favourites.
**Scampis**
Compostela Beach.
Tel: 922 75 32 32.
Traditional fish and chip shop and restaurant; also roast chicken, pies and sausages. Children's meals and take-away.

### *Playa de las Américas*
**Love India**
Centro Comercial California (1st floor).

Tel: 922 75 09 20.
With air conditioning. Indian tandoori specialists with special lunch menus, take-away service and free delivery. Open daily.

### *Puerto de la Cruz*
**Meson Los Gemelos**
Calle El Peñon 4.
Tel: 922 37 01 33.
Various *tapas*, fresh fish, shellfish and meats including goat and rabbit. Open daily from 9am–midnight.

## LA PALMA

**Moderate**
**Bruselas Tropical**
Avenida Maritima 55.
Tel: 922 41 20 33.
Canarian and international food, with sea views and a rooftop balcony.
**Chipi Chipi**
Los Alamos 42 (on the road between the Mirador la Concepción and Las Nieves).
Tel: 922 41 10 24.
Typical Canarian restaurant with a large garden terrace, specialising in barbecued fish and meats. Closed Wednesday.
**Llanovid**
Calle los Canarios, Fuencaliente.
Tel: 922 44 44 28.
Llanovid Bodegón, to which this restaurant is attached, is the

## Chicken Houses

Until recently the typical Canarian eating place comprised bare wooden tables in a garage beside a house or shop, with the menu (usually chicken) chalked upon the wall. Meals were invariably tasty and reasonably priced.

Regretfully only a few "chicken houses" remain. Most of the garages have been painted and smartened up, the tables have red check cloths, and prices have risen as more and more tourists seek somewhere away from the busy seafronts.

island's major wine producer, so this is the ideal place to try local wines matched with appropriate Canarian dishes. Closed Monday.
**Playamont**
On the harbour side at Tazacorte.
Tel: 922 48 04 43.
Renowned fish restaurant which is equally well-regarded for its *papas arrugadas* ("wrinkly potatoes") with *mojo* sauce.

## Price Categories

Meal for two with house wine:
**Expensive**    over £40
**Moderate**    £25–40
**Inexpensive**    under £25

## LA GOMERA

**Expensive**
**Hotel Jardín Tecina**
Lomada de Tecina,
Playa de Santiago.
Tel: 922 14 58 50.
The restaurant at this luxury hotel (built by the Fred Olsen shipping company) is the place to go for a special night out, but you can also enjoy more modestly-priced food in the snack bar.
**Parador de Gomera**
Balcón de la Villa y Puerto,
San Sebastián.
Tel: 922 87 11 00.
Enjoy typical Gomeran cooking in the well-regarded restaurant of this fine hotel high above the town, with great views and relaxing gardens.

**Moderate**
**Casa del Mar**
Avenida Fred Olsen, San Sebastián
Tel: 922 87 12 19.
Port restaurant specialising in classic Gomeran fish stew, but with lots of other choices, from seafood to pasta and pizza.

**Inexpensive**
**El Silbo**
Hermigua
No telephone
Eat solidly and well, or just enjoy a drink at this bar/restaurant with great views and a lovely flower-filled terrace.

## EL HIERRO

**Moderate**
**Casa Juan**
Valverde
Tel: 922 55 80 02
Excellent seafood, guaranteed to be fresh from the water.
**Parador del Hierro**
Las Playas.
Tel: 922 55 80 36.
International and Canarian dishes in the comfort of the seaside *parador*.
**Punta Grande Hotel**
Las Puntas, Frontera.
Tel: 922 55 90 81.
Sample good local fish if you are visiting this pretty village.

## Drinking

Tenerife and the other islands have cheaper prices for alcoholic drinks than mainland Spain and the rest of the EU. It is usually wise to ask specifically for a brand name as the cheap Spanish alternatives may not be to your liking.

There is an incredible selection of spirits, but be warned that measures are triple or quadruple British measures. The *ron* (rum) is a white spirit made on Tenerife from sugar cane. It is consumed by the locals who often drink it with coffee. *Ron miel*, a dark liqueur, is a mixture of rum and honey – warming on a cool evening. Or you could try the unique sweet flavour of the banana liqueur *cobana*. This makes an unusual souvenir as it is sold in a bottle shaped like a bunch of bananas.

International makes of canned beers are now widely available, such as Skol, Worthington and even Guinness. The local lager "Dorada" comes on tap and in cans and is quite thirst-quenching. *Sangria* is a mixed drink often chosen by tourists. It is served in a big glass jug with lots of fruit and ice. Beware – this attractive-looking drink can be very alcoholic. More innocuous is *zumo*, which is freshly squeezed fruit juice. Try a mixture of *naranja* (orange), *limón* (lemon) and *melocotón* (peach).

## Bars and Cafés

Bars and their owners change more often than the British weather, so it is not really practical to recommend them. However, a few have stood the test of time.

### Bajamar
**Café Melita**
Carretera Gral. Punta del Hidalgo. Tel: 922 54 08 14.
In the northwest, overlooking the sea, this German café and cake shop was opened in 1968. Mouth-watering pastries and gateaux (including diabetic choices) make this a compulsory stopping place.

### Los Cristianos
**Desperate Dans**
Opposite Los Cristianos Market (near Hotel Arona Palace).
With harbour views and a friendly atmosphere. Enormous breakfasts and a full menu. Karaoke, quiz nights, satellite TV. Moderate prices

### Playa de las Américas
**Lineker's Bar**
Calle Starco 405.
Popular cheery bar with lots of drinks and football matches shown on TV. Food from 12 noon– 6pm. Good DJs until late. Moderate prices. Open 12 noon–3am.

## Canary Island Wine

*Vino* (wine) is produced on all the islands and is increasing in quantity and quality – so much so that it is also gaining awards on the continent.

It is worthwhile making a visit to La Baranda, near El Sauzal in the north of Tenerife, to the **Wine House Museum** (tel: 922 57 27 25). In a restored 17th-century farm-house, the history and tradition of wine production over the ages is fully explained.

Visitors have the opportunity to taste various wines and make purchases, then have a meal in the adjoining restaurant, Casa del Vino (*see Restaurants*).

### Puerto de la Cruz
**Casa Abaco**
Calle Casa Grande, El Durazno. Tel: 922 37 01 07.
Near the Botanical Gardens. Go for exotic cocktails in this romantic old mansion full of antique furniture. Rather expensive. Open 10.30am–1.30pm, then 3pm–5.30pm for folk shows and fruit drinks. Evenings 8pm–2am (closed Sun/Mon).

### Santa Cruz
**Bar Olimpo**
Plaza España. On the northwest corner of the plaza, upstairs on the first floor.
A good central meeting place, also a restaurant with an international menu at moderate prices.
**Oh La La**
Duque de Santa Elana. Seafont east of Plaza España.
Clean fast service, café food at reasonable prices.

# Culture

## Culture

### ART GALLERIES AND MUSEUMS

Tenerife has a large number of art galleries and museums with diverse collections of archaeological, ethnographical, historical and scientific exhibits – the major ones are detailed in the text of the Places section.

### MUSIC AND THEATRE

There are also a number of concert halls, and in Santa Cruz there is a well-supported opera season. Every year the **Teatro Guimera** here has a full programme of visiting performers with the Symphony Orchestra of Tenerife – one of the best in Spain – giving regular concerts.

La Laguna is the cultural capital of the island and has an **annual international theatre festival** and a **jazz festival**, which are always well attended.

### CINEMA

The Canarios are keen cinema-goers. However, foreign films are dubbed into Spanish, and there is presently no English cinema on the islands. Every November, Puerto de la Cruz has an **International Festival of Ecological Cinema**, when films associated with ecological or enviromental issues are shown and discussed.

# Nightlife

It is easy to fall into the relaxed lifestyle and leisurely pace of life in Tenerife, but if you would like a more varied holiday there is an eclectic nightlife characterised by laid-back attitudes and an ever-changing variety of venues and people.

The general adage of safety in numbers applies to Tenerife nightlife, where there is far less trouble than in many European resorts.

The throbbing hearts of Tenerife nightlife are in Puerto de la Cruz in the north and Playa de las Américas in the south, although Santa Cruz can attract party animals too, especially in summer when the *Carpas de Verano* – open-air discos – are worth a visit.

New venues come and go; the following does not pretend to be an exhaustive list, but simply mentions some of the venues that have kept their popularity for some time.

### Santa Cruz
Young people tend to start the night in Avenida Anaga on the harbour front of Santa Cruz. Disco bars here include **Nooctua** and **Noh**. Many stay open until the early hours. The other popular venues are **Ku**, which is very large, and **Nooctua** (parent of the Santa Cruz bar) on the Gumasa turning near Los Rodeos airport. The latter caters for all age groups and tastes, with different rooms for salsa, flamenco and dance, and various bars and cafés.

### Puerto de la Cruz
British families make for **Molly Malone** and **The Buccaneer** bars (near the harbour and Calle La Hoya respectively). The young locals head for **Pakalolo** (near Plaza del Charco), which is always very full and is famed for its German beer

and late-night *mett* – minced beef on rye bread. Alternatively, groups tend to congregate near the Lago Martiánez or La Paz and later go to **Brahms and Liszt** on Avenida Generalísimo or **El Coto Up and Down**, located under the Oro Negro apartments, next to the Melia San Felipe Hotel. To finish off the evening, try **Joy** on Avenida Generalísimo.

**Vampis** is a mixed club (gay and straight). It has a great devil-may-care atmosphere and is open until about 7am – NOT for the faint-hearted.

## PLAYA DE LAS AMÉRICAS

Here the lights are even brighter than elsewhere in Tenerife and every taxi driver will be happy to take you to the colourful area known simply as "Veronicas, in the centre of town." Veronicas is a disco centre which, along with the Starco Centre at the opposite side of the road, has around 100 bars and discos to choose from. Plenty of taxis are always available late at night, so returning home is no problem and your wallet will not suffer as much as your head.

Young and old alike frequent the karaoke pubs along the seafront, where competition for your custom ensures that every bar offers "happy hours" or reduced rates. It is not unusual to be enticed into places by attractive staff who will even get you a free drink (entrance fees are rarely charged). It is important to pace yourself, especially if you plan to last until dawn, as measures of spirits are far larger than in Northern Europe.

The first club to stop at in Playa de las Américas is **Soul Train** (under the famous Lineker's Bar, opposite Veronicas), which plays the best in soul, rythmn and blues and hip hop. Then move on to **Busbys** or **Bobbys** (both in Veronicas) for the latest in dance music. The **Kangaroo Bar**, situated practically on the beach, is also very impressive.

When these clubs finally close around 5.30–6am the party

continues well into the morning in **Paradise** (also in Veronicas) – only for those with lots of energy. At daylight there are plenty of places to meet, if you got parted from your companions, and to refuel. Then, after a quick daytime sleep, you are ready to do it all again – that's nightlife in Tenerife.

## Places to Visit at Night

**Castillo San Miguel**
Signposted off the *autopista* south at San Miguel
Tel: 922 70 02 76.
Medieval tournament in pseudo castle with much cheering while dining, then dancing and the Drifters Show. Good family entertainment. Every evening at 8pm.

**Isla del Largo Show**
Avenida Colón, Puerto de la Cruz.
Tel: 922 38 38 52.
International artistes and showgirls present fast-moving, slick, colourful and spectacular performances every evening. The restaurant opens at 8pm and the doors to the theatre at 9.45pm, with the show commencing at 10.30pm.

**Exit Palace**
San Eugenio, Playa de Las Américas.
Tel: 922 79 73 30.
Gala performances include Magic World, Gaucho Cowboys, Spanish ballet, plus singers and a live orchestra every evening. Restaurant opens 8pm. Show at 9.30pm.

## The Smaller Islands

There is nothing very exciting in the way of evening entertainment on the smaller islands of La Gomera, La Palma and El Hierro. They all have modest discos for the locals but otherwise only the few four-star hotels have entertainment. Some bars and restaurants do have background music and TV.

The best time to see local **folk dancing and singing** is when there is a fiesta or at carnival time in February.

# Attractions

**Jardín Botánico (Botanical Garden)**
Careterra del Botánico, La Paz,
Puerto de la Cruz.
Tel: 922 38 35 72.
Famous tropical gardens with large
fine collection of subtropical and
tropical trees and plants. Open daily
9am–6pm.
**Casa Iriarte**
Calle Iriarte/San Juan, Puerto de la
Cruz.
Birthplace of the author and poet
Thomas Iriarte y Nieves-Ravello. A
beautiful 18th-century building. Now
houses a naval museum upstairs,
with a souvenir shop below. Open
daily, hours vary
**Casa de los Balcones**
Calle San Francisco 3, La Orotava.
Tel: 922 33 06 29.
Well-preserved old house with fine
wood-carved balconies around a
pretty courtyard. Lace and hand-
embroidered table linen. Many
souvenirs. Open Mon–Fri
8.30am–7pm; Sat 8.30am–3pm.
**Parque San Roque**
Vilaflor (by Mirador).
Tel: 922 70 91 24.
Close to the highest village on
Tenerife, this Mexican *hacienda* and
*taberna* restaurant has a museum
depicting Guanche life with live

re-enactments. Mexican music and
splendid riding exhibitions.
**Tenerife Pearls**
A Member of the World Pearl
Organisation, located in the
southwest corner of Tenerife at
Armenime on the road to Los
Gigantes.
Tel: 922 74 12 50.
Watch beautiful pearl jewellery
being made and see if you are lucky
enough to find a real pearl in an
unopened oyster shell. The pearls
make beautiful lightweight gifts or
souvenirs to take home.
Refreshments are served in the
licensed tea house (open daily
9am–9pm).

## Animal Parks

**Loro Parque**
Calle Bencomo Punta Brava, Puerto
de la Cruz.
Tel: 922 37 38 41.
 Allow a full day. Enjoy the parrot
and dolphin shows (they perform
four times a day). See the huge
gorillas, lively penguins, magnificent
tigers, agile monkeys, colourful
flamingos and many other
creatures, all in a highly cultivated
tropical park. Free train ride from
Playa Martiánez to Loro Parque.
Daily 8.30am–5pm.
**Zoolandia**
On the northern *autopista* east of
Puerto de la Cruz.
Tel: 922 33 35 09.
Great fun for children at a well-kept
zoo. Pony rides and chimpanzee
show. Free bus from Playa
Martiánez. Daily 9am–6pm
**Octopus Aquapark**
Urbano San Eugenio Alto, Playa de

las Américas.
Tel: 922 71 52 66.
Water park with great slides that
will keep children happy all day. Sun
terraces and a restaurant. Take
sunhats, dark glasses and lots of
barrier cream, and drink plenty of
fluids. Free bus from Playa de las
Américas and Los Cristianos. Daily
10am–6pm.
**Parque Ecologico Aguilas del
Teide**, 3 km along the Los
Cristianos–Arona road.
Tel: 922 75 30 01.
Large tropical gardens, home to a
huge array of birds of prey, including
condors and eagles. Daily and
nightly shows in the five
amphitheatres. Watch the penguins
and crocodiles being fed. Free bus
from Playa de las Américas and Los
Cristianos.
**Camel Park**
Autopista (South) exit 27, La
Camela.
Tel: 922 72 10 80
Fax: 922 72 11 21.
On a Canarian farm with friendly
animals. Camel rides and a
breeding centre. Local cultivation
and handicrafts. Typical wines and
produce are for sale. Free bus from
Playa de las Américas and Los
Cristianos. Daily 10am–5pm.

## Attractions for Children

Children of all ages are well
catered for on Tenerife with plenty
of things to see and do.
    The **beaches** are a prime
attraction. For many young
children a bucket and spade for
building sandcastles still reigns
supreme. Do not be put off by the
black sand – it brushes off as
easily as the golden stuff.

    A number of hotels have
**children's clubs** geared for
different age groups, where
trained staff entertain the
youngsters during part of the day
– giving parents time for relaxation.
    **Animal parks** are always
popular: *see the listings in this
section.*

# Sport

Tenerife has plenty to offer in the way of sports and outdoor activities. The islands of La Gomera, La Palma and El Hierro have some excellent walking regions, with a limited amount of swimming, diving and fishing.

## Diving

There are a number of diving schools, mainly in the south of the islands, where experienced divers and beginners will get qualified instruction. The waters around the islands are warm all year and the archipelago has interesting volcanic rock formations with coral reefs, wrecks and much marine life, which make sub-aqua diving and snorkelling fascinating pastimes.

## Diving Schools

**Asociación de Centros de Buceo de Tenerife**, Ten-Bel Hotelpark, Las Galletas. Tel/fax: 922 73 09 81.
**Park Club Europe**, Playa de las Américas. Tel: 922 75 27 08.
**Atlantik**, Hotel Maritím, Los Realejos, Puerto de la Cruz. Tel: 922 34 45 01; fax: 922 37 90 37.
**San Borondon**, La Marina 10, Playa San Juan. Tel/fax: 922 86 56 14.

## Fishing

This is a regular pastime of Canarians and for some it is an important way of life. Tourist areas have rocks and jetties suitable for rod and line fishing, and local shops have plenty of tackle. Deep sea fishing is becoming an increasingly popular sport, with smart boats in the new marina. It is an expensive and very exciting hobby, with the fast boats capable of chasing huge marlin, tuna, shark and swordfish. Hotels and newspapers advertise details of charter fishing trips.

### Sports Fishing Boat Hire
**Golden Marlin SL**, Puerto Colón.
Tel: 922 60 20 40
Fax: 922 76 54 71.
**Nauti Sport**, Puerto Los Cristianos.
Tel: 922 79 14 59
Fax: 922 79 36 71.

## Flying

At Los Rodeos airport there is an Aero Club where light aircraft can be hired. It is very busy at weekends. Tel: 922 25 79 40.

## Go-Karting

Hotel receptions and travel agents will have the latest details of free bus services to these venues.
**Karting Club Tenerife**, Arona.
Tel: 922 78 66 20.
**Karting Club**, Las Américas, Adeje.
Tel: 922 71 00 96.
**Karting Club**, La Esperanza.
Tel: 922 25 70 38.

## Horse Riding

Probably because of the rough terrain, there are few riding centres. In the south there is the **Amarilla Golf Riding Centre**, San Miguel de Abona (off the motorway at exit 24, follow signs for Amarilla Golf). Tel: 922 78 75 77. Beach rides and mountain treks.

## Mountain Biking

Hire of bikes and excursions are arranged from the Hotel Tigaiga, Puerto de la Cruz. Tel: 922 38 35 00. Bikes can also be hired from Alquiler in Puerto de la Cruz, tel: 922 38 29 17.

## Swimming

The sea temperature is never very cold so bathing is possible all year round. Several man-made beaches have been created with breakwaters which make for safer swimming. But sometimes the currents and roller waves can be very strong with a dangerous undertow. Watch for the red flag warning that it is not safe to swim.

## Tennis

Many of the larger hotels have tennis courts that can be hired by the public. Some are floodlit at night.
**Tenisur**, San Eugenio, Las Américas (next to Octopus Aquapark).
Tel: 922 79 61 67.
A large sports centre that has three courts and a tennis teacher. Equipment can be hired, tournaments are held every Wednesday.

## Walking

Excellent walks can be enjoyed in the mountains or inland in the forests and along the coasts of all the islands. However, the terrain can be very rough and the weather variable, so caution is required. A

## Golf is Big Business

● Golf is very much on the increase in Tenerife, and is popular with both Canarians and visitors.
● Not only are new golf courses being planned, but they include large developments of apartments and adjacent supermarkets, shops, bars and restaurants.
● Three of the golf courses on the island are of championship standard:
**Club de Golf el Peñón**, Tacoronte (off northern motorway, exit Gumasa). Tel: 922 25 02 40. Non-members welcome weekdays between 9am and 1pm. 18 holes.
**Golf del Sur**, San Miguel de Abona (off motoway south at Los Abrigos exit). Tel: 922 73 10 70. 27 holes.
**Golf Club Amarilla**, San Miguel de Abona. Tel: 922 78 57 77. 18 holes.

good map plus the right equipment is necessary. Also it is sensible, if walking alone, to inform someone of your intended route and expected time of return. Tourist offices have pamphlets giving details of the walks; some guided walks are available in El Teide National Park. There is no charge for these, but reservations are needed. For information, tel: 922 25 64 40 or 922 25 99 03. Maps and walking books can be bought in the resort shops.

If you want to arm yourself with walking guides in advance of your visit, Noel Rochford's *Sunflower Guide to Tenerife* is the best guide to the island, with clear maps and reliable public transport details. It is one of a series of guides that cover all the Canary Islands: full details can be found on the Sunflower Guide website: www.sunflowerbooks.co.uk. Lots of tour companies offer guided walks in Tenerife, including Canarias Trekking, tel: 922 20 10 51.

## Waterskiing

Waterski schools are mainly in the south where the seas are calmer. Tuition for beginners is advertised in local papers and hotels. Details from: **Heiko Mehn**, Barco *Crazy Girl*, Puerto Colón. Tel: 922 79 39 11.

## Whale Watching

These days the number of whale-watching boats licensed to take tourists out is strictly limited. The habitat of the pilot whales and dolphins is off the Los Gigantes/Los Cristianos coastline. Details from: **Nostramo Whalewatch Cruise**, tel: 922 75 00 85.

## Windsurfing

Championship competions are held regularly at Playa de la Médano, creating both a participant and a spectator sport. Details from: **Sunwind**, Avenida Islas Canarias, El Médano. Tel/fax: 922 17 61 74.

# Shopping

In the tourist resorts many souvenir shops and larger supermarkets are open 9am–8pm without a break, but in Santa Cruz, La Laguna and the inland towns and villages, shops close from 1–4pm then re-open until about 7.30pm. English is understood in the resorts and at the sites of major attractions, but a Spanish/English dictionary may be useful elsewhere.

Although there are many signs proclaiming "Duty Free Shopping", things are not as cheap as might be expected, due to the 4 percent value added tax (Impuesto General Islas Canarias, or IGIC). Tax is not always included in the figure on the price tag. Watch out for fake watches, cameras, hi-fi and electrical goods, and also counterfeit perfumes sold by street traders.

Good buys include handmade lace tablecloths and napkins, local dressed dolls and articles made from palm or banana leaves. Colourful pottery imported from Spain and local ornaments and cookware – although fragile – make lovely souvenirs. Alcoholic drinks, tobacco, cigarettes and perfume can be cheaper than in the UK.

## Tourist Markets

Outdoor markets selling clothing, jewellery, handicrafts, leatherwork and African goods are colourful places to visit. They are always busy, so care must be taken to avoid pickpockets. Most markets open 9am–1.30pm (enquiries, tel: 922 75 36 81).

In Santa Cruz, the long-running **Rastillo** (Flea Market) is held along Avenida de Anaga, by the port. In the south of the island, there is a market at **Plaza del Lano**, Alcala

(near Los Gigantes) on Monday, one at **Torviscas**, Playa de las Américas, on Thursday and Saturday, and another next to the **Arona Grand Hotel**, Los Cristianos, on Sunday.

## Music and Videos

Canarians love to make music and the local bands make commercial recordings, especially at carnival time when tapes are sold to benefit various charities. Music shops are plentiful and stock a broad selection including latest chart hits.

Video shops are now quite numerous even in the villages. In the tourist resorts there is a wide selection of English videos, both for sale and hire.

## Exports

Unless you are a Spanish resident wishing to take goods to mainland Spain, there are no restrictions on exports from the Canary Islands. There will, however, be restrictions on imports into your country of origin. You are entitled to import fewer duty-free items into your own country from the Canaries than from mainland Spain and other EU countries, because in the Canaries VAT is not prepaid. No one is allowed to export more than 500,000 pesetas from the Canaries without declaring it.

## Duty Free

The Canary Islands are not considered full members of the EU. This affects the Duty Free Allowance which is (for people aged 17 and over):

● **Alcohol** Over 38.8 proof: 1 litre; or under 38.8 proof: 2 litres; or fortified or sparkling wine: 2 litres; plus still table wine: 2 litres.
● **Tobacco** 200 cigarettes or 100 cigarillos or 50 cigars or 250gm tobacco.
● **Perfume** 60cc or 250cc toilet water.
● **Gifts** Up to the value of £145 sterling.

# Language

Spanish (or Castilian) is the national language of the Canary Islands, but there are some regional differences, as well as a distinctive accent. There are similarities with the Spanish spoken in many parts of South America, probably due to the the islands' important past role in trade with the New World.

For example, *patatas* are always called *papas*; and the islanders never use the expression *Vosotros*, the plural form for "you", but always say *Ustedes*, an idiom which the peninsular Spanish use only for addressing strangers. Canarios don't lisp the letter "z" as mainland Spaniards do, but but pronounce it as an "s", like their South American cousins.

Other expressions derive from British influence on the islands: *naife* is a Canarian knife, *chóni*, a foreigner, comes from the English "Johnny" and a *queque* is a cake. There are oddities, too: *baifo*, the word for a goat kid is said to come from the ancient Guanche language.

Spanish – like French, Italian and Portuguese – is a Romance language, derived from the Latin spoken by the Romans who conquered the Iberian peninsula more than 2,000 years ago. The Moors who settled in the peninsula centuries later contributed a great number of new words (*see panel*). Following the discovery of America, Spaniards took their language with them to the four corners of the globe. Today, Spanish is spoken by 250 million people in north, south and central America and parts of Africa.

In addition to Spanish, which is spoken throughout the country, some regions have a second language. Catalan (spoken in Catalonia), Valenciano (Valencia), Mallorquín (the Balearics) and Gallego (Galicia) are all Romance languages, unlike Euskera, the language of the Basques, which is notoriously complex and difficult – it is unrelated to any other European tongue, and experts are not even sure what its origins are.

Unlike English, Spanish is a phonetic language: words are pronounced exactly as they are spelt, which is why it is somewhat harder for Spaniards to learn English than vice versa (although Spanish distinguishes between the two genders, masculine and feminine, and the subjunctive verb form is an endless source of headaches for students). The English language is one of Britain's biggest exports to Spain. Spaniards spend millions on learning aids, language academies and sending their children to study English in the UK or Ireland, and are eager to practise their linguistic skills with foreign visitors. Even so, they will be flattered and delighted if you make the effort to communicate in Spanish.

## The Alphabet

Learning the pronunciation of the Spanish alphabet is a good idea. In particular, learn how to spell out your own name. Spanish has a letter that doesn't exist in English, the ñ (pronounced "*ny*"). **a** = *ah*, **b** = *bay*, **c** = *thay* (strong th as in "thought"), **ch** = *chay*, **d** = *day*, **e** = *ay*, **f** = *effay*, **g** = *hay*, **h** = *ah-chay*, **i** = *ee*, **j** = *hotah*, **k** = *kah*, **l** = *ellay*, **ll** = *ell-yay*, **m** = *emmay*, **n** = *ennay*, **ñ** = *enyay*, **o** = *oh*, **p** = *pay*, **q** = *koo*, **r** = *erray*, **s** = *essay*, **t** = *tay*, **u** = *oo*, **v** = *oovay*, **w** = *oovay doe-blay*, **x** = *ek-kiss*, **y** = *ee gree-ay-gah*, **z** = *thay-tah*

## Basic Rules

English is widely spoken in most tourist areas throughout the Canary Islands, but even if you can speak no Spanish at all, it is worth trying to master a few simple words and phrases. The local people are sure to appreciate you using them, and you will probably get a lot of satisfaction out of it as well.

As a general rule, the accent falls on the second-to-last syllable, unless it is otherwise marked with an accent (´) or the word ends in D, L, R or Z.

Vowels in Spanish are always pronounced the same way. The double LL is pronounced like the y in "yes", the double RR is rolled, as in Scots. The H is silent in Spanish, whereas J (and G when it precedes an E or I) is pronounced like a guttural H (as if you were clearing your throat).

## Moorish Connections

The Moors arrived in Spain in 711, and occupied parts of the peninsula for the next eight centuries. They left behind hundreds of Arabic words, many related to farming and crops, as well as place names including those of towns (often identified by the prefix Al-, meaning "the" or Ben-, meaning "son of") and rivers (the prefix Guad- means "river"). Some of these Arabic words passed on to other languages, including French, and from there into English.

Among those present in both Spanish and English are:

sugar (*azúcar*), coffee (*café*), apricot (*albaricoque*), saffron (*azafrán*), lemon (*limón*), cotton (*algodón*), alcohol (*alcohol*), karat (*kilate*), cipher (*cifra*), elixir (*elixir*), almanac (*almanaque*), zenith (*cenit*), and zero (*cero*).

## Words & Phrases

**Hello** *Hola*
**How are you?** *¿Cómo está usted?*
**How much is it?** *¿Cuánto es?*
**What is your name?** *¿Cómo se llama usted?*

My name is... *Yo me llamo...*
Do you speak English? *¿Habla inglés?*
I am British/American *Yo soy británico/norteamericano*
I don't understand *No comprendo*
Please speak more slowly *Hable más despacio, por favor*
Can you help me? *¿Me puede ayudar?*
I am looking for... *Estoy buscando*
Where is...? *¿Dónde está...?*
I'm sorry *Lo siento*
I don't know *No lo se*
No problem *No hay problema*
Have a good day *Que tenga un buen día, or Vaya con Diós*
That's it *Ese es*
Here it is *Aquí está*
There it is *Allí está*
Let's go *Vámonos*
See you tomorrow *Hasta mañana*
See you soon *Hasta pronto*
Show me the word in the book *Muéstreme la palabra en el libro*
At what time? *¿A qué hora?*
When? *¿Cuándo?*
What time is it? *¿Qué hora es?*
yes *sí*
no *no*
please *por favor*
thank you (very much) *(muchas) gracias*
you're welcome *de nada*
excuse me *perdóneme*
hello *hola*
OK *bién*
goodbye *adiós*
good evening/night *buenas tardes/noches*
here *aquí*
there *allí*
today *hoy*
yesterday *ayer*
tomorrow *mañana (note: mañana also means "morning")*
now *ahora*
later *después*
right away *ahora mismo*
this morning *esta mañana*
this afternoon *esta tarde*
this evening *esta tarde*
tonight *esta noche*

## On Arrival

I want to get off at... *Quiero bajarme en...*
Is there a bus to the museum?

## Slang

*¡Guay!* Swell!
*Bocata* Sandwich
*Litrona* a litre-bottle of beer
*Guiri* foreigner
*Kilo* one million pesetas
*Duro* five pesetas (eg. *veinte duros* is 100 pesetas)

*¿Hay un autobús al museo?*
What street is this? *¿Qué calle es ésta?*
Which line do I take for...? *¿Qué línea cojo para...?*
How far is...? *¿A qué distancia está...?*
airport *aeropuerto*
customs *aduana*
train station *estación de tren*
bus station *estación de autobuses*
metro station *estación de metro*
bus *autobús*
bus stop *parada de autobús*
platform *apeadero*
ticket *billete*
return ticket *billete de ida y vuelta*
hitch-hiking *auto-stop*
toilets *servicios*
This is the hotel address *Ésta es la dirección del hotel*
I'd like a (single/double) room *Quiero una habitación (sencilla/doble)*
... with shower *con ducha*
... with bath *con baño*
... with a view *con vista*
Does that include breakfast? *¿Incluye desayuno?*
May I see the room? *¿Puedo ver la habitación?*
washbasin *lavabo*
bed *cama*
key *llave*
elevator *ascensor*
air conditioning *aire acondicionado*

## Emergencies

Help! *¡Socorro!*
Stop! *¡Alto!*
Call a doctor *Llame a un médico*
Call an ambulance *Llame a una ambulancia*
Call the police *Llame a la policia*
Call the fire brigade *Llame a los bomberos*
Where is the nearest telephone?

*¿Dónde está el teléfono mas próximo?*
Where is the nearest hospital? *¿Dónde está el hospital más próximo?*
I am sick *Estoy enfermo*
I have lost my passport/purse *He perdido mi pasaporte/bolso*

## On the Road

Where is the spare wheel? *¿Dónde está la rueda de repuesto?*
Where is the nearest garage? *¿Dónde está el taller más próximo?*
Our car has broken down *Nuestro coche se ha averiado*
I want to have my car repaired *Quiero que reparen mi coche*
It's not your right of way *Usted no tiene prioridad*
I think I must have put diesel in my car by mistake *Me parece haber echado gasoil por error*
the road to... *la carretera a...*
left *izquierda*
right *derecha*
straight on *derecho*
far *lejos*
near *cerca*
opposite *frente a*
beside *al lado de*
car park *aparcamiento*
over there *allí*
at the end *al final*
on foot *a pie*
by car *en coche*
town map *mapa de la ciudad*
road map *mapa de carreteras*
street *calle*
square *plaza*
give way *ceda el paso*
exit *salida*
dead end *calle sin salida*
wrong way *dirección prohibida*
no parking *prohibido aparcar*
motorway *autovía*
toll highway *autopista*
toll *peaje*
speed limit *límite de velocidad*
petrol station *gasolinera*
petrol *gasolina*
unleaded *sin plomo*
diesel *gasoil*
water/oil *agua/aceite*
air *aire*
puncture *pinchazo*
bulb *bombilla*

## On the Telephone

**How do I make an outside call?**
*¿Cómo hago una llamada exterior?*
**What is the area code?** *¿Cuál es el prefijo?*
**I want to make an international (local) call** *Quiero hacer una llamada internacional (local)*
**I'd like an alarm call for 8 tomorrow morning** *Quiero que me despierten a las ocho de la mañana*
**Hello?** *¿Dígame?*
**Who's calling?** *¿Quién llama?*
**Hold on, please** *Un momento, por favor*
**I can't hear you** *No le oigo*
**Can you hear me?** *¿Me oye?*
**He/she is not here** *No está aquí*
**The line is busy** *La línea está ocupada*
**I must have dialled the wrong number** *Debo haber marcado un número equivocado*

## Shopping

**Where is the nearest bank?**
*¿Dónde está el banco más próximo?*
**I'd like to buy** *Quiero comprar*
**How much is it** *¿Cuánto es?*
**Do you accept credit cards?**
*¿Aceptan tarjeta?*
**I'm just looking** *Sólo estoy mirando*
**Have you got...?** *¿Tiene...?*
**I'll take it** *Me lo llevo*
**I'll take this one/that one** *Me llevo éste/ese*
**What size is it?** *¿Que talla es?*
**size (clothes)** *talla*
**small** *pequeño*
**large** *grande*
**cheap** *barato*
**expensive** *caro*
**enough** *suficiente*
**too much** *demasiado*
**a piece** *una pieza*
**each** *cada una/la pieza/la unidad* (eg. melones, 100 ptas la unidad)
**bill** *la factura (shop), la cuenta (restaurant)*
**bank** *banco*
**bookshop** *librería*
**chemist** *farmacia*
**hairdressers** *peluquería*
**post office** *correos*
**department store** *grandes almacenes*

---

### MARKET SHOPPING

Supermarkets (*supermercados*) are self service, but often the best and freshest produce is to be had at the town market (*mercado*) or at street markets (*mercadillo*), where you place you order with the person in charge of each stand. Prices are usually by the kilo, sometimes by gramos (by the gram) or by unidad (by the piece).

**fresh** *fresco*
**frozen** *congelado*
**organic** *biológico*
**flavour** *sabor*
**basket** *cesta*
**bag** *bolsa*
**bakery** *panadería*
**butcher's** *carnicería*
**cake shop** *pastelería*
**fishmonger's** *pescadería*
**grocery** *verdulería*
**tobacconist** *estanco*
**market** *mercado*
**supermarket** *supermercado*
**junk shop** *tienda de segunda mano*

## Sightseeing

**mountain** *montaña*
**hill** *colina*
**valley** *valle*
**river** *río*
**lake** *lago*
**lookout** *mirador*
**city** *ciudad*
**small town, village** *pueblo*
**old town** *casco antiguo*
**monastery** *monasterio*
**convent** *convento*
**cathedral** *catedral*
**church** *iglesia*
**palace** *palacio*
**hospital** *hospital*
**town hall** *ayuntamiento*
**nave** *nave*
**statue** *estátua*
**fountain** *fuente*
**staircase** *escalera*
**tower** *torre*
**castle** *castillo*
**Iberian** *ibérico*
**Phoenician** *fenicio*

## Numbers, Days and Dates

| NUMBERS | | | | DAYS OF THE WEEK | MONTHS |
|---|---|---|---|---|---|
| 0 | *cero* | 15 | *quince* | 500 *quinientos* | **DAYS OF THE WEEK** | **MONTHS** |
| 1 | *uno* | 16 | *dieciseis* | 1,000 *mil* | **Monday** *lunes* | **January** *enero* |
| 2 | *dos* | 17 | *diecisiete* | 10,000 *diez mil* | **Tuesday** *martes* | **February** *febrero* |
| 3 | *tres* | 18 | *dieciocho* | 1,000,000 *un millón* | **Wednesday** *miércoles* | **March** *marzo* |
| 4 | *cuatro* | 19 | *diecinueve* | | **Thursday** *jueves* | **April** *abril* |
| 5 | *cinco* | 20 | *viente* | **SAYING THE DATE** | **Friday** *viernes* | **May** *mayo* |
| 6 | *seis* | 21 | *veintiuno* | **20 October 1999,** | **Saturday** *sábado* | **June** *junio* |
| 7 | *siete* | 30 | *treinta* | *el veinte de* | **Sunday** *domingo* | **July** *julio* |
| 8 | *ocho* | 40 | *cuarenta* | *octubre de mil* | | **August** *agosto* |
| 9 | *nueve* | 50 | *cincuenta* | *novecientos* | | **September** *septiembre* |
| 10 | *diez* | 60 | *sesenta* | *noventa y nueve* | **SEASONS** | **October** *octubre* |
| 11 | *once* | 70 | *setenta* | (no capital letters | **Spring** *primavera* | **November** *noviembre* |
| 12 | *doce* | 80 | *ochenta* | are used for days | **Summer** *verano* | **December** *diciembre* |
| 13 | *trece* | 90 | *noventa* | or months) | **Autumn** *otoño* | |
| 14 | *catorce* | 100 | *cien* | | **Winter** *invierno* | |
| | | 200 | *doscientos* | | | |

**Roman** *romano*
**Moorish** *árabe*
**Romanesque** *románico*
**Gothic** *gótico*
**museum** *museo*
**art gallery** *galería de arte*
**exhibition** *exposición*
**tourist information office** *oficina de turismo*
**free** *gratis*
**open** *abierto*
**closed** *cerrado*
**every day** *diario/todos los días*
**all year** *todo el año*
**all day** *todo el día*
**swimming pool** *piscina*
**to book** *reservar*

## Dining Out

In Spanish, *el menú* is not the main menu, but a fixed menu offered each day at a lower price. The main menu is *la carta.*

**breakfast** *desayuno*
**lunch** *comida*
**dinner** *cena*
**meal** *comida*
**first course** *primer plato*
**main course** *plato principal*
**made to order** *por encargo*
**drink included** *incluida consumición/bebida*
**wine list** *carta de vinos*
**the bill** *la cuenta*
**fork** *tenedor*
**knife** *cuchillo*
**spoon** *cuchara*
**plate** *plato*
**glass** *vaso*
**wine glass** *copa*
**napkin** *servilleta*
**ashtray** *cenicero*
**waiter, please!** *camarero, por favor*

## Liquid Refreshment

**coffee** *café*
  **black** *sólo*
  **with milk** *con leche*
  **decaffeinated** *descafeinado*
**sugar** *azúcar*
**tea** *té*
**herbal tea** *infusión*
**milk** *leche*
**mineral water** *agua mineral*
**fizzy** *con gas*
**non-fizzy** *sin gas*

## Table Talk

**I am a vegetarian** *Soy vegetariano*
**I am on a diet** *Estoy de régimen*
**What do you recommend?** *¿Qué recomienda?*
**Do you have local specialities?** *¿Hay especialidades locales?*
**I'd like to order** *Quiero pedir*
**That is not what I ordered** *Ésto no es lo que he pedido*
**May I have more wine?** *¿Me da más vino?*
**Enjoy your meal** *Buen provecho*

**juice (fresh)** *zumo (natural)*
**cold** *fresco/frío*
**hot** *caliente*
**beer** *cerveza*
  **bottled** *en botella*
  **on tap** *de barril*
**soft drink** *refresco*
**diet drink** *bebida "light"*
**with ice** *con hielo*
**wine** *vino*
**red wine** *vino tinto*
**white** *blanco*
**rosé** *rosado*
**dry** *seco*
**sweet** *dulce*
**house wine** *vino de la casa*
**sparkling wine** *vino espumoso*
**Where is this wine from?** *¿De dónde es este vino?*
**pitcher** *jarra*
**half litre** *medio litro*
**quarter litre** *cuarto de litro*
**cheers!** *salud*
**hangover** *resaca*

## Menu Decoder

### BREAKFAST AND SNACKS

*pan* **bread**
*bollo* **bun/roll**
*mantequilla* **butter**
*confitura* **jam**
*pimienta* **pepper**
*sal* **salt**
*azúcar* **sugar**
*huevos* **eggs**
  *cocidos* **boiled, cooked**
  *con beicon* **with bacon**
  *con jamón* **with ham**
  *fritos* **fried**
  *revueltos* **scrambled**

*yogúr* **yoghurt**
*tostada* **toast**
*sandwich* **sandwich in square slices of bread**
*bocadillo* **sandwich in a bread roll**

## MAIN COURSES

### Meat/Carne

*buey* **beef**
*carne picada* **ground meat**
*cerdo* **pork**
*chorizo* **sausage with paprika**
*chuleta* **chop**
*conejo* **rabbit**
*cordero* **lamb**
*costilla* **rib**
*filete* **steak**
*jamón* **ham**
*jjsalchichón* **sausage**
*solomillo* **fillet steak**
*ternera* **veal or young beef**
*a la brasa* **charcoal grilled**
*a la plancha* **grilled**
*asado* **roast**
*bién hecho* **well done**
*en su punto* **medium**
*Poco hecho* **rare**

### Fowl

*faisán* **pheasant**
*pavo* **turkey**
*pato* **duck**
*perdiz* **partridge**
*pollo* **chicken**

### Fish/Pescado

*almeja* **clam**
*anchoas* **anchovies**
*atún* **tuna**
*bacalao* **cod**
*bogavante* **lobster**
*boquerones* **fresh anchovies**
*caballa* **mackerel**
*calamar* **squid**
*cangrejo* **crab**
*gamba* **shrimp/prawn**
*jlangostino* **large prawn**
*lenguado* **sole**
*mariscos* **shellfish**
*mejillón* **mussel**
*ostra* **oyster**
*peregrina* **scallop**
*pez espada* **swordfish**
*pulpo* **octopus**
*rsalmón* **salmon**
*sardina* **sardine**
*trucha* **trout**

## VEGETABLES/CEREALS/SALADS

*vegetables* **verduras**
*ajo* **garlic**
*alcachofa* **artichoke**
*apio* **celery**
*arroz* **rice**
*berenjena* **eggplant/aubergine**
*cebolla* **onion**
*champiñon* **mushroom**
*col* **cabbage**
*coliflor* **cauliflower**
*crudo* **raw**
*ensalada* **salad**
*ehabichuela* **bean**
*lechuga* **lettuce**
*lenteja* **lentil**
*maíz* **corn/maize**
*menestra* **cooked mixed vegetables**
*patata* **potato**
*pepino* **cucumber**
*pimiento* **pepper**
*puerro* **leek**
*tomate* **tomato**
*zanahoria* **carrot**

## FRUIT AND DESSERTS

*fruta* **fruta**
*aguacate* **avocado**
*albaricoque* **apricot**
*cereza* **cherry**
*ciruela* **plum**
*frambuesa* **raspberry**
*fresa* **strawberry**
*granada* **pomegranate**
*higo* **fig**
*limón* **lemon**
*mandarina* **tangerine**
*manzana* **apple**
*melocotón* **peach**
*melón* **melon**
*naranja* **orange**
*pera* **pear**
*piña* **pineapple**
*plátano* **banana**
*pomelo* **grapefruit**
*sandía* **watermelon**
*uva* **grape**
*Postre* **Dessert**
*tarta* **cake**
*pastel* **pie**
*helado* **ice cream**
*natilla* **custard**
*flan* **caramel custard**
*queso* **cheese**

# Further Reading

## General

Dicks, Brian. *Lanzarote, Fire Island* (Dryad, London, 1988).
Fernandez-Armesto, Felipe. *The Canary Islands after the Conquest* (Clarendon, Oxford, 1982).
Hayter, Judith. *Canary Island Hopping* (Sphere, London, 1982).
Mason, John and Anne. *The Canary Islands* (Batsford, London, 1976).
Mercer, John. *The Canary Islanders* (Collins, London, 1980).
Yeoward, Eileen. *Canary Islands* (Stockwell, Ilfracombe 1975).
*Warm Island Walking Guide*; *Tenerife South Walking Guide*; *Tenerife North Walking Guide*; *Tenerife West Walking Guide*; *Plants and Flowers Field Guide, Tenerife* (Discovery Walking Guides Ltd, 10 Tennyson Close, Northampton NN5 7HJ).
Noel Rochford. *Sunflower Guide to Tenerife* (Sunflower Books, 12 Kendrick Mews, London SW7 3HG).

## Other Insight Guides

*Insight Pocket Guide: Tenerife* by Nigel Tisdall (Apa Publications). Itinerary-based guide to help you get the most out of Tenerife during a short stay. The tours are supported by full-colour maps and photographs. A superb pull-out with plotted routes accompanies the book – and this can also be used independently.

*Insight Compact Guide: Tenerife* (Apa Publications). A conveniently sized yet comprehensive guide to the island with suggested routes, maps and practical information.

*Insight Guide: Gran Canaria.* (Apa Publications). A guide to Gran Canaria, Fuerteventura and Lanzarote, with history and background features, itineraries linked to full-colour maps, and a wealth of information on travel arrangements, accommodation, and much more.

## Maps

All the tourist information centres and most hotels provide free maps of all the islands. These are detailed enough for most tourists, although they can be unreliable in more remote areas. For those planning walking holidays, it is possible to buy more detailed maps published by the Spanish Government and military, available from bookshops.

*Insight Flexi Map: Tenerife* provides clear cartography, bite-size travel information and has a hard-wearing laminated finish.

# ART & PHOTO CREDITS

**INSIGHT GUIDE**
## Tenerife

*Cartographic Editor* **Zoë Goodwin**
*Production* **Stuart A Everitt**
*Design Consultants*
**Carlotta Junger, Graham Mitchener**
*Picture Research*
**Hilary Genin, Monica Allende**

# Index

*Numbers in italics refer to photographs*

# INSIGHT GUIDES

*The world's largest collection of visual travel guides*

## Insight Guides – the Classic Series
## that puts you in the picture

Alaska
Alsace
Amazon Wildlife
American Southwest
Amsterdam
Argentina
Asia, East
Asia, South
Asia, Southeast
Athens
Atlanta
Australia
Austria

Bahamas
Bali
Baltic States
Bangkok
Barbados
Barcelona
Bay of Naples
Beijing
Belgium
Belize
Berlin
Bermuda
Boston
Brazil
Brittany
Brussels
Budapest
Buenos Aires
Burgundy
Burma (Myanmar)

Cairo
Calcutta
California
California, Northern
California, Southern
Canada
Caribbean
Catalonia
Channel Islands
Chicago
Chile

China
Cologne
Continental Europe
Corsica
Costa Rica
Crete
Crossing America
Cuba
Cyprus
Czech & Slovak
   Republic
Delhi, Jaipur & Agra
Denmark
Dominican Republic
Dresden
Dublin
Düsseldorf

East African Wildlife
Eastern Europe
Ecuador
Edinburgh
Egypt
England

Finland
Florence
Florida
France
Frankfurt
French Riviera

Gambia & Senegal
Germany
Glasgow
Gran Canaria
Great Barrier Reef
Great Britain
Greece
Greek Islands
Guatemala, Belize &
   Yucatán

Hamburg
Hawaii

Hong Kong
Hungary

Iceland
India
India's Western
   Himalayas
India, South
Indian Wildlife
Indonesia
Ireland
Israel
Istanbul
Italy
Italy, Northern

Jamaica
Japan
Java
Jerusalem
Jordan

Kathmandu
Kenya
Korea

Laos & Cambodia
Lisbon
Loire Valley
London
Los Angeles

Madeira
Madrid
Malaysia
Mallorca & Ibiza
Malta
Marine Life ot the
   South China Sea
Mauritius &
   ·Seychelles
Melbourne
Mexico City
Mexico
Miami
Montreal

Morocco
Moscow
Munich

Namibia
Native America
Nepal
Netherlands
New England
New Orleans
New York City
New York State
New Zealand
Nile
Normandy
Norway

Old South
Oman & The UAE
Oxford

Pacific Northwest
Pakistan
Paris
Peru
Philadelphia
Philippines
Poland
Portugal
Prague
Provence
Puerto Rico

Rajasthan
Rhine
Rio de Janeiro
Rockies
Rome
Russia

St. Petersburg
San Francisco
Sardinia
Scotland
Seattle
Sicily

Singapore
South Africa
South America
South Tyrol
Southeast Asia
   Wildlife
Spain
Spain, Northern
Spain, Southern
Sri Lanka
Sweden
Switzerland
Sydney
Syria & Lebanon

Taiwan
Tenerife
Texas
Thailand
Tokyo
Trinidad & Tobago
Tunisia
Turkey
Turkish Coast
Tuscany

Umbria
USA: Eastern States
USA: Western States
US National Parks:
   East
US National Parks:
   West

Vancouver
Venezuela
Venice
Vienna
Vietnam

Wales
Washington DC
Waterways of Europe
Wild West

Yemen

**Complementing the above titles are 120 easy-to-carry Insight Compact Guides, 120 Insight Pocket Guides with full-size pull-out maps and more than 60 laminated easy-fold Insight Maps**